014504025

not in BCL
au in BCL

W9-AHQ-367

WITHDRAWN
NDSU

The
WIDENING
CIRCLE

The Twentieth Publication in

THE HANEY FOUNDATION SERIES
University of Pennsylvania

The
WIDENING
CIRCLE

Essays on the Circulation of Literature in Eighteenth-Century Europe

ROBERT DARNTON

BERNHARD FABIAN

ROY McKEEN WILES

Edited by
PAUL J. KORSHIN

UNIVERSITY OF PENNSYLVANIA PRESS
1976

Copyright © 1976 by The University of Pennsylvania Press, Inc.

All rights reserved

Library of Congress Catalog Card Number: 76-20161
ISBN: 0-8122-7717-1

Printed in the United States of America

Z
1003.5
E9
D37

Contents

Introduction

Paul J. Korshin

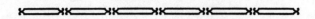

The 1974 A. S. W. Rosenbach Fellowship in Bibliography at the University of Pennsylvania was devoted to the Fifth Annual Meeting of the American Society for Eighteenth-Century Studies. The Rosenbach Fellowship, founded by the late A. S. W. Rosenbach in 1931, has traditionally consisted of several lectures by a single scholar on an aspect of descriptive bibliography, in the specialized sense. The Fellowship had never before been applied to the gathering of a learned society whose aims were primarily interdisciplinary and largely unbibliographical. For the 1974 meeting of the Society, therefore, the choice of an interdisciplinary topic with broad appeal to specialists in various disciplines yet consistent with the bibliographical motif of the Fellowship seemed appropriate. The theme of the lectures was "Literacy and the Reading Public in the Eighteenth Century." The Society invited the three contributors to conceive of literacy in a sense more general than any which it bears in common usage, to make use of original primary materials, and to cover, if possible, an area previously uncharted by other scholars. The only other requirement was that each contributor should focus on publishing, reading, and the diffusion of printed materials in a different country.

The three contributors, Robert Darnton, the late Roy McKeen Wiles, and Bernhard Fabian, are already widely known as specialists in aspects of eighteenth-century reading and publishing. Professor Darnton has written about publishers and the reading public during the Old Regime. Professor Wiles was the world's leading authority on the eighteenth-century English newspaper.[1] And Professor Fabian specializes in eighteenth-century German bibliography and scholarship and in Anglo-German literary relations. The contributors are not, therefore, occupied with identical aspects of "literacy." Indeed, it might properly be said that they are not occupied with the concept of literacy but with the history of books and their eighteenth-century readers and with methods of evaluating these phenomena, the diffusion of printed materials, and the growth of reading.

"Literacy" in its conceptual sense is taken by many historians to mean no more than an ability to read and write. The lower limit of literacy, in this sense, is usually easy to ascertain. Considerable evidence is available to document the lower threshold of literacy, in parish registers, legal deeds and conveyances, wills, and marriage contracts. The records of educational institutions help to establish the proportion of the population, at a given time in the historical past, that learned to read and write, but they tell us comparatively little about *what* they read. We already know a good deal about the lower level of literacy in the eighteenth century, thanks to the studies of Lawrence Stone, Roger Schofield, and Kenneth A. Lockridge.[2] Their work, like much of that dealing with literacy, has focused principally on an ability to write, often interpreted as an ability to sign one's name. Signatures form a quantifiable body of evidence, worthy of evaluation, from which it may be possible to draw valuable conclusions about a large

portion of a population. The study of who could produce a legible signature, however, while it may furnish a rough guide to the lower limit of literacy in a given
century, is of small value in telling us who could read. Yet the identity of who
could read, of a body of readers or a reading public, is important not only for
the social historian but for the student of literature as well. What people in the
eighteenth century read and how much of it they demanded, how tastes in
reading changed, and how high the upper limit of literacy reached and in which
social classes have important implications for the intellectual, political, and social
history of eighteenth-century countries and peoples.

Until recently, much of the study of the higher limit of reading has been
left to bibliographers, who have made useful contributions in such areas as the
size of editions of eighteenth-century books and the growth, in terms of sheer
numbers, in the demand for printed materials. In the study of English reading and
publishing, for example, there is much scattered evidence concerning number of
copies printed of various books, and some information about the average size of
printings at different times, but the evidence is too disparate to be useful.
Efforts to ascertain the number of books (*book* may be taken to mean any printed
work with a separate title page, even a single broadsheet) actually printed in
eighteenth-century Europe, such as Project LOC or short-title catalogues of all
printed works, are still in a preliminary stage, and are unlikely to produce
significant results for many years.[3]

Bibliographical studies have been the inspiration behind examinations of
other kinds of evidence that shed light on reading and reading publics. The
reprinting of eighteenth-century auction and library catalogues, for example, has
made available a major body of evidence concerning what was collected and
read by selected individuals, who are almost always identifiable as to profession
and social class.[4] The analysis of quantitative data from almost ten thousand
book sale catalogues has barely begun, but there can be no doubt that by the
end of the decade we will have learned much from this source. A similar and
more ingenious quasi-bibliographical study is that involving book subscription
lists.[5] So far, this study involves only the two thousand or more books published
by subscription in eighteenth-century England for which lists of subscribers
survive. The project, which is computer assisted, has already started to furnish
projections on the kinds of people who subscribed to (and, presumably, read)
thousands of books of all kinds. Many, if not most, people whose names appear
on eighteenth-century subscription lists can be identified by social class or
profession. The directors of the Book Subscription List Project believe that they
will ultimately be able to prepare a compilation with data concerning the reading habits of a million subscriber names on thousands of subscription lists. These
materials are especially interesting with regard to books published in provincial
cities, where the study of reading, publishing, and the audience for books has
lagged behind that conducted for large cities. For it may be that in the provinces
more meaningful results can be obtained, since the population in, say, Newcastle
would be more stable and homogeneous than in a metropolis such as London,
Paris, or Berlin. It should be clear, then, that the materials about reading publics

and reading habits gathered through these new, mainly bibliographical studies will greatly assist social and political historians.[6]

Another important, established area of investigation for students of reading, publishing, and audiences is traditional literary history. For a somewhat later period in England, the paradigm is Richard D. Altick's *The English Common Reader: A Social History of the Mass Reading Public, 1800–1900.*[7] And studies of magazines and periodicals, newspapers, popular or "street" literature, and the book trade during the eighteenth century have provided much commentary on the world of books, yet without always asking the vital questions about who the readers of the time were and what, exactly, they read.[8] Often the studies of individual branches of literature, such as the early scientific magazine or popular pamphlets, have disappointed in that they only describe and catalogue their materials, with little attempt to assess the broader implications of these works upon an audience or, indeed, any thought about who that audience was. Sometimes, too, as Robert Darnton has shown, the evidence is misinterpreted through the introduction of sweeping generalizations.

Perhaps one answer, then, to the problems that face the student of eighteenth-century literacy is to seek new areas of inquiry, new and previously untouched sources, and controlled, easily reifiable topics. A topic as broad as the English book trade in the eighteenth century is simply not a feasible area of inquiry anymore, although less than fifty years ago A. S. Collins could write several leisurely volumes on this very subject.[9] Rather, the more specialized study of a topic where the major portion of the evidence can be readily commanded is likely to make the larger contribution today. The scrutiny of publishers and their business history, publishers' archives and booksellers' records, surviving correspondence between authors and publishers, the records of circulating libraries and reading societies, studies of previously ignored genres like book reviewing: these newer areas may yield more important information about trends in reading and on the expansion of literacy than the older, more established scholarship has done.

Our contributors, as I said above, are concerned with widely differing aspects of the history of literacy and reading, with the printed word and its audience, and with the methodologies of bringing printed works to a particular public. Here I might note that the marketing and economics of bookselling, printing, and publishing often play a major role in recent studies of reading and reading publics. Nowhere is this more true than in Robert Darnton's essay, "Trade in the Taboo: The Life of a Clandestine Bookseller in Prerevolutionary France." By studying the business of one clandestine dealer, Professor Darnton explores the general milieu of the shady characters in the literary underworld. So the story of Bruzard de Mauvelain, tied up with accounts of smugglers, hack-writers, swindlers, scoundrels, and confidence men, presents a human element that is lacking in standard studies of the eighteenth-century book trade. Mauvelain's dealings with the large and important Swiss firm, the Société typographique de Neuchâtel, during the early 1780's, would have been unlikely if not unnecessary in a less repressive era than the Old Regime. The numerous acts and decrees

dealing with censorship, forbidden books, and matters like libel which charac-
terize the literary scene in eighteenth-century France are by no means unique
to that country. No eighteenth-century society was wholly free from some
restraints on the freedom of the press. Undoubtedly, however, the clandestine
book trade flourished more around the borders of France than elsewhere in
Europe. Clandestine booksellers, as Professor Darnton shows, drove a dangerous
trade, for not only did they import prohibited books, whether obscene, libelous,
politically radical, or blasphemous, not only did they circulate cheap piracies of
established literature, but they also constantly violated customs regulations by
smuggling their wares across borders, bribing corrupt officials into secrecy or
connivance. The papers of the Société typographique survive at Neuchâtel. Close
study of them suggests how valuable the analysis of booksellers' and publishers'
archives will be for students of the history of bookselling and reading in the
future. The hero (perhaps antihero would be better) of Professor Darnton's
account, the impecunious and diseased clandestine bookseller Mauvelain, is
human indeed. His pyramiding of credit may be small in comparison to that
of the great financial swindler Ivar Kreuger, but his mental and physical agonies,
his grandiose yet flawed literary schemes, his financial peculations and unpaid
bills furnish an interesting aspect to the study of literacy that is almost wholly
absent from bibliography and literary history.

Traditional bibliography and literary history have usually turned their
gaze on polite literature and the tastes of the educated reader.[10] The world of
Grub Street has been glimpsed mainly from the perspective of the eighteenth-
century writers who looked down scornfully at the "prostitute scribblers" (to
borrow a phrase from Swift) inhabiting it. The map of this literary underworld
(if it is an underworld) has not been easy to draw. It is easier to plot the day-by
day literary career of Pope or Voltaire than of Defoe or Mauvelain.[11] Yet
chroniques scandaleuses, salacious gossip of all kinds, cheap, pirated duodecimos
were an important part of the literary scene in eighteenth-century France, as they
were, too, in England (though in a slightly different guise). Mauvelain was just
one of many clandestine booksellers and the fact that he operated in provincial
France, in a cultural backwater where adult literacy was low, suggests that the
market for the literature of protest did not flourish only in the country's metropolis
and main towns.

One consequence of the repressive official attitude toward social criticism
during the Old Regime was that news of all kinds, especially news accounts
which tended to be critical of the governmental establishment, traveled to the
provinces via an underground route. There was a trade in banned books in
England, too, but actual censorship was confined mainly to obscene works (such
as Cleland's *Memoirs of a Woman of Pleasure*, Wilkes's *Essay on Woman*).[12] As
Roy McKeen Wiles's essay shows, an impressive array of provincial newspapers
readily promoted the transmission of news in eighteenth-century England. A
methodological characteristic of many studies of English publishing and reading
habits has been the tendency to make broad generalizations about the nation's
literary taste from what we know (or can surmise) about the demand for "polite"

literature in the country's metropolis. But London is not the only constituent of the field of eighteenth-century English literacy: the fallacy of taking the part for the whole has long prevented scholars from making an accurate assessment of the English reading public. While Professor Wiles admits that a fund of solid, quantifiable evidence is difficult to obtain, his essay, "The Relish for Reading in Provincial England Two Centuries Ago," demonstrates that much suggestive material is available, and that from it judicious conclusions may be drawn about what people in provincial England read during the latter half of the eighteenth century. The number of provincial newspapers increased by a factor of four between 1712—the year of the Stamp Tax, which tended to retard the growth of the provincial press—when there were nine, and 1780, when there were thirty-seven. Scanty surviving publishers' records show that by 1776 the readership of some provincial newspapers was computed at more than 10,000. More significant, perhaps, than circulation figures are the advertisements which populate the pages of the provincial press, as thick as leaves in Vallombrosa, and as varied and interesting. Indeed, the study of newspaper advertisements on a broad, systematic basis may well provide more insight into eighteenth-century reading habits than any other scrutiny undertaken previously. The length of Professor Wiles's essay does not permit him the luxury of cataloguing and classifying the thousands of advertisements placed in the provincial press by London booksellers and publishers, circulating libraries and reading societies, book auctioneers, and local educational establishments which taught reading.[13] Such close analysis, however, is certain to be undertaken by other scholars in the near future, for suggestive historical evidence seldom lies fallow for long. The importance of Professor Wiles's contribution is that, although it does not pretend to demonstrate statistically what proportion of the eighteenth-century English population could and did read, it emphasizes the existence of a wealth of unstudied material concerning reading habits and the reading public. From the unchallengeable facts concerning literacy which he assembles, statistical projections will ultimately be made.

Reading, publishing, and the audiences for books are both national and international phenomena. These phenomena, as we have seen in the study of Mauvelain in the 1780's, may involve the transfer of printed materials from one country to another, the translation of popular works from one language into another, and the establishment of outposts of one national culture in another country. We find less transference of a foreign literary culture to France and England than we do to eighteenth-century Germany. The German literary community and certainly the German publishing industry were more dispersed in the eighteenth century among various intellectual centers than were those of France or England. Leipzig was the dominant publishing city, but Berlin, Frankfort, and Hamburg were by no means insignificant. The lack of a unified governmental structure and, especially, the lack of a strong German literary tradition are doubtless responsible for the great influence that foreign literatures enjoyed during the eighteenth century. In the first half of the century, the major influence was France; English influence grew in the latter half of our period. In his "English Books in Eighteenth-Century Germany: An Outline

Sketch," Bernhard Fabian finds primary evidence concerning the spread of literacy in a foreign language that is unavailable in other countries and that, for Germany, has hitherto been overlooked or only partially understood. Most publishers' archives and many institutional and private libraries in Germany were destroyed during World War II, so one kind of evidence that has been invaluable to students of French and English reading publics is quite scarce. Professor Fabian, however, while relying mainly on printed sources, shows that the traditional "literary" bibliographies, long regarded as standard, are far from complete, that printed books outside of the *humaniora* class have been little noticed, and that some printed evidence, such as the catalogues of the Frankfurt Book Fairs, have barely been used at all.

The study of the ability to read a foreign language has interesting implications as a "control" in the study of the audience for literature. Once again, statistical projections are difficult to obtain, but the mass of evidence about the reading of a foreign language in Germany suggests the existence of similar phenomena in France, England, and other eighteenth-century societies. Professor Fabian's systematic methodology is a model for such studies in other cultural milieux: he defines the Anglo-German literary tradition and its reading public in terms of such categories as bookselling, publishing, book reviewing, book collecting, and reading. Each of these categories requires the evaluation of a different kind of primary evidence, such as booksellers' and publishers' advertisements, tabulations of book reviews, auction and library catalogues, and, to a lesser extent, the records of circulating libraries. The picture that emerges is striking. We learn how well organized the international German book trade was in the later eighteenth century. Some publishers employed agents in London who scouted out likely titles for rapid translation. Others simply imported English books which a substantial English-reading German public devoured as fast as they could be made available. Hamburg even had an English bookshop. Translations of popular English authors (such as Shakespeare, Pope, Edward Young, Laurence Sterne, and, naturally, Ossian) were numerous: one Mannheim publisher printed some 300,000 copies of these reprints between 1778 and 1785. The popularity of English fiction in Germany was unusually great, especially that of such middle-class authors as Defoe and Samuel Richardson. Almost as many copies of Richardson's least popular novel, *Sir Charles Grandison,* were sold in Germany as in England. The German moral weeklies, which imitated the English periodical essay, form a large and important genre. As Professor Fabian demonstrates, the expansion of a reading public must be studied over a period of many years (half a century is a useful span): the gradual accumulation of evidence about the wide spectrum of general readers who could and did demand books in English or by English authors indicates a tremendous growth of ordinary German literacy. If we assign a more specialized value or taste to literacy in a foreign language than we do to that in a native language, then the growth of the reading public for English books in eighteenth-century Germany tells much about that public's taste and sophistication in other matters. The "control" which I mentioned earlier becomes a device useful for determining the degree of sophistication of an audience. The German audience was clearly highly literate, given to extensive rather than intensive reading, and much interested in the literature which was transforming the rest of Europe, especially in England and France.

The identity of the audience for literature and the history of reading publics are difficult to reconstruct. Our perception of both has for long focused principally on questions of who could read and write (literacy in the traditional sense) or what books were popular (literary history in its traditional sense). The questions which the three essays collected here ask are different and in some ways revolutionary for the history of reading and the study of audiences. For to determine what a given audience read is to help lay the groundwork for the studies of the intellectual historian, the social historian, and the student of politics and revolutions. The essays that follow, by employing new, often untouched materials in their quest for solutions to these old problems, make a notable contribution to our understanding of the eighteenth-century reading public and to the methodologies for its study.

NOTES

1. Roy M. Wiles died on 9 March 1974, after completing his essay but before he had finished his documentation, which was undertaken by his colleague, Richard Morton, of the Department of English, McMaster University. I am grateful to him for preparing the final draft of Professor Wiles's essay.

2. See Lawrence Stone, "Literacy and Education in England, 1640–1900," *Past & Present*, No. 42 (1969), 69–139, a classic in its field. See also Roger Schofield, "The Measurement of Literacy in Pre-Industrial England," in *Literacy in Traditional Societies*, ed. Jack Goody (Cambridge, 1968), pp. 311–25, and Kenneth A. Lockridge, *Literacy in Colonial New England: An Inquiry into the Social Context of Literacy in the Early Modern West* (New York, 1974), *passim.*

3. Project LOC is a computer-assisted undertaking which has as its goal a catalogue of all pre-1801 printed books in the British Library (L), the college and departmental libraries of Oxford (O) and Cambridge (C) universities, the Bodleian Library, and the Cambridge University Library. Work on the project has languished in recent years. An eighteenth-century *Short-Title Catalogue* is thought feasible, at least for English books, but the work is still in the planning stage. Estimates of the number of books printed in England between 1701 and 1800 vary from 350,000 to 750,000; I am unaware of similar projections regarding France or Germany.

4. The reprinting of eighteenth-century sale catalogues began with *Sale Catalogues of Libraries of Eminent Persons,* under the general editorship of the late A. N. L. Munby (London, 1971–); there have been nine volumes to date. University Microfilms has announced a complete series of all Sotheby's sale catalogues (beginning with 1733) in microfilm. Georg Olms Verlag, of Hildesheim, Germany, plans to reprint fifty English and European sale and library catalogues of the eighteenth century, under the editorship of Bernhard Fabian and Paul J. Korshin.

5. The Book Subscription List Project, directed by P. J. Wallis and F. J. G. Robinson of the University of Newcastle, has been active since 1970, and has started to issue a series of pamphlets and volumes derived from their extensive collection of data, including, most recently, F. J. G. Robinson and P. J. Wallis, *Book Subscription Lists: A Revised Guide* (Newcastle upon Tyne, 1975).

6. See, for instance, Pat Rogers, "Book Subscriptions among the Augustans," *Times Literary Supplement,* 15 December 1972, pp. 1539–40, and P. J. Wallis and F. J. G.

Robinson, "The Potential Uses of Book Subscription Lists," in *The Art of the Librarian,* ed. A. Jeffreys (Newcastle, 1973), pp. 133–39.

7. Chicago, 1957. Altick's introductory chapter, on trends in reading during the eighteenth century, is important for the student of literacy.

8. There has been much literature on these subjects. For example, see Leslie Shepard, *The History of Street Literature* (Newton Abbot, 1973), unfortunately a popular account; David Pottinger, *The French Book Trade in the Ancien Régime* (Cambridge, Mass., 1958); and Robert Darnton, "Reading, Writing, and Publishing in Eighteenth-Century France: A Case Study in the Sociology of Literature," *Dædalus,* 100 (1971), 214–56.

9. Collins' two books, *Authorship in the Days of Johnson . . . 1726–1784* (London, 1927) and *The Profession of Letters . . . 1780–1832* (London, 1928), should still be consulted, but they are entertaining rather than instructive.

10. A recent exception to this trend is Pat Rogers, *Grub Street: Studies in a Subculture* (London, 1972).

11. Defoe, as Rogers makes clear (see *Grub Street,* pp. 311–27), spent much of his life and literary career engaged in clandestine activity; unlike Mauvelain, he was never a bookseller, but his career in England's literary underworld is just as elusive and difficult to trace.

12. Studies of obscene literature are numerous. Consult David Foxon, *Libertine Literature in England, 1660–1745* (New York, 1965). Less accessible to the general reader is Charles R. Dawes, "A Study of Erotic Literature in England" (unpub. Ms., British Museum, 1943). David Tribe, *Questions of Censorship* (London, 1973), pp. 47–69, contributes a brief historical account of English censorship.

13. On the eighteenth-century library, see Paul Kaufman, *Libraries and Their Uses: Collected Papers in Library History* (London, 1969), *passim,* and "Readers and Their Reading in Eighteenth-Century Lichfield," *The Library,* 5th ser., 28 (1973), 108–15.

Trade in the Taboo:
The Life of a Clandestine Book Dealer
in Prerevolutionary France

Robert Darnton

Although the clandestine book trade of the Old Regime has received its share of scholarship,[1] no one has been able to discover very much about the actual books that circulated "under the cloak" or the shady characters who handled them. The literary underground has been studied only from the perspective of the state—inevitably so, because the documentation has come almost entirely from the bureaucracy charged with suppressing illegal books. But in the papers of the Société typographique de Neuchâtel, one of the most important publishers of the late eighteenth century, the clandestine book dealers emerge as full-blown personalities, grappling with very human problems—disease, debt, loneliness, failure, and above all the frustrations of a difficult trade. By exploring the world of one of them, this essay is meant to show how the underground operated and what material it conveyed to ordinary readers in an ordinary town.

PART ONE: BRUZARD DE MAUVELAIN

Early Relations with the STN: Author-publisher, Publisher–Book Dealer

The Société typographique de Neuchâtel, Switzerland (STN), was one of many publishing houses that grew up around the borders of France in order to supply Frenchmen with books that could not be produced legally or safely within the kingdom. Some of these publishers specialized in *livres philosophiques*, as they were known in the trade—obscene, irreligious, or seditious works. Others printed cheap, pirated editions of books that French publishers had marketed with a *privilège*, a kind of copyright. The STN did a little of each, and it often received manuscripts from obscure authors who wanted their work printed cheaply and safely in Neuchâtel, then smuggled back to them in France for distribution through underground channels. One such proposal arrived in a letter from Tonnerre dated 14 April 1781 and signed "De Mauvelain, écuyer." Mauvelain wanted to print "une petite brochure sur les moines" in duodecimo format at a pressrun of 600 copies. The STN had been recommended to him by a friend, Jacques-Pierre Brissot de Warville, the future leader of the Girondists, who was then struggling to establish himself as a man of letters and had hired the STN to print his first philosophic works. In order to get a favorable reception, Mauvelain stressed his intimacy with Brissot: "Le nom de M. de Warville . . . sera ma caution vis à vis de vous." He offered to pay the STN's standard charge of one sou for every sheet printed, and he promised to make half the payment upon receiving the edition and half six months later.[2] The STN accepted, although

13

somewhat reluctantly, because the small size of the printing would reduce its profit margin (it preferred pressruns of at least 750 copies). Mauvelain wrote back that he was delighted to establish relations with them. He would expand his pamphlet with a "lettre sur les maisons de force en France," and that was only the beginning of his plans for publishing: "Nous avons beaucoup de projets, M. de Warville et moi. Je me propose d'aller fixer mes tabernacles auprès de lui à Paris dans le courant de l'année et de travailler de concert. Nous avons formé conjointement celui d'aller à Genève et auprès de vous, Monsieur, en septembre ou octobre."[3] Mauvelain's next letter, dated 5 June 1781, promised the manuscript within a month or two and explained that he philosophized so assiduously that he had damaged his health: "Etre trop longtemps assis rend les humeurs stagnantes; les couloirs s'engorgent; de là naissent les maux de tête, les dérangements d'estomac, en un mot le délabrement de tout le physique." He announced that he drank only water and had taken up gymnastics.[4]

At this point the correspondence broke off. When it resumed a year later, Mauvelain had settled in Troyes and signed "Bruzard de Mauvelain, avocat." He had dropped his plan to print the anticlerical pamphlet with the STN and now was writing to recommend a local lawyer called Millon, who wanted to print a philosophical treatise, *L'Interprète apologétique et politique de la nature:* "Des gens auxquels je me suis adressé et qui s'y connaissent m'ont assuré que c'était pour l'esprit un très plat seigneur et très mince génie; point d'aménité dans les moeurs et dans la société, ce qui n'est point étonnant, étant fils d'un cabaretier. Voilà son personnel. Il a de la fortune, et l'on ne risque rien de traiter avec lui, en sorte que si vous avez, Monsieur, des intérêts pécuniaires avec lui, vous ne devez avoir aucune crainte là-dessus. On m'a dit qu'on préférait ses billets au porteur à ses billets à Cloris—ses titres pécuniaires à ses titres littéraires."[5] This philosophic "écuyer" sounded rather grand, but there was no reason to suspect that he was putting on airs, because letters of recommendation like this abounded in the correspondence of eighteenth-century publishers, who relied on them for protection against confidence men. The clandestine book trade suffered more from the debtors and swindlers within its own ranks than from the police, and so the term "confiance" recurs like a leitmotiv in the letters of book dealers. They extended and withdrew confidence like credit, in carefully measured doses according to the reliability of their clients.

Mauvelain returned to the role of a recommender in his next letter, which he wrote in favor of a certain Bouvet, whom he described as one of the region's most important booksellers. He was renting part of Bouvet's house, he explained, and the bookseller, who was eager to increase his stock, had asked to be recommended to the STN. "Je le fais avec plaisir," Mauvelain wrote, "parce que c'est un brave garçon qui vous payera bien et très bien. Je vous promets de veiller à ce que les remises se fassent exactement."[6] Mauvelain made it clear that he was only a gentleman author doing a favor for a plebeian friend. His status showed more prominently in his next letter, which announced that he soon would send off a manuscript for the STN and gave the publishers a foretaste of his facility in belles-lettres: "Me trouvant ces jours derniers avec une belle dame de cette ville qu'on appelle par surnom la princesse, elle lâcha qu'elle aimait beaucoup *les politesses;* et moi *les compliments,* repris-je aussitôt, ce qui était deux polissoneries gazées. La princesse disait vrai. On m'engagea à mettre cela en couplet que voici, et que je lui envoyai le lendemain.

Etrennes à Mde . . .

En ce jour, Madame, entre nous,
Lequel des deux préférez-vous,
D'un compliment, ou d'une politesse. . .
Vous hésitez belle princesse!
Le compliment est de mon goût,
Si la politesse est du vôtre,
Nous voilà d'accord sur le tout.
Remplissez votre rôle, et nous ferons le nôtre."[7]

But the salon lion also sounded like a businessman. Having heard from the STN that it would supply Bouvet (it did a largé wholesale trade in all kinds of books), Mauvelain replied that he was delighted and that he would make sure that it had not misplaced its confidence. He would watch his landlord like a hawk and even would withhold the rent if Bouvet failed to pay the STN on time. So ardently did he desire to be of service that he would handle all the STN's affairs with Bouvet: he would communicate Bouvet's orders (it turned out that Bouvet was barely able to write anyhow), would see to their payment, and even would receive the shipments of books, because crates addressed to a respectable gentleman would not arouse the suspicions of the police. As a favor to some friends, Mauvelain occasionally would order some books himself. In fact, he wanted thirty-eight works right away. They concerned a variety of subjects—belles-lettres, history, natural history—and they included a half-dozen prohibited books, like *Les Fastes de Louis XV* and *L'Espion dévalisé,* which Mauvelain slipped casually into his order, as if he were testing the STN's willingness and ability to provide them. Bouvet's order, which Mauvelain wrote out in an accompanying letter, contained a larger proportion of *livres philosophiques: Thérèse philosophe, Anecdotes sur Madame DuBarry, Les Fastes de Louis XV, Le Système de la nature, Vénus dans le cloître, La Fille de joie, Dom B. . . , portier des Chartreux, Les Trois Imposteurs,* and many others. Bouvet needed the books in time for the fair that would open in Troyes on 15 March; and if this first shipment could be slipped past the authorities successfully, Mauvelain announced, "nous pourrons faire de grosses affaires par la suite."[8]

A few days later Mauvelain sent a supplementary order of his own, "parce que mes amis m'en demandent," and asked for the STN's list of "tous les livres prohibés ou non."[9] Like many publishers and wholesalers, the STN listed the prohibited books in its stock in anonymous, handwritten catalogues entitled "livres philosophiques," which it circulated secretly among its customers. It printed only a few of these books itself, but it procured them from other Swiss publishers (Fauche of Neuchâtel, Mourer of Lausanne, Gallay, Cailler, Bardin,

Nouffer, and Téron of Geneva), who specialized in the genre and who traded their publications for those of the STN. In this way, the STN unburdened itself of large proportions of its own editions and acquired a large enough inventory of *livres philosophiques* to fill orders from booksellers whose clients clamored for underground literature.

Mauvelain's early letters did not imply that his "friends" had any special desire for such books. He asked for only a few prohibited works in his second and third orders. But now, without saying so directly, he indicated that he planned to engage in the book trade by himself, and his letters discussed commercial matters in detail. His first order had reached him without mishap, he informed the STN on 9 April 1783, but it had taken too long and cost too much. Actually, the crate had left Neuchâtel on 6 February and had arrived at Troyes on 12 March, which was not bad for a clandestine shipment of about 210 miles, much of it through mountainous terrain. And the handling charges were not excessive: 18 livres 9 sous for the 71 volumes in the combined orders of Mauvelain and Bouvet.[10] So Mauvelain probably found this first experience encouraging. He began to pile order on order, gradually increasing the proportion of prohibited works, and neglecting each time to send a bill of exchange. By 9 April when he sent in his fourth order, he could avoid the subject of payment no longer. The most convenient way of paying for him, he explained, was to let his debts accumulate until he could discharge them all by a single bill of exchange on Paris. "Ne soyez pas inquiet, je vous prie, tout s'arrangera pour le mieux. . . . Procurez-moi, je vous prie, les livres défendus. . . ."[11]

"De Mauvelain, écuyer," treated financial affairs with aristocratic casualness. Instead of supplying the promised bill of exchange, he sent the STN a boar's head, "encore chaude," on 3 May with elaborate instructions on how to prepare and eat it. It traveled by coach (Mauvelain explained that such things kept for three months in winter and for six weeks in summer), and it weathered the trip as well as the books had done. Having received it "en bonne santé," the Neuchâtelois ate it "en bonne compagnie."[12] So it served Mauvelain's purpose, which, he said, his tone becoming constantly more intimate, was to cement his friendship with the publishers. His letters avoided the distasteful topic of his growing debts and concentrated instead on the unscrupulous activities of Bouvet. For Mauvelain had discovered that Bouvet could not be trusted after all: he duped his suppliers, picking quarrels in order to avoid payment and to entangle them in endless litigation. Mauvelain reproached himself for having put the Swiss in contact with such a man, but he would intervene to prevent foul play. The STN should suspend all shipments to Bouvet. It should send Mauvelain its legal "procuration," empowering him to collect Bouvet's bills in its name. And Mauvelain himself would be glad to handle its business in Troyes. He was especially eager to receive copies of Linguet's *Mémoires sur la Bastille*.[13]

On 23 May, Mauvelain sent in an order for six *Fastes de Louis XV*, six *Espion dévalisé*, six *Suite de l'Espion anglois*, and six *Lettres de cachet*. Two weeks later he ordered another half dozen of each and also six *Mémoires sur la Bastille* and a *Vie privée de Louis XV*. Clearly he was buying in bulk, not merely procuring a few odd volumes for friends. And now he offered to serve as the STN's middleman for all its shipments through Champagne. Writing in an off-hand manner as one gentleman who took pleasure in obliging another, he suggested that the director of the STN send everything bound for Paris and vicinity directly to him. He would have the crates relayed safely to their destination: "Mettez-les tout bonnement à mon adresse. C'est l'affaire de mon domestique et voilà tout."[14] At the same time, Mauvelain seemed especially eager to discredit Bouvet, whom he now described as an unregenerate scoundrel. Bouvet had bought his house on credit, Mauvelain explained, and was now so deep in debt that he had moved to a miserable "bicoque" in order to rent the rest of it. He might flee from his creditors at any moment. "Il va faire le métier de libraire roulant: ainsi il n'aura plus de boutique à Troyes, et on craint qu'il ne s'en aille un de ces jours."[15]

Of course Mauvelain did not mean to give the impression that he was destroying the STN's confidence in Bouvet in order to replace him. On the contrary, while stepping up his orders of prohibited books, Mauvelain increased his emphasis on his role as a man of letters. He continued to drop Brissot's name, and he proclaimed his admiration for the abbé Raynal, who had passed through Neuchâtel in the summer of 1783, having had to flee from France because of the scandal aroused by the 1780 edition of his *Histoire philosophique et politique de l'établissement des Européens dans les deux Indes.* "C'est notre maître à tous," Mauvelain exclaimed. "Devant lui nous devons baisser pavillon. Dites-lui combien je l'honore et le respecte au-delà de toute expression et que je soupire ardemment après la nouvelle édition."[16] "Nous" obviously meant "we philosophes." Mauvelain wanted to be associated with France's leading literary figures and kept close track of them: "Est-il vrai, Monsieur, comme il en court le bruit ici, que Mercier est mort entre les bras de l'abbé Raynal, qui s'est dit-on marié?"[17] There was no mistaking where his sympathies lay, and he also made sure that there were no misimpressions about the company he kept. His letters frequently mentioned notables and aristocrats, suggesting that he philosophized as a gentleman and not as one of the obscure, impoverished "pauvres diables" satirized by Voltaire. Mauvelain informed the STN that the marquis de Florian, then visiting Ferney, was one of his relatives and that he had a brother who was a magistrate at Semur-en-Auxois. Not that Mauvelain had any absurd respect for titles. Quite the contrary: a friend had recently written a "Histoire de la ville de Bar-sur-Aube," and Mauvelain had persuaded him to give the printing job to the STN. But the friend would not hand over the manuscript until an expected title had been bestowed on him, because he wanted his name to look as grand as possible on the title page, "comme si le titre d'homme de lettres n'était pas le plus honorable et le plus distingué de tous," Mauvelain commented scornfully. "Je le préfère à tous. . . . O curas hominum, ô quantum [est in] rebus inane!"[18]

So, despite his distinguished social position, Mauvelain was content to be known as a man of letters; that was a central theme in his correspondence. In June 1783 he announced that he was finishing a two-volume "Histoire de Châlons-sur-Marne," which had been delayed only because of "une douleur sur les yeux que m'a causé la lecture de vieilles chartes."[19] He planned to hire the STN to do the printing, of course, but in August he warned of a further delay: the Academy of Châlons wanted to make him a member, and he ought to hold back the prospectus of the book until he had joined the academy. In April 1784, he sent the copy for the prospectus, promising that the text would follow in "quelques mois." But, like all of Mauvelain's projects, this work somehow evaporated before it reached the STN's presses. He ceased to mention it in his letters and instead dangled other proposals before the printers.[20]

The Marquis de Thyard, one of Mauvelain's well-born friends, had written a biography of an ancestor, Pontus de Thyard, a bishop of Châlons in the seventeenth century, and Mauvelain had persuaded him to let the STN print it— an attractive commission, since the marquis would pay for everything and Mauvelain would act as intermediary, handling the distribution of the book. After inspecting the manuscript, the STN said that it was too short to form a volume. Mauvelain offered to flesh it out by providing a genealogy of the Thyard family, and the STN executed the work in late 1784, apparently to the satisfaction of everyone (more on this later). In November 1783, Mauvelain said that he himself had begun work on a history of the *contrôleurs-généraux* of France. He evidently intended to write a political tract, which would capitalize on the polemics aroused by Necker's recent ministry and on the interest in the increasingly sensitive subject of state finance. "Cela sera piquant et se vendra bien," Mauvelain explained, adding that of course it would have to be anonymous.[21] But he wanted to be paid for the manuscript; and the STN preferred to pirate not to purchase its copy, so it refused. Six months later Mauvelain announced that he would soon supply the STN with "un petit roman et une plaisanterie sous le nom d'un capucin."[22] They never materialized, however; nor did two other novels, which he later claimed to have ready for press.[23] Eventually he began to sound somewhat like an underground literary agent rather than a gentleman philosophe. He had procured a spicy, irreligious manuscript from one of his contacts, he wrote on 16 June 1784: "Le livre est bon, l'ouvrage excellent, et sape tout ce que la Bible, la Genèse enseignent sur la création. Il se vendra bien, je vous le promets." An accompanying memorandum (now missing) outlined the work at length. The STN would advance all the printing costs; and once they had been covered by the sales, it would split its profits with the author. "Je me réserve pour mon droit six exemplaires de chaque manuscrit [procured for the STN]," Mauvelain added.[24] The STN did not bite. It also refused Mauvelain's offer of "Pièces érotiques," an anthology of obscene Latin and Italian literature, which had been compiled and translated by "un de mes amis." The unnamed friend would not pay one sou for the printing, but he would supply the manuscript free of charge, or rather in exchange for a few dozen printed copies, which was a common form of payment for hack writers, who often peddled their own works. Mauvelain strongly endorsed the project: "Il y a des choses charmantes; cela se vendra,"[25] and campaigned insistently for it: "Cela se vendra, croyez-moi. Ces livres là sont de débit."[26] The man of letters had evolved into a clandestine businessman.

Faivre and the "Insurance" Business

By that time—the summer of 1784—Mauvelain had corresponded so long with the STN and had sent in so many orders for prohibited books that there was no need to hide the fact that he dealt heavily in the illegal book trade. This role, too, emerged openly in 1784, and it greatly overshadowed his occasional ventures as a manuscript salesman.

But just as they began to involve regular, large-scale transactions, Mauvelain's relations with the STN became embroiled in a crisis that was disrupting the underground book business throughout France.[27] Before the summer of 1783, foreign suppliers did not have to overcome insurmountable obstacles to get their books into France, because they could count on allies among the provincial bookdealers. For a century, the provincials had suffered from the monopolistic practices of the great publishing houses in Paris. They were happy, therefore, to trade with foreign publishers, who could provide cheap pirated and prohibited works; and they favored that trade by neglecting to detect the illegal books that flowed through their provincial guilds and by cooperating with smugglers, usually through the fraudulent discharge of an *acquit à caution,* a customs permit that the state used to regulate book imports. But on 12 June 1783 the government ordered that all *acquits* be discharged after the books were inspected in the Parisian booksellers' guild, no matter what their destination. The order meant that shipments to the provinces would have to make an enormous detour through the capital, that the Parisian booksellers would reinforce the government authorities in cracking down on the illegal trade in the provinces, and that many of the old smuggling techniques would no longer work. Like other foreign publishers, the STN considered the order a disaster, "l'équivalent d'une prohibition absolue," for its French trade.[28] It had learned this lesson the hard way, because in August 1783, soon after the order of 12 June had gone into effect, a border patrol of the Ferme Générale near Pontarlier had seized a shipment from the STN to Lépagnez of Besançon, one of its closest customers in the provinces. In issuing the order, the government had announced its intention of stopping the flow of prohibited works into France. It clearly meant what it said, and the Pontarlier route, which was the STN's favorite and one of the most important in the underground traffic from Switzerland to France, looked especially dangerous.

Mauvelain's shipments had all taken this route, and they had succeeded so well that, as mentioned, he had proposed to act as the STN's agent for all of its traffic through Champagne. The order of 12 June dashed those plans, for in July the STN reported that it could no longer get any books to him. Throughout the summer of 1783, however, he held on to the hope that "les nouvelles entraves ne peuvent pas durer." He absolutely had to get his books, he lamented, or he would be "tourmenté par mes amis."[29] Perhaps the STN had exaggerated the seriousness of the crisis. He had heard that the latest edition of *Le Tableau de Paris* was circulating in Paris, despite the government's attempts to confiscate it,[30] and two new prohibited works, *Les Muses du foyer de l'Opéra* and *La Chronique scandaleuse*, had just appeared on the market. He ordered them on 6 August and kept his ear to the ground, hoping that some way could be found to restore communications with Neuchâtel.[31]

By the end of the summer, it seemed that Mauvelain's perserverance would be rewarded. On 16 August 1783, the STN signed a contract with Faivre of Pontarlier for smuggling its books across the French border. Faivre was a typical entrepreneur of the underground book trade. His origins can not be traced, but he had worked for a while in the book business in Neuchâtel, where the STN had known him as "un homme fort actif, intrigant même, mais qui ne possède rien au-delà de son savoir-faire."[32] In 1771 he established himself as a bookseller in Pontarlier and immediately took up smuggling books across the border for ten livres the quintal. He did not do well enough to avoid bankruptcy in 1773; but he put his business together again in 1776, working out of Pontarlier as a traveling salesman—not an impoverished *colporteur,* it seems, but a semi-indigent *libraire roulant* with horse and carriage, who also sent his wife and daughter around the countryside on "missions." When the crisis of June 1783 put a premium on professional smuggling, Faivre was happy to offer his services to the STN. His contract provided that he should get its crates fom Les Verrières, on the Swiss side of the border, to Pontarlier for fifteen livres per quintal in *assurance.* Such smuggling was literally a kind of insurance. The smuggler or "assureur" bound himself to reimburse his client for the full value of any books that might be seized by the agents of the Ferme Générale who administered the customs stations and policed the borders. Faivre occasionally managed to bribe some customs officers in his area, but he generally relied on teams of *porteurs* who carried the books on their backs in loads of about fifty pounds (*poids de marc*). After a free drink in a tavern at Les Verrières, Switzerland, they would pick up their packs at a secret warehouse and make their way at night along mountainous trails to Faivre's hidden stockrooms in or near Pontarlier, France.

Mauvelain was delighted to learn that the STN had rebuilt its clandestine route to France. On 1 September, he sent in a new order for the usual array of prohibited books and, in an expansive mood, he asked the STN to include a few dozen Neuchâtel cheeses, which he would repay with "des hures, langues et fromages de cochon de Troyes."[33] By this time his letters had revealed that he was an enormously fat man, who enjoyed all the pleasures of life and especially the local *charcuterie,* which still makes Troyes a paradise for the visiting researcher. Nothing had arrived by November, however, when Mauvelain's patience began to run out. His customers had threatened to cancel their orders, he complained. Many prohibited books had already begun to circulate again in Troyes, but his shipments were still stuck in Switzerland. Nothing had reached him by the end of the year, and he consoled himself only with the thought that the Garde des Sceaux, the top official in charge of the book trade, was rumored to be dying.[34]

Meanwhile, Faivre was having difficulty in recruiting porters for his smuggling operation: "Jusques à présént, je n'ai pas pu trouver qui que ce soit pour faire passer votre balle qui est aux Verrières que des gueux d'ivrogne où il n'y a pas a se fier sur le passage," he wrote to the STN on 4 October 1783. "Je ne peux rien vous promettre. Les ordres sont si forts que je ne peux rien gagner sur l'esprit de qui que ce soit pour me donner la main pour le passage des balles."[35] By the end of 1783, however, he had bribed a customs agent and had put together a team of porters, although at a greater expense than he had anticipated: "Je vous préviens," he wrote to the STN, "que je ne peux pas être assureur de vos balles à 15 livres [per quintal], parce qu'il me faut payer aux porteurs 15 livres du cent pesant. Il me faut [donner] à ces porteurs du vin et 8 louis d'or à ceux avec qui je me suis abouché. Mais avec ces 8 louis, je veux entrer 50 à 60 balles et plus."[36] The STN refused to accept any increase in the insurance and began haggling over other terms in the arrangement; so its crates remained in Les Verrières, while Faivre smuggled successfully for other Swiss firms, notably Fauche fils aîné, Favre et Witel, a new publishing house in Neuchâtel. Finally, the STN sent an agent to settle with Faivre; and on 23 January 1784 they signed a new contract, which maintained the old rate of 15 livres per quintal but also stipulated that Faivre could act as a middleman in the lucrative business of forwarding the STN's legal shipments.

Informed at last that the route was definitely open, Mauvelain agreed to pay the insurance costs, as the STN required; and once again he began to pile up his orders, asking for more and more prohibited books. He apparently used the STN as his major source of supply for everything he thought would sell in his region, for he did not merely order from its catalogues but told it to procure books that it did not have in stock from other Swiss firms and to send legal and illegal books together by their new route, "en faisant assurer le tout à 15 livres pour cent pesant, car 400 livres pesant ne feront que 60 livres de frais, ce qui sera 3 sols par volume. C'est une bagatelle, au lieu que le voyage par Paris, sans compter les frais, causera un retard considérable."[37] In fact, the high proportion of *livres philosophiques* in Mauvelain's orders showed that they made up the bulk of his business—and soon he began to do business in bulk.

The great jump in the size of Mauvelain's orders came in the spring of 1784, when Faivre finally succeeded in getting the first shipments through to him. Heavy snows had made the mountain trails impassable until April, and even then, Faivre wrote to the STN, "Les amas de neiges qu'il y a encore ont beaucoup fatigué mes porteurs. Ils m'ont passé 6 balles cette nuit, tant de Lausanne que de chez vous et de Berne. Ils viennent de se remettre en route pour en entrer autant."[38] By 22 April, his men had carried eighteen crates over the mountains—dangerous, back-breaking work, which had not been made easier by the STN's packers: "Mes porteurs vous prient de faire les balles par la suite qu'elles ne pesent les plus gros 60 livres et des petites de 40 livres," Faivre wrote.[39] And at last on 26 April, he reported, "Vos balles pour Troyes en Champagne marqués MT 183, BM 13, tous les deux pour M. Bruzard de Mauvelain avocat à Troyes, sont parties ce matin pour Besançon pour y prendre la route par Langres et la Champagne."[40]

The two crates arrived safely at Troyes on 7 May 1784. Although he found the insurance and transport costs steep (60 livres in all), Mauvelain was overjoyed: the new route worked, and he immediately placed a gigantic order for all sorts of books, including *Les Petits Soupers du Comte de Vergennes* and *Le Passe-temps d'Antoinette,* two of the latest libels about the queen and the ministers. These were the very works that the government had attempted to suppress by its order of 12 June 1783. Only someone deeply involved in the literary underground would have known that they existed in the spring of 1784. Mauvelain, who hoped to sell them in large numbers, clearly specialized in such literature. He chided the STN for failing to supply all the prohibited books he had ordered: it should get what it lacked from other Swiss houses and should not send merely pirated editions of inoffensive works. "Je vous dirai franchement, Monsieur, que mes amis sont fâchés de ne recevoir que des livres courants en France, qu'il est inutile, disent-ils, de faire venir de si loin [ce] qui leur coûtent aussi cher par les frais et peut-être plus qu'ils ne seraient en France. Ils veulent en être dédommagés par des livres prohibés, qui sont rares et qu'on se procure plus difficilement ici."[41]

Mauvelain did not send a bill of exchange upon reception of the merchandise, as was customary in the book trade; but he offered to send the STN a gift of another boar's head and some tongues, and the tone of his letters became still more intimate: "Soyons amis, Monsieur, je vous prie."[42] On 10 May, he had written to F. S. Ostervald, who handled the correspondence of the STN, that he wanted to come to Neuchâtel "vous embrasser. C'est un désir violent qui me tourmente." On 17 May, he announced that he would make the trip in September, bearing money and *charcuterie.* Meanwhile, he would see to the collection of Bouvet's debt, which had gone unpaid for a year.

The STN had supplied Bouvet with two shipments of books in early 1783. Far from being "un des plus fort libraires de ce pays,"[43] as Mauvelain had first described him, Bouvet seems to have been a marginal type, who teetered on the brink of bankruptcy and gambled in the risky but profitable trade of prohibited books as a means of saving himself. In September 1783, Mauvelain told the STN that it would not get a sou out of Bouvet unless they took him to court. In December he reported that two or three of Bouvet's creditors had had him condemned for nonpayment, and he advised the STN to do the same by making out a bill of exchange to him (Mauvelain) drawing on Bouvet so that he could force the collection of the debt. The STN sent the bill of exchange, but Mauvelain then decided not to require its payment, "par complaisance pour sa femme," as he explained mysteriously.[44] He said that he favored negotiation, and by July 1784 it looked as though that strategy might succeed, for Bouvet had decided to sell his house (Mauvelain had moved out of it long ago) in order to pay his debts. The STN could make sure that it got its share of the money from the sale, Mauvelain wrote, if it sent another bill of exchange on Bouvet in Mauvelain's name; he would insist on its payment this time. The STN complied, and in August Mauvelain reported that the maneuver was working.[45] But then he dropped the subject. The STN did not discover what had become of its bills of exchange until the spring of 1785, when it was too late to rescue them.

In the autumn of 1784, after Mauvelain's letters had ceased to mention Bouvet, their main subject was the duplicity of the other booksellers of Troyes and Mauvelain's determination to save the STN from getting swindled by them. This theme was calculated to get a warm response in Neuchâtel, because the STN had been burned in its dealings with Sainton and André, two other Troyens who specialized in the illegal book trade. Sainton had done business with the STN in a small way since 1776, when he had said that he was eager to trade with them if they were good at smuggling: "Je prends beaucoup d'ouvrages philosophiques. Ainsi envoyez m'en une note."[46] He had not paid his bills by July 1784. So the Neuchâtelois hardly needed Mauvelain's warning: "Ne faites point d'affaires avec Sainton. Il est très difficulteux et très difficile au paiement."[47] Mauvelain also told the STN not to trust André, who had the dubious distinction of being Bouvet's brother-in-law and who had refused to pay the STN for a copy of its pirated edition of the *Description des arts et métiers*, because it had been seized by the police. The two booksellers were "coquins," Mauvelain explained: they purposefully entangled their affairs so as to avoid paying, but he would cut through their defenses and force them to honor their debts.[48] In his later letters, he talked militantly of lawsuits: "Les Bouvet, les André, les Sainton sont des fripons avec lesquels il n'y a rien à faire qu'avec justice."[49] But he never collected any money, or at least he never sent any to Neuchâtel. He did, however, win the STN's gratitude for helping it against "la race tortue et perverse des libraires de Troyes"[50]—no small success, as far as he was concerned, for it indicated that he was gaining its "confidence."

The confidential tone of Mauvelain's letters increased throughout the last six months of 1784. He suffered from occasional deafness, he wrote on 9 July. Could he prevail upon Ostervald, in the name of their friendship, to solicit a written "consultation" from Auguste Tissot, the famous doctor of Lausanne? Mauvelain would gladly reimburse Ostervald for Tissot's fee; and soon he would send yet another boar's head with some tongues. The deafness had improved a few weeks later; but, Mauvelain complained, "Mon estomac est délabré et ma machine souffrante."[51] Familiar remarks about his health, his devotion to Ostervald, and *charcuterie* garnished the rest of Mauvelain's letters—without slackening the growth in his orders for books. Meanwhile, Faivre's smuggling continued to go well. On 22 July, he informed the STN that another batch of crates, which probably included some for Mauvelain, had crossed the border and were en route to customers in the provinces. Mauvelain made an open bid to become a clandestine distributor for the STN: "Je puis beaucoup étendre votre commerce et vous procurer un gros débit, ayant beaucoup de facilités pour faire entrer chez moi beaucoup de ballots, ayant une porte de derrière isolée et commode, des remises fermantes, greniers où tous vos paquets seront en sûreté."[52] Two weeks later he wrote that a publisher near the STN (presumably the house of Samuel Fauche) had offered to supply him with "tous les livres possibles." But he had refused because he would only deal with the STN: "Vous pouvez comptez sur moi à la vie et à la mort."[53] On 9 August, he explained that the STN's competitor might be able to undersell it by charging a flat rate of 3 sols per pound (*poids de marc*) for smuggling and transport. But if the STN reduced its handling charges and made him its agent, he could extend its business enormously. "Connu et répandu comme je suis, je puis vous procurer un débit immense. En m'envoyant beaucoup de livres dont je vous compterai à mesure que je les placerai, je vous en ferai vendre en Bourgogne et en Champagne."[54] The STN should supply him with an inventory of books; he would stock them in his hiding places; and he would market them throughout northeastern France, paying the STN as his sales progressed.

Mallet and Mirabeau: An Underground Press

This plan was interrupted by the arrival in Troyes of a man who personified yet another aspect of the underground book trade. Jacques Mallet, typesetter, peddler, police spy, and publisher, turned up in Mauvelain's apartment a year after having been released from the Bastille, where he had been imprisoned for selling prohibited books. By good fortune, the police record of his interrogation has survived (it is printed at the end of this essay). As Mallet confessed almost everything he knew and as he knew almost everything that there was to be known about the book trade out of Neuchâtel, his confession is worth studying in detail. It provides some rare glimpses of a clandestine publishing operation and the milieu of operators like Mauvelain.

On 20 July 1782, Mallet told the police, he became a partner in Fauche fils aîné, Favre et Witel, a publishing house which had been established recently in Neuchâtel and which specialized in printing prohibited books. At that time, the firm had a contract with Mirabeau for the publication of everything he could send to it from the prison of Pontarlier, where he was awaiting trial for his celebrated abduction and seduction of the marquise de Monnier. Mirabeau's adventures had provided him with plenty of material for books about prisons and sex, and he supplied the Neuchâtel publishers with the manuscripts of three works: *Des lettres de cachet et des prisons d'Etat, Le Libertin de qualité ou ma conversion,* and *Errotika Biblion.*[55]

Mallet described the production of *Des lettres de cachet* in glorious detail. Mirabeau doled out the manuscript page by page from his cell, where he also corrected the proof as it was sent to him sheet by sheet. The publishers had no worries about being disturbed by the prison guards (the better sort of eighteenth-century prisons seem to have been great centers of literary production), but they wanted to make sure that the municipal authorities of Neuchâtel would not object to the printing of such a radical work; so they also sent the proofs to some leading citizens in the town. Not only did the Neuchâtelois approve of the text, they suggested ways to improve it and passed it around as if they enjoyed getting a preview of a book that was bound to create a sensation in Paris. Having agreed to a compromise settlement of his case, Mirabeau himself then arrived in

Neuchâtel and was feted all over town. But he got a cold reception from his printers. They had paid him 150 louis (3,600 livres) for *Des lettres de cachet*—an enormous sum for a publishing venture in the eighteenth century—and they wanted to bring down the cost of the other two manuscripts.[56] Mallet and his associates protested at the danger and the expense of publishing such radical and pornographic works, but Mirabeau would not bargain. He insisted on receiving a security deposit of 100 louis (2,400 livres) before he let the manuscripts out of his hands; and once he had collected the deposit, he refused to permit the publishers even to examine the manuscript of the *Errotika biblion* until they had paid for it in advance. That may not have been an altogether outrageous demand in a trade where manuscripts were often stolen or copied furtively for pirating, but it was too much for Fauche fils aîné, Favre et Witel, who broke off negotiations and took the dispute to arbitrators. As a result of the arbitration, the publishers finally got the *Errotika biblion* and *Le Libertin de qualité*, but they had to give Mirabeau another 1,000 livres in books, which he was to choose from their stock.[57]

They had built up this stock from the inventory of Witel's earlier bookselling business (it included well-known prohibited works like *Les lauriers ecclésiastiques, La Réduction de Paris, La Vérité rendue sensible à Louis XVI,* and *L'Espion dévalisé*), from commerce with the neighboring houses of Samuel Fauche and the STN, and from trades with other Swiss publishers. Mallet could only recall one of these trades: 50 of his firm's *Lettres de cachet* for 50 *Fastes de Louis XV,* one of the best-selling anticourt libels, which was provided by a dealer in Basel. But Witel handled the trading. Mallet was the traveling salesman of the firm, and in December 1782 he left on a trip through Switzerland and France, evidently carrying sample volumes and handwritten catalogues of *livres philosophiques* drawn up from the catalogues of Samuel Fauche and the STN as well as from the inventory of his own stock. First, Mallet called on some Swiss publishers and wholesalers of prohibited French books. In Lausanne, he sold *Lettres de cachet* to La Combe, Heubach, Grasset, Des Combes, Pott, and Mourer (even though Mourer was already printing a pirated edition of it). He found no buyers in Geneva. But in Lyons, he sold *Lettres de cachet, L'Espion dévalisé,* and other works to several dealers: Jacquenet, Rosset, Grabit, Los Rios, Barret, LeRoy, Bernuset. "Il ne leur a pas été difficile de les faire entrer, parce qu'ils sont presque tous de la Chambre syndicale (the local booksellers' guild)," Mallet explained to the police. Next stop, Paris: Desauges and Hardouin, disreputable dealers who traded heavily in prohibited books, ordered a variety of works from him, but the shipments, which apparently followed the Pontarlier route from Neuchâtel, were seized in Besançon. Mallet said that he did not do very well with the other Parisian booksellers, but he sold an allotment to Poinçot, one of the most important clandestine dealers in Versailles, where the greatest entrepôts of prohibited books were located. On his way back, Mallet failed to do any business with Mailly, an important dealer in Dijon, and sold only a few books to Chamboz of Dôle, who preferred to order his forbidden books from Samuel Fauche. In

Besançon, he mainly dealt with Lépagnez, the bookseller who oversaw the smuggling operations of Fauche fils aîné, Favre et Witel, and in Pontarlier he sold a great many *Lettres de cachet* to Faivre, the smuggler of the STN.

In short, Mallet made a clandestine, literary *tour de France,* and he described every stop of it to the police with full details about the names of the bookdealers and the books they ordered. This information proved to be crucial in the government's decision to maintain and enforce the order of 12 June 1783, despite impassioned protests by the booksellers. During Mallet's *embastillement,* the directeur de la librairie received a memorandum from one of his subordinates which argued that the order should not be revoked, because it provided the most effective way of checking the flow of prohibited books. To sustain this argument, the memorandum went into a full discussion of the techniques of book smuggling and noted pointedly, "Il y a maintenant à la Bastille un particulier associé avec des libraires de Neuchâtel, qui par ses aveux et déclarations confirme l'usage que l'on fait de tous ces moyens."[58]

When he arrived back in Neuchâtel in the early spring of 1783, Mallet had no idea that touring of this sort would lead him to the Bastille; but soon after he returned, his partners sent him on a fatal mission to Paris. This time he was to check on their supply routes and to handle some financial affairs. While passing through Besançon, he told Lépagnez to take more care with his smuggling, because the publishers planned to send their new edition of the *Tableau de Paris* through Besançon and all but one of their previous shipments by that route had been confiscated. The successful shipment had contained about 150 *Lettres de cachet,* 4 to 6 *Fastes de Louis XV,* 6 *Espion anglois,* 21 *Espion dévalisé,* and 200 *Errotika biblion.* After he arrived in Paris, Mallet learned that the underground traffic was flowing more smoothly than he had expected. In early June he received twelve crates of prohibited books at his secret stockpile near Bourg-la-Reine. He transferred them into small packages and then transported them, a few at a time, into Paris simply by taking them with him on the public coach, which was not searched at the customs barrier, because it served the local traffic between Bourg and the capital. In this way Mallet supplied various Parisian booksellers with 270 copies of a Lausanne edition of Linguet's *Mémoires sur la Bastille,* 50 *Histoire de Suzon,* and an "assortissement" of other prohibited works, including the *Lettres de cachet.* But he took a false step in early July, and soon he was confessing everything to the lieutenant-general of police: "Je supplie très humblement Monseigneur de ne pas me perdre. Tout ce que j'ai fait dans le commerce de la librairie, je n'en connaissais pas les dangers; c'est plutôt par ignorance que par intérêt ou méchanceté. Tous les livres que j'ai vendus, je ne les ai jamais lus. Je suis extrêmement borné dans ce genre de commerce. Daignez, Monseigneur, avoir quelques égards pour ma petite famille: au nom de l'Etre Suprême, ne me perdez pas. Je fais serment que je ne ferai jamais plus le commerce de librairie, ni en France ni dans l'étranger. . . . Notre maison est entièrement ruinée et discréditée par les pertes considérables que nous avons essuyées cette anneé et le retard de faire mes paiements que me cause ma détention."

A year later, Fauche fils aîné, Favre et Witel was still fighting off bankruptcy, and Mallet, who had extricated himself from the Bastille and no longer had any connection with the firm, unexpectedly appeared before Mauvelain. "Il m'a été amené depuis ma dernière," Mauvelain informed the STN, "un homme sortant de la Bastille qui a, m'a-t-il dit, une maison de commerce dans votre ville en librairie qui a ou cessé ou manqué absolument. Il assure avoir encore dans votre ville sa maison avec beaucoup de livres qu'il voudrait en faire venir, il sait comment. Ces renseignements pourront vous faire reconnaître le personnage, qui, pour en revenir à lui, m'a fait beaucoup solliciter de lui livrer des anecdotes rares manuscrites venant d'un homme en place sur la cour qu'il voulait joindre à ce livre intitulé *Entretiens de feu Louis XV et de ses ministres* qu'il avait et dont il voudrait faire deux volumes au lieu d'un. Il avait aussi des *Barjac* [i.e., the obscene novel *Le Vicomte de Barjac*], des *Diables dans un bénitier* [another anticourt libel that the government was trying especially hard to suppress] dont je n'ai point voulu. J'ai refusé net ces anecdotes (que je garde pour vous), en disant que je les avais rendues. . . . Je l'ai pris pour un espion. Ai-je eu tort? Expliquez-moi tout cela."[59] A week later, Ostervald of the STN replied with a description of Mallet that made him seem rather less naive and repentant than he did in his confession to the police: "Voici son portrait pour le physique et le morale. Il se nomme Mallet, est agé d'environ 35 ans, maigre, cheveux noirs, parlant assez mal, taille tout au plus de 5 pieds. Travaillant à Lyon comme ouvrier compositeur, il fit la connaissance de la femme d'un paumier ayant quatre enfants avec laquelle il partit pour Genève. Là, ayant été chagriné par la police, il l'a conduite ici, où elle a trouvé et trouve encore à faire usage de sa beauté. Une circonstance assez plaisante, c'est qu'après un assez long séjour dans notre ville, Mallet voulait bien la restituer moyennant qu'on lui payât sa pension. Mais le paumier, un homme sage, a laissé ici la femelle et a gardé son argent. Elle s'est associée avec d'autres et a eu assez de crédit pour monter une petite imprimerie. Mallet a fait un voyage à Paris et fut mis à la Bastille pour avoir offert publiquement des ouvrages licentieux. De retour ici, il s'est brouillé avec ses associés et les a quittés. Ils disent hautement que c'est un coquin. Il s'est aussi flatté d'être espion de la police, condition sous laquelle il dit avoir obtenu son élargissement. On dit qu'il a établi une imprimerie dans votre ville ou aux environs et qu'il vient d'imprimer *Le Libertin de qualité*, ce livre qui fait tant de bruit en France et ici. C'est un fait dont il me serait très important d'être certioré. Tel est, entre nous, le personnage. Défiez-vous de lui et tâchez de vous défaire d'un aussi mauvais voisin."[60]

Mauvelain did not need to be prompted to keep his eye on such a dangerous competitor. Soon he reported that Mallet had installed a printing press in a country house outside of Troyes and already was marketing an impressive selection of prohibited books: *La Tentation de Saint Antoine, Histoire de Marguerite, Anecdotes de la vie d'Ambroise Borelly, Conversations du Comte de Mirabeau avec le Garde des Sceaux, La Muse libertine, La Cassette verte mauvaise, Ma conversion* (with 6 plates), *Essais historiques et critiques, Le Vol plus haut ou l'espion des principaux théâtres de la capitale, Supplément à l'Espion dévalisé, Réforme du clergé, Amusements d'un bon Picard, Muses du foyer de l'Opéra, Contes géologiques, La Vérité rendue sensible à Louis XVI.* "Si vous voulez un exemplaire de chacun de ses livres," Mauvelain added suggestively, "Je vous en enverrai un. Vous les imprimerez."[61] Ostervald replied that he, too, felt threatened by Mallet's activities: "Je suis bien aise d'être maintenant assuré par les détails que vous m'en donnez qu'il s'imprime d'aussi bonnes drogues dans le coeur du royaume, et je tirerai bon parti d'une telle découverte. Vous savez que jamais rien de licentieux n'a souillé nos presses; mais comme on en demande souvent, il nous convient de pouvoir au besoin en trouver autour de nous. . . . Presque tous ces chefs-d'oeuvre dont vous m'indiquez les titres sont encore inconnus ici. Mais l'honnête Mallet ne manquera pas sans doute d'en assortir ses correspondants en Suisse; et s'ils en débitent, la France jettera les hauts cris et continuera de proscrire toute typographie venant de notre pauvre ville. Voilà comment les choses vont dans ce meilleur des mondes."[62]

Ostervald was not referring to the general crackdown on the foreign book trade since June 1783 but to special measures against the printing of prohibited books in Neuchâtel. The French government had learned that a later edition of *Le Libertin de qualité ou ma conversion* was being printed in Neuchâtel, and it had exerted diplomatic pressure to get the printing stopped. One reason for the flourishing of the publishing industry in this small corner of Switzerland was that Neuchâtel had been a Prussian principality since 1707. For printers of *livres philosophiques,* it would be difficult to find a better sovereign than Frederick II, who did little to correct the laxness of the municipal executive authority called the Quatre Ministraux. Although the Quatre Ministraux occasionally felt obliged to investigate printing shops, they always arrived too late to find incriminating evidence. In response to a request from the French ambassador at Soleure, they searched the town for *Le Libertin de qualité* in August 1784 and, as usual, found nothing. But the ambassador had information derived from Mallet's confession in the Bastille and perhaps also from later reports by Mallet, if indeed he had become a police spy. So the ambassador insisted that the Quatre Ministraux look harder and in particular that they seek out Mallet's wife, who was reported to have had the manuscript of the book in her possession the previous winter. With most of the detective work being furnished from Paris, the Quatre Ministraux at last managed to find the trail of *Le Libertin de qualité.* "Madame" Mallet told them that indeed she had had the manuscript more than a year ago, while her husband was in Paris, and that she had given it to Fauche fils aîné, Favre et Witel, who had printed it. Favre then admitted to having bought the manuscript from Mirabeau but claimed that Mallet had made off with it and had published it himself. Since Mallet had gone underground in France, the investigators could not question him. Their inquiry dragged on until June 1785, when Fauche fils aîné, Favre et Witel were found guilty and had their shop closed. Meanwhile, the affair gave Ostervald a scare, because as he explained to one of his correspondents, "Quoique notre petit pays soit bien indépendant, nous avons les plus grands ménagements à garder vis-à-vis de la France, à cause de nos fabriques, du commerce, et du voisinage."[63] A correspondent in Paris had warned him that Neuchâtel was swarming with spies of the French police, and Ostervald must have

known how in 1764 the police had raided three publishers in Bouillon, another
small and defenseless principality on the French border, which was a center for
the production of prohibited books.[64] The giant across the Jura could, if sufficiently
aroused, crush the STN's trade in France and even hurt the STN in Neuchâtel.

It was at the height of this crisis during the summer and autumn of 1784
that Ostervald learned, to his delight, that Mallet had turned up in Troyes. Perhaps Mallet's secret presses had produced the very works that the French expected to confiscate in Neuchâtel or Pontarlier. "Puisque Mallet vous assortit
ainsi de mauvais livres," he wrote to Mauvelain on 19 October, "marquez-moi, je
vous prie, s'il s'en trouve un qui ait pour titre le *Libertin de qualité* en un volume
octavo. J'ai grand intérêt à le savoir." The point, of course, was to prove to
Versailles that it would do better to turn its police onto territory closer to home.
Ostervald made his motive perfectly clear in his next letter to Mauvelain:
"L'affaire du *Libertin de qualité* dont je vous parlais dans ma dernière fait
toujours beaucoup de bruit. La cour de France continue à se plaindre de ce que
l'on diffère trop de punir ceux qui ont mis sous presse ce mauvais livre. C'est ce
qui me fait désirer de savoir si Mallet en débite autour de vous."[65] Mauvelain
replied obligingly, "Le sieur Mallet débite, puisque vous voulez le savoir, et
inonde le pays du *Libertin de qualité*. Il a changé le titre en celui de *Ma conversion*. Il y a 6 estampes dans le livre que j'ai lu. Tout le monde l'a ici. . . . Il
en a des ballots, à ce qu'on m'a assuré, gros comme des lits. . . . Vous pouvez
tenir le fait sûr. On m'a offert de me les faire voir. J'ai refusé."[66] That was
exactly the information he needed, Ostervald replied. "J'en ai fait usage où il
convenait. Les libraires qui, dit-on, l'ont imprimé n'ont point été inquiétés jusqu'à
présent, et je suppose que notre gouvernement aura répondu au ministère de
France en réclamant notre indépendance."[67]

After the crisis had passed, the references to Mallet dropped out of the
correspondence between the STN and Mauvelain until February 1785, when
Mauvelain complained vehemently that the STN had let his confidential information leak out and that Mallet had learned of all their dealings. "Cela va me
compromettre avec un étourdi que je ne connais ni ne veux connaître. . . . Il sait
tous nos secrets. . . . Je suis au désespoir qu'un homme comme moi passe par
la langue d'un homme de cette espèce."[68] Mauvelain found it unnerving to know
that his clandestine book business had been discovered by a man who was both
a competitor and reputedly a police spy. But the STN reassured him that it had
protected his secrecy, and soon he was convinced that Mallet had lied to him
about the leak, presumably as a ruse to ellicit some compromising information
about the Neuchâtel trade. "Je le ferai pincer un de ces jours," Mauvelain concluded. "J'ai des amis du crédit. Je n'en suis point embarrassé. Je vous vengerai
de lui et de toutes le faussetés qu'il débite ici sur votre compte."[69] Whether or not
Mauvelain ever succeeded in getting this dangerous neighbor back into prison
and whether or not Mallet really was a double agent can never be known, because
at this point his name disappears from the archives.

In corresponding about Mallet, the STN and Mauvelain clarified their
roles in the illegal book trade. Mauvelain emerged as an active distributor of

prohibited books and he showed himself to be well informed about the tricks of the trade. In fact he offered to provide the STN with the latest *livres philosophiques* so that it could produce its own editions of them, and he even offered to supply it with a manuscript libel. The STN refused to print such extreme works, but it admitted that it stocked them and sold them in large numbers. A new note of frankness came into the exchanges of letters, and Ostervald began slipping into the intimate mode of discourse favored by Mauvelain. He expressed sympathy for Mauvelain's perpetual ailments; and although he failed to get the requested "consultation" out of Tissot, he sent some written advice from a doctor in Geneva. Meanwhile, Mauvelain was in the most active phase of his efforts to force the bookdealers of Troyes to pay their debts to the STN. Having virtually become an agent of his Swiss "friends," Mauvelain was now the only person in Troyes with whom they still did business. His relations with them reached a peak of cordiality in the autumn of 1784. He had captured their confidence.

A Smuggling Circuit: Cost and Effectiveness

The Mallet episode also affected the flow of books between Neuchâtel and Troyes. While applying diplomatic pressure to get the Neuchâtel authorities to suppress the production of prohibited books, the French government ordered its customs agents to prevent their distribution by maintaining a special alert along the French-Swiss border near Pontarlier. In August 1784 the agents arrested five porters carrying crates full of *Le Libertin de qualité* and other prohibited works, which were being smuggled into France for Fauche fils aîné, Favre et Witel. This disaster produced consternation up and down the Pontarlier route. Although he had had no part of it, Faivre immediately warned the STN to suspend all shipments. "Depuis ce malheureux moment tous les employés des fermes sont nuit et jour en alerte," he lamented.[70] His porters, who could be sent to the galleys if they were caught, would no longer take the slightest risk; and the STN's crates were not even safe in their secret entrepôt in the home of François Michaut, Faivre's relay man at Les Verrières, on the Swiss side of the border, "parce qu'il y a des espions et des coquins aux Verrières, qui vendent les autres."[71] Faivre ordered Michaut to hide the books on top of a nearby mountain until the crisis passed and the clandestine route could be rebuilt. The STN notified Mauvelain that the breakdown of the smuggling operation had caused six of his crates to be stranded near the border, "en attendant que l'orage soit un peu calmé. . . . Il n'en résultera que quelques retards. Notre homme [Faivre, whom they never mentioned by name in their letters to France] sait son métier et est intéressé lui-même à bien prendre ses mesures."[72] The news upset Mauvelain, because he had made advance sales of some of the books to army officers, who soon would be transferred from Troyes. Others were destined for local customers, who had grown so impatient that they were threatening to cancel their orders. And a third group had been promised to Parisians, who were about to return to the capital after spending the summer months near Troyes and so would probably refuse to accept the books, "le moment de la vogue étant passé et les trouvant partout à bon marché."[73] A great deal of damage had been done to Mauvelain's market by early October, when at last he received an encouraging letter from the STN: "Notre assureur commence à se *rassurer,* comme il paraît par une lettre reçue de lui il y a huit jours. En conséquence, nous garnissons toujours de plus en plus le dépôt. L'approche de l'hiver et de ses neiges nous sera favorable."[74]

Faivre had counted on overcoming his porters' fears of arrest by increasing their wages and by bribing some of the customs agents. On 14 October 1784, he reported to the STN, "Samedi prochain vos balles entreront. J'ai tant fait et promis à ces porteurs que je leur donnerait de quoi boire et qu'ils seront contents, ce qui les a ranimés à retourner. . . . Je suis au moment de traiter avec un employé des fermes pour nous laisser passer librement la nuit et m'indiquer les chemins où l'on doit passer en sûreté." Five days later, the STN tried to pacify Mauvelain with the news that "notre homme" was about to conclude "un arrangement solide" for the smuggling. And on 21 October, Faivre reported that the first crates had got through successfully and that future shipments would be helped if the STN could provide him with three copies of an erotic novel for his allies among "ces Messieurs de la ferme du roi." His main difficulty came from his labor force: "Les porteurs me rançonnent. Ils m'ont augmenté de 6 deniers par livre, et ce qu'il me faut payer d'un autre côté [à] ceux qui me donnent la main [i.e., his bribes], le temps perdu pour les voyages, après tout compté, j'en suis pour le mien."[75] Five crates arrived in Faivre's stockrooms on the night of 12 November, and he forwarded them on to Mauvelain soon afterward. Another shipment came through safely on 18 November.[76] So at last the way was clear for smooth and regular trading, when new difficulties arose, this time on Mauvelain's end.

As soon as the STN learned that "notre homme de la frontière" had got Mauvelain's first two crates through the new route, it sent the good news to Troyes: "Voilà donc enfin les derniers obstacles levés." It also requested Mauvelain to send payment for the shipments he had received before the route had closed—unless he still planned to bring the money with him on a trip to Neuchâtel that year.[77] Mauvelain had avoided the subject of payment. Whenever he mentioned it, he said that he would settle his bills during his visit, which he kept postponing. On 11 October 1784 he announced that he could not make the journey at present, owing to the deterioration of his health. Physically, he traced his trouble to "l'humeur fébrile"; morally, to his sensitivity: "Un homme qui a l'âme sensible est plus malheureux qu'un autre. La méchanceté des ses semblables l'attristent." But Mauvelain could not remain insensitive to the STN's requests for payment after November, when the new shipments arrived. At this point the tone of his letters suddenly changed. He began to quibble over costs, to complain about the way the crates were shipped, and to haggle like a man who needed pretexts for refusing to pay his bills. This was the classic defense of the toughest customers in the illegal trade, as the STN had just mentioned in a letter to Mauvelain about his attempts to collect its debts from the other booksellers of Troyes: "Il est à remarquer que ces bonnes gens ne commencent à faire des

objections que quand on leur demande des espèces."[78] Mauvelain's bickering made
theirs seem mild, and it is especially interesting, because it contains a great deal
of information about the economics of the underground book trade. Since there
has never been any economic analysis of this kind of commerce, it merits a short
digression.

Smuggling books was a complicated business. The merchandise was bulky,
dangerous, and easily damaged, because most publishers like the STN sent their
books in the form of unfolded, printed sheets (a sheet of a quarto volume containing eight printed pages, an octavo sixteen pages, and so on), which its packers
stuffed into crates, using straw and spoilt sheets (*maculature*) to protect against
friction and damp. Mauvelain required that his books be folded and stitched,[79]
and they had to be sent in small crates of 50 or 60 pounds, so that Faivre's
porters could carry them. (Faivre complained that the STN tended to make its
crates too heavy, and he once divided a large crate into two, "parce qu'un homme
ne peut pas porter 110 livres sur son corps.")[80] The crates left Neuchâtel on horse-
drawn wagons and made their way up the difficult roads of the Val de Travers
to the secret storehouse of François Michaut, Faivre's agent in Les Verrières, the
last town on the Swiss side of the border. The porters then back-packed them at
night along mountain trails near the French customs station of Frambourg,
where Faivre had bribed the agents of the Ferme to slacken their vigilance, and
deposited them in Faivre's clandestine warehouse in or near Pontarlier. Faivre
then consolidated them into large crates, loaded them onto wagons, and sent
them off to Besançon as if they were ordinary domestic shipments (only foreign
books had to make the detour to the Parisian booksellers' guild). In Besançon
they were unloaded and stored by a shipping agent called Péchey, a well-known
figure in the underground book trade, who worked hand-in-glove with local
bookdealers, notably Lépagnez. Péchey paid the waggoner who delivered the
crates to him for all the expenses, including the insurance, that they had accu-
mulated since their departure from Neuchâtel. When he found a place for them
on a wagon bound for Troyes, he added those expenses, his own, and those of
the last stage of the journey together in a single bill, which the waggoner had to
collect before he could unload the merchandise into Mauvelain's hidden store-
rooms. The waggoner—Claude Carteret of Langres in the case of Mauvelain's
largest shipment—would present Mauvelain's bill of exchange to Péchey on a
return trip and would receive payment in cash for his own services.

It is thus possible to reconstruct this clandestine circuit in detail, following
the books and the accumulation of their expenses as they passed from agent to
agent in the network linking Neuchâtel and Troyes. Map 1 shows how one
shipment progressed along the route, stage by stage and day by day:

March–June 1784: Mauvelain sends in his orders in a series of four letters.
26 July (approximately): The STN sends off the seven crates numbered BM 107–110,
   BT 120, and BM 121–22, weighing 440 livres (poids de marc) in all.
4 October: Faivre reports that all of the crates have been stalled at Michaut's storehouse in Les Verrières, owing to the critical new conditions at the border.
14 October: Faivre writes that he has reconstructed his smuggling system: the customs
   agents at Frambourg have been won over, and his porters will resume work soon.

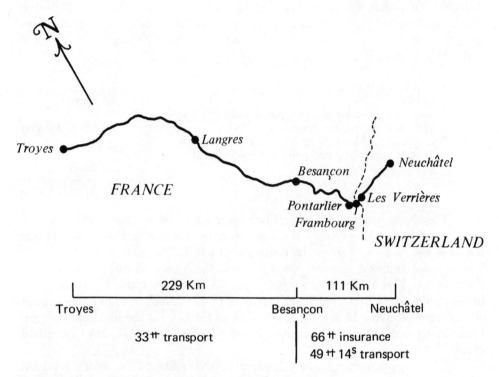

12 November: The first five of Mauvelain's crates cross the border.

18 November: The other crates arrive safely in Pontarlier and will be forwarded by Faivre to Péchey in Besançon the next day.

Early December: Péchey's waggoner, Claude Carteret, loads the seven crates on his cart in Besançon and sets off for Troyes.

31 December: Mauvelain acknowledges reception of the crates, which arrived at some previous date, probably soon after 13 December.

By making wagon drivers double as bill collectors, this system prevented persons from refusing to pay the shipping charges, as they frequently did when it came to paying the manufacturer. But it was slow and expensive. Mauvelain's books took five months to cover the 210 miles between him and the STN—not an uncommon delay for the smuggling industry, where a single confiscation or the transfer of one corrupt customs agent could back up traffic for weeks. The total cost of the shipment (148 livres 14 sous), came to 15 percent of its wholesale value (1019 livres 11 sous). And worst of all, the system of c.o.d. payments offered great possibilities for peculation to the middlemen. The consignment note (*lettre de voiture*) mentioned only two charges: the total cost of the Neuchâtel-Besançon leg of the journey (115 livres 14 sous) and the costs between Besançon and Troyes (33 livres). Mauvelain had to pay both. He could understand the latter, because the note informed him that the seven crates weighed 440 pounds in all and that the carrying rate from Besançon to Troyes was 7 livres 10 sous per quintal. But he had no way of knowing the real costs of the first stage of the shipment. Of course the insurance cost him 15 livres per quintal, or 66 livres, which he could subtract from the 115 livres 4 sous in order to estimate the handling charges between Neuchâtel and Troyes (49 livres 14 sous). So he could make the following calculations:

Insurance for the border crossing (15 livres per quintal)	66 livres
Transport & handling charges, Neuchâtel to Besançon (rate per quintal not given)	49 livres 14 sous
Transport & handling, Besançon to Troyes (7 livres 10 sous per quintal and some minor additional charges)	33 livres
	148 livres 14 sous

Clearly it was the Neuchâtel-Besançon stage, where the crates changed hands many times, that offered the most opportunities for padding costs. It was the most mountainous part of the route, but it was half as long as the Besançon-Troyes stage and cost twice as much; so something seemed to be wrong, especially as the STN said that it normally paid 3 livres per quintal for shipments between Besançon and Neuchâtel. At that rate, Mauvelain would have been overcharged 36 livres 12 sous, or 24 percent of the bill for the handling charges. Considering that insurance accounted for 45 percent of that bill, Mauvelain had reason to complain.

The complaints began in a letter of 15 November 1784, which reported that crates number 105 and 106, the first two to be sent through the new route, had arrived on the previous day. But the wagon driver had demanded so much in carrying expenses that Mauvelain had decided to hold back his payment to the STN for the actual purchase of the books. In the first place, he argued, he had had to wait almost a year for some of them, and he did not know whether his own customers would honor their orders after such a delay. But more important, the carrying charges were outrageous. They came to 51 livres for two crates weighing 150 pounds together, which was the equivalent, according to Mauvelain's calculations, of 6 sous per volume. The STN had assured him, he claimed, that the extra charges would not amount to more than 3 sous per volume. Since he planned to sell the books at prices varying from one to three livres, this unforeseen expense would cut badly into his profit. Less scrupulous dealers would not pay anything at all; so the STN would have no right to complain if he waited a year before sending his bill of exchange. He planned to make his long-delayed trip to Neuchâtel some time in 1785 and would bring the money with him then.

Mauvelain was equally difficult about the shipment of the seven crates, which Faivre had smuggled across the border and forwarded on toward Troyes by 19 November. The STN had informed Mauvelain that the shipment was on its way in a letter of 16 November, but he had not received anything by 13 December, when he complained bitterly, "Eh bien, vanterez-vous encore, mon très honoré ami, l'efficacité de vos mesures? La diligence, l'exactitude, le zèle, les soins, la finesse de votre homme de la frontière?" His customers were disgusted with the STN, and, frankly, so was he, because his competitors, who were supplied by the other Neuchâtel publishers, received quicker and cheaper service and got better assortments of books (Mauvelain especially resented the STN's failure to provide him with the desired quantity of political tracts like *Les Fastes de Louis XV*). If the STN did not improve, he would take his business to its neighbors (i.e., Samuel Fauche or Fauche fils aîné, Favre et Witel). Mauvelain had fallen into a foul humor. Illness had driven him almost into his grave. Doctors were no help: he had spent a fortune on them, and they merely told him to take special baths. Finally, one of them had given him some relief by draining "un pot de chambre de pus" out of his genital area. It had been a ghastly operation: "J'étais enflé comme un boeuf qu'on va tuer"—and he was still bedridden. The doctors' fees had consumed all the cash at his disposal. He had not sold half the books and had not received payment for the other half. So the STN would have to be patient: it was their turn to wait, anyhow, and to fortify their patience he soon would send another boar's head.[81]

Dénouement

As the shrill tone of Mauvelain's letter suggests, his arguments had little validity. In the book trade, as in other forms of commerce, customers were supposed to send a promissory note or bill of exchange upon receipt of their merchandise. To be sure, the notes often did not become due for six or twelve months, but they legally bound the debtor to make the payment on the pre-scribed date. Mauvelain merely promised vaguely to produce the money in the spring of 1785, when he expected to make the Neuchâtel journey that he already had postponed several times. And aside from the shipments that Faivre smuggled to him in the winter of 1784–1785, he owed 805 livres 9 sous for all his earlier orders, which went back to February 1783. He had been receiving books from the STN for almost two years and had sent nothing in return, except expressions of friendship and *charcuterie*.

Ostervald replied generously that he would let Mauvelain postpone the financial settlement until the spring journey. As to the shipment of the seven crates, he denied any negligence in its handling. He had written about the delay to Faivre; Faivre had checked with Péchey; and Péchey had reported that all seven crates had arrived safely in Troyes long ago. Ostervald assured Mauvelain that the STN had not overcharged him for the earlier shipment of crates 105 and 106. The insurance had been levied in an honest, businesslike manner, and the transportation costs should have been moderate: the STN usually paid 3 livres per quintal for the haul from Neuchâtel to Besançon, twenty mountainous leagues, and the fifty easy leagues from Besançon to Troyes should cost only 6 livres per quintal. If Mauvelain had paid more, he had been swindled by the

middlemen. He could protect himself in the future simply by refusing to pay the
waggoner until he received a detailed account of the costs, whose rate should be
fixed "comme le prix du pain chez le boulanger. Je conclus de tout cela, Monsieur, que ne connaissant pas la rapacité des commissionnaires et des voituriers,
vous [vous] êtes comme bien d'autres laissé trompé par ces gens là, qui vous
font payer en gros une somme à titre de remboursement et voiture etc. Après
avoir passé moi-même par leurs mains, voici le parti que j'ai pris. Lorsque je
soupçonne que le compte de ces gens là est enflé, j'exige avant que de payer un
compte détaillé de tous frais, et alors la volerie saute aux yeux et le rabais s'en
suit."[82]

Mauvelain acknowledged his reception of the seven crates on 31 December
1784, but he complained vehemently that their handling charges still came to
6 sous per volume, a rate so "effrayant" that it would price the books out of the
local market. He illustrated his point with some precise economic analysis: "En
voici un exemple. *Barjac* [*Le Vicomte de Barjac,* an obscene work] que vous
vendez 25 sols, 6 sols de port, font 31 sols; 3 sols de brochage 34; au moins un
sol ou deux de faux frais et ports de lettres: 36 sols. On le donne ici à ce prix-là,
petit format avec la clé. . . . Personne ne veut du *Libertin de qualité* à 6 livres.
On donne ici *Ma conversion,* qui est la même chose, à 3 livres." But Mauvelain
could not have been as discontented as he sounded, because he followed his
complaints with another huge order for many of the same books, including *Le
Vicomte de Barjac.* He would pay for everything, he added, upon his arrival in
Neuchâtel at some future date.[83]

In his next letter, Mauvelain returned to the attack, accusing the STN
itself of collaborating in the attempt to swindle him on the transportation costs:
"Je vous dirai franchement que tout le monde croit ici que c'est une astuce de
votre part et que vous partagez le gateau avec vos correspondants." He complained
that the STN's shipments generally took six months and arrived long after more
efficient suppliers had sated the market. And as if that were not infuriating
enough, the STN failed to provide all of the books (especially the *livres philosophiques*) that he wanted, and it filled the gaps in his orders with unsellable
works "qui dorment chez moi en attendant la Résurrection." Slipping into the
first person plural, which was the usual style in formal commercial correspondence, Mauvelain concluded with some blunt business talk: "Vous ne pouvez
disconvenir que si nous ne trouvons pas au moins un tiers de bénéfice sur le prix
des livres que nous tirons de chez vous, et que si vous ne nous fournissez que les
livres qui se trouvent partout, et que nous n'ayions pas les nouveautés les premiers
et à leur aurore, il est inutile que nous courrions les risques de la saisie, de la
gâte, les frais de port de lettres et tous les autres inconvénients auxquels nous
nous exposons en faisant des affaires avec vous. Or il s'en faut bien que nous
ayons eu 5 sols par volume de bénéfice. Nous avons été mal et lentement servi."
Then he ended on a personal note: although he had lost some weight and felt
a little better, he was still very ill and would not be able to make it to Neuchâtel
until June. He would be forty-five on 6 March.[84]

Ostervald replied that Mauvelain's accusation was too ludicrous to be offensive, since it was well known that "tous les fabriquants et négociants n'ont pas de pires ennemis que les commissionnaires, qu'il faut continuellement les surveiller, et que ce serait à nous la plus grande de toutes les bêtises de nous entendre avec eux, parce que pour l'appétit d'un chétif bénéfice nous perdrions infailliblement tous nos pratiques." Mauvelain should inquire about the normal handling charges from local merchants; he should compare them with the charges on the consignment note ("lettre de voiture") accompanying the next shipment; and if there were a disparity, he should have the crates sequestered and refuse payment until the shipping agent sent a detailed account. "Vous n'aurez pas pris une seule fois ce soin là que vous verrez votre homme devenir juste, raisonnable, et coulant pour toujours afin de ne pas perdre son crédit et ses pratiques. *Experto crede Roberto.* Nous avons passé jadis par les griffes de ces drôles-là, et aujourd'hui il n'y en a pas un seul qui, sachant que nous épluchons leur affaire et que nous connaissons les prix ne nous fournisse son compte en détail sans se faire tirer l'oreille." Now Ostervald showed some signs of uneasiness about Mauvelain's own financial practices. The STN needed to gather funds for some heavy payments to be made at the beginning of June, he wrote. Since Mauvelain would not arrive in Neuchâtel before the end of May, he should pay his debts by mail sometime soon.[85]

Mauvelain answered that he would pay right away—that is, as soon as he could collect from his own customers. Meanwhile, he badly needed to receive his last order by the end of February, because it contained a great many books for some guards officers, who were to be transferred from Troyes at that time. He would send Ostervald a boar's head for Easter . . . but above all, he needed that February shipment. March came, with no payment from Mauvelain and no shipment from the STN. But Mauvelain continued to beg for the books: if they arrived by the beginning of April, he could still sell them to the guards. To dispose the STN more favorably to this appeal and probably also to divert more of its traffic in his direction, he announced, "J'ai découvert une mine d'or pour vous" and outlined a plan to smuggle huge quantities of books for the STN from Troyes to Paris. A friend of his who supplied the Hôtel Dieu with boatloads of provisions had agreed to take up to four thousand pounds of books on each barge, without any cost or risk for the STN, since the barges unloaded in the center of the capital without passing through customs. Mauvelain closed with the usual remarks about his health. Now he was suffering from "une humeur rhumatismale goutteuse" which had caused a new abscess in his thigh and had kept him bedridden for the last two weeks. He was unable to walk and had grown very fat.[86]

In a letter of 8 March, written by a clerk instead of by Ostervald, the STN began to get tough. It needed money, not advice about smuggling; and it would not send the new shipment until Mauvelain had paid for the old ones. "Il n'entre point dans notre système de commerce d'accumuler partie sur partie. Nous bornons vis-à-vis de tous nos correspondants notre confiance à un certain point. Vous ne cessez de nous faire de nouvelles demandes, et vous n'envoyez point d'argent." Mauvelain adopted a tone of outraged innocence in his reply. Of course he could not pay just now, because he had spent a fortune on doctors, who had kept him in bed for five months, preventing him from selling his books and collecting his bills. To try to squeeze money out of him at this critical moment was the height of inhumanity: "On ne tient pas le pistolet sous la gorge des gens. . . . Cette maladie m'ayant coûté des sommes immenses, je me trouve très court d'argent. J'ai d'ailleurs 400 volumes qui ne sont point encore placés que je vais faire emballer et vous renvoyer. Je n'aime pas les malhonnêtetés. . . . Je commence à croire ce que dit Mallet, que vous êtes des gens aussi avides qu'intéressés et qui ne faites que des vilainies à ceux qui ont affaire à vous. . . . Je vois que vous n'êtes point accoûtumés à traiter avec des gens comme il faut. Je suis très piqué du trait que vous venez de me faire et m'en souviendrai longtemps. . . . Je suis piqué, voilà mon dernier mot."[87]

Mauvelain sounded so overwrought because not only had his debts piled up while his health collapsed, but also three subplots in his affairs with the STN had begun to unravel. The first concerned a manuscript "Histoire naturelle physiologique médicinale" by one of his friends, a Dr. Housset. Mauvelain had said that he had persuaded Housset to hire the STN to do the printing. But the manuscript never arrived, and the STN suspected that Mauvelain had secretly given it to Fauche in an attempt to ingratiate himself with a competing supplier of prohibited books behind the STN's back.[88] Whether Fauche finally did print the manuscript cannot be determined; but the allusions to him, to Fauche fils aîné, Favre et Witel, and to Mallet in Mauvelain's correspondence suggest that Mauvelain did more business with the other printers in Neuchâtel than he wanted to admit to the STN. Second, the STN learned that Mauvelain had collected 194 livres 5 sous of the old debt owed to it by Bouvet and had secretly kept the money: that was the explanation of his strange silence about their bills of exchange.[89] And third, it discovered that the printing job for the Marquis de Thyard had gone astray. As mentioned above, the STN printed Thyard's "Vie de Pontus de Thyard" in 1784 and sent the edition to Mauvelain, who had negotiated the whole affair. After waiting in vain for Mauvelain to send the payment for the printing, the STN mailed a bill directly to the marquis at his estate near Semur-en-Auxois. Thyard replied on 7 March 1785 that he had sent Mauvelain 168 livres for the printing in early January and had received Mauvelain's acknowledgment for the money on 25 January. But on 30 January, Mauvelain had written to the STN that the shipment of the edition had been delayed and so Thyard would not be able to pay for it in the immediate future. Actually, as Thyard told the STN, he had received the books in early January and had given one hundred of them to Mauvelain as compensation for his services.[90]

The STN had pieced together these swindles by the time it received Mauvelain's tirade of 12 March. Its only reply was that it had learned the truth about the Thyard affair and that it had instructed a lawyer in Troyes called Gérard to collect Mauvelain's entire debt—a matter of 2,136 livres 8 sous in addition to the payments Mauvelain had received from Bouvet and Thyard. There was little Mauvelain could say by way of reply. He had reached the end of a confidence game that he had kept going with a good deal of wit and bravura for two years. To be sure, he had had a good run for his money. He had received several hundred hot-selling books in exchange for the payment of some shipping expenses, five dozen letters, and a boar's head. But he had failed to build a successful book business, he was desperately ill, and he was penniless. Instead of attempting to concoct a defense, he answered melodramatically that he was about to die, a "fièvre catarrhale" having compounded his earlier ailments. He acknowledged the STN's legitimate claim to a share in his estate; and to facilitate its future efforts to collect its due, he included a promissory note for 2,535 livres 13 sous.[91] The note was worthless, because it did not specify any date of payment; so the STN sent it to Gérard with instructions to force Mauvelain to pay everything he owed. Gérard confronted Mauvelain and received a flat refusal with the explanation that "pour de l'argent, il n'en avait point ni n'en pouvait avoir." The STN could always sue, Gérard wrote, but it was a hopeless case.[92]

Writing from the depths of this hopelessness on 27 May 1785, Mauvelain dropped his disguise and told the story of his life. "Je suis Bourguignon. Je m'appelle Bruzard de Mauvelain. Une malheureuse affaire d'honneur que j'eus en 1785 [a slip for an earlier date], dans le temps que j'étais député de ma province aux états, m'a ruiné. Insulté par deux particuliers, je donnai un soufflet à l'autre, qui était un homme en place. Toute la France l'a su; et si je n'avais eu autant d'amis puissants, j'aurais subi . . . [missing word] jours de prison suivant les ordonnances pour un homme de robe qui donne des coups de baton. J'allai voyager en Hollande, en Angleterre pendant qu'on arrangeait mon affaire, qui m'a coûté ma charge de président, lieutenant criminel, et ma fortune pour payer des dommages, intérêts, ensorte que je ne vis actuellement que d'une pension alimentaire que me fait ma famille, parce qu'elle le veut bien sans y être obligée.

"Vous allez me dire, Messieurs, 'Comment serons-nous payés de votre billet en le gardant?' J'attends de moment à autre la succession de mon beau-père, qui a 300,000 livres et plus et est très vieux, celle d'un frère garçon qui est conseiller et qui est toujours malade, dont je suis héritier. Voilà, je crois, de quoi m'acquitter.

"Je suis venu me retirer à Troyes en attendant les successions. J'y suis aimé et chéri, vivant avec ce qu'il y a de mieux dans la ville; et avant ma maladie je ne soupais jamais chez moi. Pendant me maladie, qui dure toujours, toute la ville s'est intéressée à mon sort. Les gens les plus distingués ne m'ont pas quitté; et sans cette chienne de maladie où j'ai tous les jours un medécin et un chirurgien gardes, vous seriez payés, puisque tout l'argent qui est passé là vous était destiné.

"Venons au fait. Si vous me faites assigner, qu'en arrivera-t-il? Nous plaiderons, je contesterai, vous aurez sentence dans un an, 18 mois, peut-être plus tard. Qu'en ferez-vous de cette sentence? N'ayant point de bien, n'ayant qu'un appartement garni, vous ne pourrez être payé, et ce sera le moyen de ne l'être jamais. Mon beau père qui apprendra ces poursuites ainsi que mon frère se mettront de mauvaise humeur, substitueront le bien qu'ils laisseront, et malgré ma bonne volonté, je ne pourrai vous payer, étant dans l'impuissance de le faire. Et ce sera votre ouvrage dont vous ne tirerez d'autre avantage que d'avoir appris à ceux qui ignoraient que j'étais gêné, ma misère. Vous me ferez perdre la protection d'un puissant archévêque de France, qui m'assiste de sa bourse et qui cherche à me procurer une place un peu comme il faut à un homme bien né et avec les revenus de laquelle je pourrais vous payer, si je l'obtiens."

In short, Mauvelain was a déclassé, and he was broke. By way of assets, he had only some unsold books from the STN, an incomplete draft of a history of Châlons (which he offered as a down payment on his bill), the hope that his relatives would die, and the possible protection of an archbishop. He did not defend his conduct, but he clung to his pride. He was, he concluded, "un galant homme à qui ses malheurs, sa misère n'ont pas fait perdre l'estime et l'amitié des gens distingués qui m'écrivent sans cesse et m'aiment. Au reste, Messieurs, permettez-moi de vous rappeler un proverbe qui dit 'qu'on ne peigne pas un diable qui n'a point de cheveux.' Je suis pour le moment dans ce cas."

On the same day and in the same desperate state, Mauvelain wrote another letter to the STN specifying that his protector was Loménie de Brienne, Archbishop of Toulouse, and reiterating his determination to defend himself to the death (or even longer) in the courts: "J'ai été homme de loi, et vous ne devez pas douter que je n'en connaisse tous les retours et détours. . . . Une fois l'assignation lâchée et l'éclat fait, je vous avertis que je plaiderai jusqu'à la résurrection glorieuse de nos corps." Ostervald hesitated for two weeks before replying to this outburst, one of the most extraordinary letters, he said, that he had ever received. In the end, and after Gérard had confirmed the futility of resorting to the courts, he decided to let Mauvelain chase windfalls for twelve months. But Mauvelain would have to send a proper promissory note for his total debt of 2,405 livres, including 5 percent interest, to be paid in a year. Mauvelain sent the note and also 93 livres' worth of books, which were all he had. He also announced that he was going to Paris, where (he claimed) the archbishop had offered him an apartment and a "M. La Fond de Fressinet, habile chirurgien" promised to cure him in six weeks.[93]

Mauvelain evidently left for Paris at the end of July, but it is impossible to know what became of him, because his last letters mix falsehoods and fantasies in a way that suggests he was trying to escape either the STN or reality. He would rebuild his life in Paris, he wrote: "M. de Toulouse m'y donne un apartement où je serai, me mande-t-il, comme chez moi: Médecins, chirurgiens, et dans l'intervalle des remèdes. Je travaillerai à un ouvrage qu'il me donne. Il dit qu'il me fera donner les plus grands soins afin que je puisse promptement guérir, ayant besoin de moi dès que je serai en santé. J'espère que sitôt que je serai guéri il me placera."[94] That sounded splendid, except that during the summer of 1785 an agent for the STN sought out Mauvelain several times at Brienne's townhouse, where the apartment was supposedly located, and was told that no one had ever heard of him. The agent, Jacob-François Bornand, also learned that Mauvelain had broken with Brissot, that he had left a wife in Paris from whom he had been separated for years, and that he had failed to pay a debt to Desauges, a Parisian book dealer who specialized in prohibited works. Concerned that, like many characters in the literary underground, Mauvelain might disappear without paying his debts, the STN wrote to him at his old address in Troyes and received an oddly buoyant reply dated from Paris on 3 October 1785.

He was indeed in Paris, Mauvelain wrote, and very happily settled, too. Bornand would have found him in Brienne's townhouse, if he had given the correct name to the porter, "qui me connaît peu, étant appelé tantôt Bruzard de Mauvelain, tantôt Mauvelain." Now he had moved to "la Maison Royale de Santé, barrière de l'Enfer, des Pères de la Charité, nouvel établissement où moyennant 200 livres par mois on est nourri, soi et son domestique, chauffé, éclairé, blanchi, fourni de remèdes, de linges, avec la faculté de retenir à manger un ami qui vous vient voir, ce qui est fort agréable. On y est mieux que chez soi. On vous y fournit tout ce que vous pouvez désirer au monde, quoiqu'il puisse côuter." The archbishop himself had chosen Mauvelain's room, came to visit three times a week, and sent a lackey to inquire about his health every day. He received the very best medical treatment: in fact, the doctors sent by the archbishop had saved his life by three operations in which they had made deep incisions into his lower abdomen. Now he felt much better—so good, in fact, that he wanted to invite Bornand over for dinner. It was at the dinner hour that Mauvelain normally received, "le matin se passant à prendre des bains. L'après dîner la maison s'assemble chez moi pour me tenir compagnie. . . . On est bien ici; c'est dommage que c'est un peu cher."[95] Far from disintegrating obscurely in some hideout or poorhouse, Mauvelain had settled into genteel retirement—or so he suggested. The STN never heard from him again and never succeeded in tracking him down. Its last attempt failed in 1787, when Ostervald inquired about him in a letter to Brissot, which explained that the STN's investigations had produced only one discovery:. "la nature peu honorable de sa maladie et la dépravation de ses moeurs."[96] Brissot replied that Mauvelain had vanished; and indeed as far as the STN was concerned, he had ceased to exist, except as a name in its account books, where he appeared until 1792 under the heading "mauvais débiteurs" for an uncollected debt of 2,405 livres. By that time he probably had died of venereal disease.

PART TWO: MAUVELAIN'S BOOKS

Sources, Charts, Graphs

Each time Mauvelain sent in an order, a clerk of the STN recorded it in a Livre de Commissions. The STN then tried to procure whatever it did not have in stock from other Swiss firms; and when it had gathered enough volumes for a shipment, it sent them off through Faivre's underground railway. Mauvelain generally passed on orders as they came in from his own customers, although he also speculated on books that he had not sold in advance but that he believed would sell, judging from his experience of the market in Troyes. He did not base his orders on the offerings in the STN's catalogues, but rather relied on the STN to supply him with most of the books he wanted. That supply did not meet the demand, because the STN had difficulty in getting some of the books that were not in its inventory and because it soon began to suspect Mauvelain of being a *mauvais payeur*. By the end of 1784 it had begun to look as though Mauvelain might never pay at all, and the STN had adopted the practice of recording his orders without trying to fill them. The Livres de Commissions therefore provide a precise record of what Mauvelain and his customers wanted, not what they received. They show what the raw demand for prohibited works was in Troyes around 1784. By analyzing them and the books they mention, it is possible to come closer than ever before to understanding the taste for the taboo in a small provincial city.

To be sure, one can not draw general conclusions from one case, but a case study of Mauvelain's business may compensate for some weaknesses in the scholarship on the literature and book trade of the Old Regime. Research on those topics has failed to come close to the actual reading habits of eighteenth-century Frenchmen, because it has been based on sources like the (censored) catalogues of library auctions or requests to the state for permission to publish a book or the incomplete inventories of private book collections in *inventaires après décès*.[97] Even if such sources give one a general sense of the literary terrain, they rarely mention books that the state considered to be ideologically offensive. Where then can one discover what those books were? By reconstructing the pattern of Mauvelain's orders, it is possible to watch the unfolding of the demand for prohibited books in Troyes, week by week, for a period of two years. Two years, one town, a thousand books—of course it would be absurd to claim that this pattern represents France as a whole. But one must begin somewhere. Mauvelain offers a good starting point, because he specialized so heavily in *livres philosophiques* and because he was so immersed in the literary underground. At this stage the method must be microscopic: it requires a close analysis of a small segment of the illegal book business. But it may open the way toward an understanding of the entire literary underground in France on the eve of the Revolution.

Chart 1 shows the evolution of Mauvelain's orders for prohibited books from January 1783 to January 1785.

The chart lists the books according to their order of appearance in the Livres de Commission, eliminating all nonprohibited books and all books that Mauvelain ordered only once or twice. Mauvelain did ask the STN to send him various works that contained nothing offensive to the state, religion, or morality, though they were usually pirated editions. However these nonprohibited books formed only a small part of his orders, and they have no bearing on the problems of analyzing the trade in prohibited works, so they have not been tabulated. But how can one tell the prohibited from the nonprohibited? That difficulty is less serious than one might think, because Mauvelain usually grouped the nonprohibited works together in his orders and because the titles usually indicate the contents of the books. *Lettres de Julie ou tableau du libertinage à Paris* is obviously pornographic and *Les Prêtres démasqués* anticlerical. Moreover, it has been possible to trace almost all the books that Mauvelain ordered frequently and in large number.

Mauvelain's orders contain 120 titles that clearly belong to the category of prohibited books (an additional half dozen might be prohibited but can not be identified). Only 48 of them appear at least three times in the Livres de Commission, but those 48 account for the great bulk of Mauvelain's requests for prohibited books: 1,004 of the 1,528 copies that he ordered. The remaining 72 titles were ordered only once or twice and in small quantity.[98] So it seemed justifiable to exclude them from the analysis (to tabulate and identify all 120 titles proved an unmanageable task) and to assume that the 48 titles on the chart show what prohibited books were in demand in Troyes, how great the demand was, and how it varied over a two-year period.

Of course the chart should not be read literally, as if it were the mirror image of the popularity of each book that appears on it. It indicates, for example, that there was considerable demand for Mercier's *Tableau de Paris* (5 separate orders for a total of 27 copies), but it does not mention the *Tableau de Paris* before 21 March 1784, about three years after it was first published. By that time the book had been reprinted at least twice and had established itself as a best seller. It would be unreasonable to conclude that there was no interest in it among Mauvelain's customers before 21 March 1784. Because Mauvelain specialized so strongly in prohibited books, his orders indicate the general character of the works that circulated underground; they do not provide an exact and complete repertory of those works.

They do, however, show a significant pattern of repetition. Retail bookdealers often ordered one or two copies of a work to see how it would sell. If it sold well, they would order three or four more, and they would continue to increase the number and size of their orders as their sales progressed. They also sent for books at their clients' request and repeated their orders according to the incidence of sales that they made in advance. Mauvelain worked in this manner, and so his orders for *Les Fastes de Louis XV, L'Espion dévalisé,* the *Mémoires secrets* of Bachaumont, and the *Histoire philosophique* of Raynal show a steady demand for those books among his clientele—a demand that probably grew, since the orders were repeated regularly and the number of volumes per order generally increased.

The pattern of Mauvelain's orders also corresponds to the evolution of his relations with the STN. At first he asked for only a few books with a discreet admixture of *livres philosophiques.* Gradually, as he gained more and more of the publisher's confidence, his orders grew larger, the proportion of prohibited books in them increased, and he ordered more copies of each work. By February 1784, when he agreed to buy Faivre's insurance service, he ceased to pretend that he was merely requesting a few volumes for friends, and he began to buy in bulk. The small orders that appear at this stage of his relations with the STN (21 December 1783, 16 April 1784, 6 September 1784, 10 January 1785) were

	29 Jan.	13 Mar.	31 Mar.	9 Apr.	28 Apr.	23 May	May 12	7 June	27 June	6 Aug.	1 Sept.	Total Copies	Total Orders
Les Fastes de Louis XV (Villefranche, 1782), 2 vols., (Buffonidor)	1	1	6	2			6	6			12	35	7
L'Espion dévalisé (London, 1782), (Baudouin de Guémadeuc)	1	1	1			2	6	6			6	23	7
L'Intolérance ecclésiastique (Neuchâtel, 1779), (Thumel and Nicolaï), 2^H 5^S	1	1										2	2
Suite de L'Espion anglois (London, 1783), 3 vols. (extracts from Bachaumont)	2		1				6	6				15	4
Aventures de la Marquise de xxx et St. François d'Assise	1											1	1
Histoire philosophique ... (Geneva, 1780), 5 vols., Raynal, 18^H			1						1		1	3	3
L'An 2440 (London, 1775), (Mercier)			1								1	2	2
Vie privée des François, 7^H 10^S					2						1	3	2
La Papesse Jeanne, poème (The Hague, 1777), (Borde)			1									1	1
Mémoires sur la Bastille (London, 1783), Linguet, 1^H			1			2		6			6	15	4
Mémoires secrets pour servir à l'histoire de la République des lettres (London, 1777–89), 36 vols. (Bachaumont)				1		1				1	1	4	4
Le Christianisme dévoilé (London, 1777), (d'Holbach) 2^H				1							1	2	2
Histoire critique de Jésus-Christ (Amsterdam, 1778), (d'Holbach), 1^H				1							1	2	2
Des lettres de cachet et des prisons d'État (Hamburg, 1782), 2 vols., (Mirabeau), 3^H				1		2	6	6			6	21	5
Vie privée de Louis XV (London, 1781), 4 vols., (Mouffle d'Angerville)									1		1	2	2
Les Muses du foyer de l'Opéra (Paris, 1783), (Imbert), 1^H								1			1	3	3
La Chronique scandaleuse (Paris, 1783), (Imbert)										3	12	15	1
Système social (London, 1774), 3 vols., (d'Holbach)										3		3	1
Erotika biblion ("Rome," 1783), (Mirabeau), 1^H 10^S													
Tableau de Paris (Hamburg, 1781–82) 4 vols., (Mercier)													
Correspondance politique, civile, et littéraire pour servir à l'histoire du XVIIIe siècle (Berlin, 1783)													
Essais historiques, critiques, littéraires et philosophiques (Geneva, 1783), (Manuel)													
Le Vicomte de Barjac (Dublin, 1784), 2 vols., (Luchet), 1^H 5^S													
Le Journal des gens du monde (Frankfurt-on-Main, 1782–85), 10 vols., (Luchet)													
Le Ciel ouvert à tous les hommes, traité théologique (1768), (Cuppé), 1^H													
Théologie portative ("Rome," 1776), 2 vols., (d'Holbach)													
Lettres sur la liberté politique et la réforme du clergé													
Le Chien après les moines (Amsterdam, 1784), (Mirabeau?)													
Les Moines après les chiens													
Le Gazetier monastique, 2 vols.													
Dialogue des morts, ou entretien entre Louis XV et ses ministres													
Vie privée, ou apologie de Mgr. le duc de Chartres (London, 1784), (Morande)													
Le Portefeuille de Mme. Gourdan dite "la Comtesse" (Spa, 1783), (Morande), 1^H 10^S													
Remarques historiques sur la Bastille													
Anecdotes du Marquis de Pombal													
Lettres iroquoises ("Irocopolis," 1752), 2 vols., (Maubert de Gouvest)													
Histoire des voyages des papes ("Vienna," 1782), (Charles Millon)													
Mémoire sur les maisons de force du royaume de France													
Requête au Roi pour la suppression des moines													
L'Art de rendre les femmes fidèles (Geneva, 1779), 2 vols.													
L'Horoscope de la Pologne, augmenté par le célèbre Cagliostro ("Cetinje," 1779), (Zannowich)													
Le Philadelphien à Genève ("Dublin," 1783), (Brissot), 1^H 10^S													
L'Observateur anglois ou correspondance secrète (London, 1777–78), 4 vols., (Pidansat de Mairobert), 4^H 10^S													
Le Désoeuvré ou l'espion du boulevard du Temple (London, 1781), (Mayeur de Saint-Paul)													
Oeuvres complètes de Lamettrie (Berlin, 1764), 4 vols., 4^H 10^S													
Oeuvres complètes d'Helvétius (London, 1781), 4 vols., 6^H													
Anecdotes du dix-huitième siècle (London, 1783), 2 vols., (extracts from Bachaumont)													
	6	3	12	6	2	7	24	31	2	7	50	150	52

	1784										1785		
	4 Oct.	21 Dec.	21 Mar.	16 Apr.	17 May	16 June	7 July	? July	6 Sept.	31 Dec.	10 Jan.	Total Copies	Total Orders
Les Fastes de Louis XV (Villefranche, 1782), 2 vols., (Buffonidor)					12	12			12	13		49	4
L'Espion dévalisé (London, 1782), (Baudouin de Guémadeuc)				2		6		6				14	3
L'Intolérance ecclésiastique (Neuchâtel, 1779), (Thumel and Nicolaï), 2ᴴ 5ˢ													
Suite de L'Espion anglois (London, 1783), 3 vols. (extracts from Bachaumont)					4	4						8	2
Aventures de la Marquise de xxx et St. François d'Assise ...										1		1	1
Histoire philosophique ..., (Geneva, 1780), 5 vols., Raynal, 18ᴴ					6	6						12	2
L'An 2440 (London, 1775), (Mercier)	1	2	2		3	6				1		15	6
Vie privée des François, 7ᴴ 10ˢ	6				6	11						23	3
La Papesse Jeanne, poème ("The Hague, 1777"), (Borde)				6								6	1
Mémoires sur la Bastille (London, 1783), Linguet, 1ᴴ		4			6	6			12	13		43	5
Mémoires secrets pour servir à l'histoire de la République des lettres (London, 1777–89), 36 vols., (Bachaumont)	2			1						12		15	3
Le Christianisme dévoilé (London, 1777), (d'Holbach), 2ᴴ			2	1	3	4				2		12	5
Histoire critique de Jésus-Christ (Amsterdam, 1778), (d'Holbach), 1ᴴ						1						1	1
Des lettres de cachet et des prisons d'Etat (Hamburg, 1782), 2 vols., (Mirabeau), 3ᴴ			2		3	6				6		17	4
Vie privée de Louis XV (London, 1781), 4 vols., (Moufle d'Angerville)	1				2	2						5	3
Les Muses du foyer de l'Opéra			12		12	6				13		43	4
La Chronique scandaleuse (Paris, 1783), (Imbert), 1ᴴ			12		12	6						30	3
Système social (London, 1774), 3 vols., (d'Holbach)												4	2
Erotika biblion ("Rome," 1783), (Mirabeau), 1ᴴ 10ˢ		6	6		2	2				2		18	5
Tableau de Paris (Hamburg, 1781–82) 4 vols., (Mercier)			6		6	6						27	3
Correspondance politique, civile et littéraire pour servir à l'histoire du XVIIIe siècle (Berlin, 1783)			6		6	6						18	3
Essais historiques, critiques, littéraires et philosophiques (Geneva, 1783), (Manuel)			6		6	6				2		20	4
Le Vicomte de Barjac (Dublin, 1784), 2 vols., (Luchet), 1ᴴ 5ˢ			6		6	6				6		24	4
Le Journal des gens du monde (Frankfurt-on-Main, 1782-85). 10 vols., (Luchet)			2		6	6						14	3
Théologie portative ("Rome," 1776), 2 vols., (d'Holbach)			2		3	6						11	3
Le Ciel ouvert à tous les hommes, traité théologique (1768), (Cuppé), 1ᴴ			2		6	6				13		27	4
Lettres sur la liberté politique et la réforme du clergé			6		6	6						18	3
Le Chien après les moines (Amsterdam, 1784), (Mirabeau?)			6		6	6						18	3
Les Moines après les chiens			6		6	6						18	3
Le Gazetier monastique, 2 vols.			6		6	6						18	3
Dialogue des morts, ou entretien entre Louis XV et ses ministres			6		6	6				13		31	4
Vie privée, ou apologie de Mgr. le duc de Chartres (London, 1784), (Morande)			6		6	6						18	3
Le Portefeuille de Mme. Gourdan dite "la Comtesse" (Spa, 1783), (Morande), 1ᴴ 10ˢ			6		6	6				13		31	4
Remarques historiques sur la Bastille			6		6	6						18	3
La Mule du pape			6		6	6						18	3
Anecdotes du Marquis de Pombal			6		6	6						18	3
Lettres iroquoises ("Irocopolis," 1752), 2 vols., (Maubert de Gouvest)			6		6	6						18	3
Histoire des voyages des papes ("Vienna," 1782), (Charles Millon)			6		6	6						18	3
Mémoire sur les maisons de force du royaume de France			6		6	6						18	3
Requête au Roi pour la suppression des moines			6		6	6				6		24	4
L'Art de rendre les femmes fidèles (Geneva, 1779), 2 vols.			2		6	6						14	3
L'Horoscope de la Pologne, augmenté par le célèbre Cagliostro ("Cetinje," 1779), (Zannovich)			6		6	6						18	3
Le Philadelphien à Genève ("Dublin," 1783), (Brissot), 1ᴴ 10ˢ				1	11	10						22	3
L'Observateur anglois ou correspondance secrète (London, 1777-78), 4 vols., (Pidansat de Mairobert), 4ᴴ 10ˢ				2	6	6		6					
Le Désoeuvré ou l'espion du boulevard du Temple (London, 1781), (Mayeur de Saint-Paul)			2		6	6						14	3
Oeuvres complètes de Lamettrie (Berlin, 1764), 2 vols., 4ᴴ 10ˢ					1	1				2	2	6	4
Oeuvres complètes d'Helvétius (London, 1781), 4 vols., 6ᴴ					1	1				1		3	3
Anecdotes du dix-huitième siècle (London, 1783), 2 vols., (extracts from Bachaumont)			6		6	6				6		18	3
	10	12	154	13	238	249		12	24	138	4	854	151

Chart 1. Mauvelain's book orders.

The Livres de Commissions mention only the short titles of the books. Other information—the authors' names, the dates and places of publication, the number of volumes,
the full titles—has been supplied from standard reference works such as Barbier's
Dictionnaire des ouvrages anonymes. Some of this information is unreliable, because
Mauvelain mainly ordered anonymous works, which have lapsed into obscurity since
his time. In attributing authorship, Barbier has been followed, except in the case of the
Holbachean works, where the best authority is Jeroom Vercruysse, *Bibliographie
descriptive des écrits du Baron d'Holbach* (Paris, 1971). The names of anonymous
authors are set off in parentheses. Dating the editions did not usually prove to be a
problem, because in most cases only one edition had appeared when Mauvelain placed
his order. But the works of Raynal, Mercier, and d'Holbach went through many editions.
In such cases the date of the latest edition at the time of Mauvelain's order has been
given, even though it is impossible to know precisely what edition he wanted. (Actually
in ordering Raynal's *Histoire philosophique* he specified that he wanted the Geneva,
1780, edition, 5 volumes in quarto.) The places of publication have been given as
they appear on the title pages, even though they were notoriously fictitious in illegal
books of the eighteenth century. The number of volumes given for each edition is
probably accurate, except in the case of the *Mémoires secrets* of Bachaumont, which
ran to thirty-six volumes by 1789. Mauvelain wanted as many volumes as had appeared
at the time of his order, but that number cannot be known. The prices (abbreviated
as ^ᴴ for livre and ^ˢ for sous) have been taken from the STN's account books and
therefore show what the STN charged the booksellers with whom it dealt, not what
retailers demanded from their customers. The STN occasionally varied the price that it
charged for the same book, and of course the different books in Mauvelain's orders had
quite different prices. It therefore is somewhat misleading to take one copy of one title
as the unit for making comparisons, as has been done throughout this essay. Clearly
Linguet's *Mémoires sur la Bastille* (one volume for one livre) and d'Holbach's *Histoire
critique de Jésus Christ* (one volume, one livre 10 sous) did not represent the same
commercial value as the *Oeuvres complètes* of Helvétius (4 volumes, 6 livres) or the
four-volume scandal sheet called *L'Espion anglois* (4 livres 10 sous). But these
expensive, multivolume works fall in all the categories, except pornography, so
categorical comparisons are not badly impaired by the unevenness of the economic
value of the books.

only postscripts or supplements to enormous orders, in which he asked for books by the half dozen or dozen (twelve copies of a book frequently entitled the buyer to a free thirteenth). So the chart illustrates one of the main themes in Mauvelain's correspondence: it shows how the tough, professional bookdealer emerged from behind the false front of the *littérateur*.

What pattern emerges as to the subject matter of these books? This is a tricky question, because a single work could be offensive in so many ways: it could revile the king, denigrate the clergy, drag the ministers through the mud, curse God, advocate utopian republicanism, and celebrate sexual deviance. Nonetheless, most prohibited books tended to concentrate their fire on one area of the spectrum of values that the regime defended, and the regime had its own way of categorizing the attacks. Edicts on the book trade and censors' reports usually distinguished offenses against the state, religion, and morality.[99] The bar graphs in Chart 2 (p. 50) represent the character of Mauvelain's books according to those three categories and a fourth, which includes books that were too general in their iconoclasm to fit under the other rubrics. Only by including this fourth category did it seem possible to avoid imposing an overly artificial schema on the raw material and to do justice to an important element in Mauvelain's orders: general treatises like Raynal's *Histoire philosophique* and general scandal sheets like the *Mémoires secrets* of Bachaumont. Of course any classification system must be arbitrary. This one was adopted after many hours spent in reading the books themselves: it suits them, and it corresponds to the way they were classified in the eighteenth century. In an effort to minimize arbitrariness, the material has been tabulated twice, once according to the total number of books ordered in each category and once according to the number of orders. Thus *Les Fastes de Louis XV*, which was a political libel attacking the king and ministers, represents a value of 84 on the second bar of the first graph and a value of 11 on the second bar of the second graph, because Mauvelain ordered a total of 84 copies on 11 different occasions. In fact, the two graphs do not differ greatly: whether one measures the overall volume of Mauvelain's orders or their pattern of repetition, the effect is the same.

It is difficult to interpret an abstract pattern like this without being able to relate the categories to the books themselves; the following list breaks down the categories according to the titles Mauvelain ordered. The first of the two numbers given after each title refers to the total number of copies ordered, the second to the number of orders.

Religion
  Satire and Polemics

L'Intolérance ecclésiastique	10/4
La Papesse Jeanne	44/6
Le Gazetier monastique	18/3
La Mule du pape	18/3
Histoire des voyages des papes	18/3
Requête pour la suppression des moines	18/3
Total	126/22

Treatises
   Le Christianisme dévoilé — 3/3
   Histoire critique de Jésus Christ — 19/6
   Le Ciel ouvert à tous les hommes — 11/3
   Théologie portative — 27/4

  Total — 60/16

  TOTAL — 186/38

Politics
  Libels
   Les Fastes de Louis XV — 84/11
   L'Espion dévalisé — 37/10
   Vie privée de Louis XV — 7/5
   Vie privée . . . de Mgr. le duc de Chartres — 18/3

  Total — 146/29

  Pamphlets and Topical Works
   Mémoires sur la Bastille, Linguet — 30/7
   Des Lettres de cachet, Mirabeau — 21/5
   Lettres sur la liberté politique — 18/3
   Dialogue des morts — 31/4
   Remarques historiques sur la Bastille — 18/3
   Anecdotes du Marquis de Pombal — 18/3
   Mémoire sur les maisons de force — 18/3
   L'Horoscope de la Pologne — 14/3

  Total — 168/31

  Treatises
   Système social — 5/3

  TOTAL — 319/63

Pornography
  Anticlerical
   Aventures de la marquise de xxx et St. François — 13/3
   Le Chien après les moines — 18/3
   Les Moines après les chiens — 18/3

  Total — 49/9

  General
   Muses du foyer de l'Opéra — 46/5
   Errotika biblion — 18/3
   Le Vicomte de Barjac — 24/4
   Le Portefeuille de Madame Gourdan — 31/4
   L'Art de rendre les femmes fidèles — 24/4
   Le Désoeuvré — 14/3

  Total — 157/23

  TOTAL — 206/32

General Works
  Chroniques scandaleuses
   Suite de l'Espion anglois — 16/5
   Vie privée des françois — 9/3
   Mémoires secrets, Bachaumont — 16/9
   La Chronique scandaleuse — 45/5
   Correspondance politique, civile et littéraire — 18/3

Essais historiques, critiques, littéraires	20/4	
Le Journal des gens du monde	14/3	
L'Observateur anglois	22/3	
Anecdotes du dix-huitième siècle	18/3	
Total		178/38
Treatises		
Histoire philosophique, Raynal	18/9	
L'An 2440	25/5	
Tableau de Paris	27/5	
Lettres iroquoises	18/3	
Oeuvres de Lamettrie	16/4	
Oeuvres d'Helvétius	3/3	
Total		107/29
TOTAL		285/67

Finally, it should be useful to establish a sort of best-seller list of the works that Mauvelain ordered in largest number and most often:

Most Wanted Books According to Number of Copies Ordered

1. *Les Fastes de Louis XV*	84
2. *Muses du foyer de l'Opéra*	46
3. *La Chronique scandaleuse*	45
4. *La Papesse Jeanne*	44
5. *L'Espion dévalisé*	37
6. *Dialogue des morts* and *Portefeuille de Mme. Gourdan*	31
7. *Mémoires sur la Bastille*, Linguet	30
8. *Tableau de Paris* and *Théologie portative*	27
9. *L'An 2440*	25
10. *Le Vicomte de Barjac* and *L'Art de rendre les femmes fidèles*	24
11. *L'Espion anglois*	22
12. *Des Lettres de cachet*	21
13. *Essais historiques, critiques, littéraires*	20

(The number of copies of all the other books ordered by Mauvelain was 18 or less per title.)

Most Wanted Books According to Number of Orders

1. *Les Fastes de Louis XV*	11
2. *L'Espion dévalisé*	10
3. *L'Histoire philosophique*, Raynal; *Mémoires secrets*, Bachaumont	9
4. *Mémoires sur la Bastille*, Linguet	7
5. *La Papesse Jeanne*; *Histoire critique de Jésus Christ*	6
6. *Suite de l'Espion anglois*; *L'An 2440*; *Des lettres de cachet*; *Vie privée de Louis XV*; *Muses du foyer de l'Opéra*; *La Chronique scandaleuse*; *Tableau de Paris*	5

The Literary Market Place, Underground

In attempting to interpret this material, the first point that stands out is the paucity of philosophy among these *livres philosophiques*. The famous, pro-

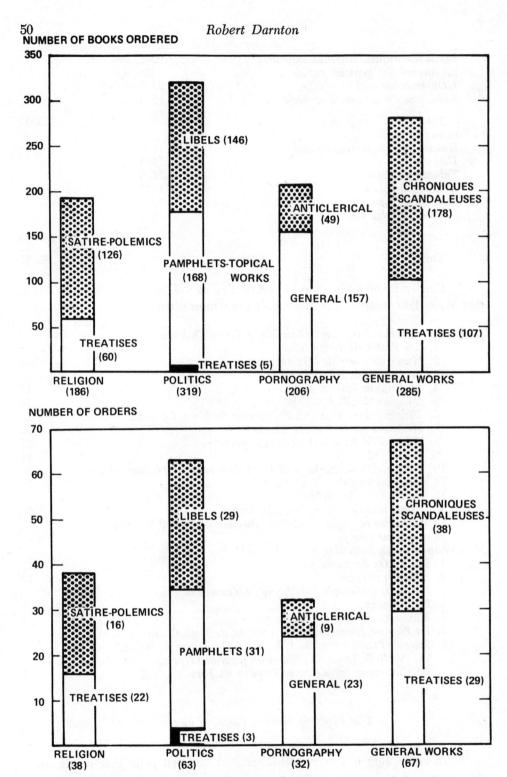

NUMBER OF BOOKS ORDERED

350

300

250
LIBELS (146)

200
ANTICLERICAL
(49)
CHRONIQUES
SCANDALEUSES
(178)

150
SATIRE-POLEMICS
(126)

PAMPHLETS-TOPICAL
(168)   WORKS

GENERAL (157)

100

50
TREATISES
(60)
TREATISES (5)
TREATISES (107)

RELIGION   POLITICS   PORNOGRAPHY   GENERAL WORKS
(186)   (319)   (206)   (285)

NUMBER OF ORDERS

70

60
LIBELS (29)

50
CHRONIQUES
SCANDALEUSES
(38)

40
SATIRE-POLEMICS
(16)

30
ANTICLERICAL
(9)

PAMPHLETS (31)

20
GENERAL (23)
TREATISES (29)

10
TREATISES (22)
TREATISES (3)

RELIGION   POLITICS   PORNOGRAPHY   GENERAL WORKS
(38)   (63)   (32)   (67)

Chart 2. Subject matter of books ordered by Mauvelain.

hibited books by the philosophes do not figure prominently among the mass of obscure works ordered by Mauvelain. Thus the graph representing books that were primarily political in content contains only a tiny portion of "treatises," that is, political theory. The list breaking the categories down by title shows that there was only one such political treatise: d'Holbach's *Système social,* which Mauvelain ordered three times for a total of five copies. And the two best-seller lists confirm this view: they are made up almost entirely of books that have been forgotten today, and they include no abstract philosophy, except d'Holbach's *Histoire critique de Jésus Christ* and Raynal's *Histoire philosophique.* Conversely, the worst sellers among all 48 titles are the books that one would associate most directly with the Enlightenment: the works of Helvétius (3 orders totaling 3 copies), the works of Lamettrie (4 orders totaling 6 copies), d'Holbach's *Système social* (3 orders totaling 5 copies), and d'Holbach's *Christianisme dévoilé* (3 orders totaling 3 copies).

Taken as a group, however, the books that express the philosophical themes of the Enlightenment constitute a significant minority of Mauvelain's orders. Their importance shows most clearly among the works attacking the Catholic religion. Two thirds of those books are polemical, anticlerical tracts directed mainly against the papacy and the monastic orders. But the other third is made up of abstract, philosophical works, which are well-known representatives of the Enlightenment at its most extreme: three of them are by d'Holbach. Philosophical writing also accounts for about a third of the books classified as general works. In this case, the "philosophy" is not abstract: Lamettrie and Helvétius fall under this category, but they make a poor showing next to Raynal and Mercier, who wrote as popularizers and rhetoricians rather than as original thinkers. Nevertheless, Raynal and Mercier expressed most of the themes of the High Enlightenment. *L'Histoire philosophique* may seem unreadable today, but Mauvelain's contemporaries found it sublime and memorized its fiercest declamations against despotism and religious superstition, in order to recite them tearfully to one another during *épanchements.*[100] Of course Raynal at his most violent was also most vague, and ostensibly his remarks applied only to societies far from France. But the text became increasingly radical as the book went through its three main metamorphoses (1770, 1774, 1780) and its thirty or more editions. By the time it appeared in Mauvelain's orders, it had become a kind of anthology of outspoken Enlightenment opinion on a wide range of subjects, notably the American Revolution, which Raynal extolled in language that made even Thomas Jefferson uncomfortable.[101] At this time it was also profiting from a *succès de scandale,* because in 1781 it was condemned by the Parlement of Paris, and Raynal was forced to flee the country. Mauvelain ordered *L'Histoire philosophique* nine times. He asked for only eighteen copies in all, but each copy contained five large volumes and cost 18 livres—far more than the other books in his orders, which normally cost one or two livres. So those *Histoires philosophiques* suggest that Mauvelain's clients had some interest in Enlightenment literature.

The same may be said of Mauvelain's orders for Mercier's two extremely popular works, *L'An 2440* and the *Tableau de Paris.* In the first, Mercier described a future utopia, which like Raynal's America served as an implicit condemnation of French institutions. The hereditary nobility, parlements, venality of office, privileges of all kinds, extremes of wealth and poverty, and even the absolute monarchy all stood condemned by Mercier's vision of the good society.[102] By contrast, the *Tableau de Paris* provided a vivid description of how bad life could be in contemporary Paris, the negative complement to Mercier's utopia. Mercier meant to depict the "physionomie morale"[103] of the capital, not to write a political diatribe; and he succeeded, for the book is a masterpiece of reportage. But by merely reporting the misery of the poor, the insolence of the rich and well-born, and the arbitrariness of the government, he wrote as an enlightened social critic. The last book in the category of general treatises, *Les Lettres iroquoises* by J.-H. Maubert de Gouvest, resembles the works by Raynal and Mercier in that it combines utopian fantasy and social criticism. It is a report on European civilization by a noble savage, and it reads like a radicalized version of *Les Lettres persanes,* though its political comments are mild in comparison with those of Raynal and Mercier. Finally, it should be noted that two of the most important books under the political rubric, Linguet's *Mémoires sur la Bastille* and Mirabeau's *Des lettres de cachet,* contain a great deal of enlightened argument. The first volume of Mirabeau's work in particular is full of political theory, mainly derived from Rousseau and Montesquieu. So it would be wrong to conclude that the preponderance of obscure, nonphilosophic books in Mauvelain's orders indicates a lack of interest in the Enlightenment.

But what sort of Enlightenment was this? Not one of the great philosophes—Montesquieu, Voltaire, Rousseau, or Diderot—appeared in Mauvelain's orders. Some minor philosophes got mentioned: Charles Borde, author of *La Papesse Jeanne* and friend of Voltaire; Pierre Cuppé, author of the Voltairian *Le Ciel ouvert à tous les hommes;* and Maubert de Gouvest, an extraordinary adventurer whose *Lettres iroquoises* (1752) expressed the main themes of the philosophic movement at mid-century. But aside from the obscure hacks who wrote most of Mauvelain's books, the names that stand out in his orders are Helvétius, Lamettrie, and d'Holbach. Although the first two accounted for only a few orders, d'Holbach seems to have been a great favorite in Troyes. He heads the list of authors who wrote two or more of the titles that Mauvelain ordered:[104]

d'Holbach:	54 total copies of 4 different books ordered on 16 separate occasions.
Mercier:	52 copies, 2 books, 10 orders.
Morande:	49 copies, 2 books, 7 orders.
Mirabeau:	39 copies, 2 books, 8 orders.
Luchet:	38 copies, 2 books, 7 orders.

Mauvelain's clients did not show an unusual interest in any single book by d'Holbach, but they indicated a strong and steady demand for d'Holbach's works in general. And since Lamettrie and Helvétius put in at least a modest appearance on Mauvelain's lists, unlike the more famous philosophes, it seems that the demand for prohibited books around Troyes had gone beyond Voltairian impiety and had extended to rank atheism of the sort that horrified Voltaire himself. Of course it would be absurd to claim that readers who wanted atheistic books were atheists. The point is that the milder forms of anti-Catholic propaganda had little place in the repertory of a dealer like Mauvelain, even though they could not circulate openly. The trade in hard-core prohibited books favored the most extreme, Holbachean version of Enlightenment thought. That kind of Enlightenment held a subordinate but significant place in the pattern of Mauvelain's orders.[105]

Mauvelain wanted immoral books about as badly as he wanted irreligious ones—that is, he wanted them in moderation, for the two categories together amounted to only two-fifths of his orders, and each of them looks rather small in comparison with the political and general works on the bar graphs. By modern standards, the pornography was restrained; and like the painting of the period, it was veiled and voyeuristic. Its character is summed up in the title of one of Mirabeau's obscene works, *Le Rideau levé:* the erotic literature of the eighteenth century seemed always to be lifting curtains, tearing off veils, glancing up skirts, and peeping through keyholes. Mauvelain favored books that would give his customers glimpses of prostitutes at work: *Les Muses du foyer de l'Opéra, Le Portefeuille de Madame Gourdan, Le Désoeuvré.* They had no redeeming social value. They were written by veterans of the boulevard and the brothel who wrote only for money, speculating on the market for sex, scandal, and sensationalism. *Le Désoeuvré ou l'espion du boulevard du Temple* by F.-M. Mayeur de Saint-Paul provided behind-the-scenes gossip about actors and call-girl actresses, which Mayeur had collected in the course of his own career as an actor and a rake. Charles Théveneau de Morande specialized in brothels. His *Portefeuille de Madame Gourdan* presented itself as the correspondance of Paris' most distinguished madame, and described the daily life of a high-class whorehouse. A typical letter:[106]

DE M. L'EVÊQUE DE M*** [to Mme Gourdan]
Paris, ce 15 décembre 1774.

Vous méritez que je vous fisse mettre à l'Hôpital [a prison for prostitutes]. J'ai reçu chez vous un fameux coup de pied de Vénus qui m'oblige de quitter la capitale pour aller rétablir ma santé dans mon diocèse. On a bien raison de dire qu'il n'y a plus de probité, et qu'on ne sait à qui se fier.

Not very flattering to the upper clergy. But Morande's main purpose was to shock and titillate in the usual manner of eighteenth-century pornography. His *Portefeuille* resembled standard works like those he listed in a fictitious letter to Mme Gourdan from a book peddlar, who offered to replenish the library of her brothel.[107]

DE M. D***, COLPORTEUR
Paris, ce 22 juin 1780

Je viens, Madame, de recevoir d'Hollande de superbes éditions, avec gravures en taille-douce: la *Pucelle,* le *Portier des Chartreux, Margot*

> *la Ravaudeuse*, les *Postures de l'Arétin*, les *Lauriers ecclésiastiques*, la
> *Fille de joie*, les *Délices du cloître*, le *Chapitre des Cordeliers*, *L'Entretien
> de deux nonnes pour servir d'instruction aux jeunes demoiselles qui
> entrent dans le monde*, *l'Ode à Priape* et la *Foutromaine*. S'il y a,
> Madame, quelques-uns de ces ouvrages qui vous conviennent, mandez-
> les-moi, avec l'heure à laquelle je pourrai vous trouver.

The archives of the STN contain many letters like this from genuine bookdealers, ordering the very same titles. The titles themselves reveal the strong element of anticlericalism in the indecent books of the Old Regime. Depraved bishops and concupicent nuns were stock figures in a tradition that went back to the Middle Ages and had reached a high point in Boccaccio. But in almost a third of Mauvelain's pornographic books the denigration of the clergy is such a dominant theme as to warrant classification as a subcategory. For example, *Le Vicomte de Barjac* and *Le Chien après les moines* both recount the adventures of a great seducer; but the former is merely an erotic, picaresque novel,[108] while the monk's tale reads like an attack on the regular clergy, even though its subject is mainly sexual. Many of Mauvelain's books had themes that overlapped and intertwined too thoroughly for them to be classified exclusively in one category. But one theme was usually dominant, and the subthemes in the erotic and irreligious books made them mutually reinforcing, whether they were obscene attacks on the church or anticlerical pornography.

No author better illustrates the tendency of one category of *livres philosophiques* to shade off into another better than Mirabeau, who wrote all kinds of prohibited works and frequently mixed the genres. *Le Libertin de qualité*, which caused such trouble for the STN's trade and for French-Swiss relations, recounts the adventures of a gigolo, but it also contains some social comment about persons of *qualité* in general. Thus after recounting his affair with a depraved duchess, the hero explains that he was replaced by a prince: "Quant au moral, ils se convenaient; pour le physique, elle eut ses laquais: c'est le pain quotidien d'une duchesse."[109] A passing quip, it was all the more effective for having been dropped unexpectedly in an obscene context. The *Errotika biblion* comes close to being "pure" pornography, but it contains many blasphemous passages about the church, the Jesuits, and even the Holy Trinity. Mirabeau also spiced it up with some political remarks which echo his *Lettres de cachet;* and the latter, an exclusively political work, complements the pornographic view of state prisons in Mirabeau's *Lettres de Vincennes*.[110] Mirabeau probably did not regard these works as distinct and unrelated any more than did his publishers, who sold them all under the same rubric, *livres philosophiques*. They sold well, too, judging from Mauvelain's orders. He never asked for many copies of *Le Libertin de qualité*, because Mallet had peddled it throughout the area. But he ordered 18 copies of *Errotika biblion* and 21 of *Des Lettres de cachet*. Mirabeau ranked fourth, just after Morande, on the best-selling authors list. And Morande himself mixed social and political comment with pornography in an even more outspoken manner. The denigration of the clergy and aristocracy in his *Cor-*

respondance de Madame Gourdan seems mild in comparison with his political libels, which contain obscene attacks on everything exalted and venerable, including the monarchy itself.[111]

The books in Mauvelain's orders that did not have a dominant motif and that contained something to offend almost everyone in authority in France belong to the third category, general works. As explained above, about a third of these books were treatises, which expressed Enlightenment thought on a wide variety of subjects. The rest can best be described as *chroniques scandaleuses*—journalistic accounts of love affairs, crimes, and sensational events. This kind of literature aimed to shock the reader, but it could be completely apolitical, as is illustrated by a typical excerpt from *La Chronique scandaleuse,* the book from which the genre takes its name:[112]

> La Dlle. de Villiers agée de 64 ans fut un jour trouvée morte dans la rue d'Orléans au marais. Le commissaire la fit exposer à la morgue; personne ne la réclama, elle fut enterrée. Un de ses parents inquiet de son sort fit des perquisitions; il reconnut les habits de sa parente, on la fit déterrer, il fut sûr de son fait. On sut que le jour de sa mort elle avait dîné chez le Chevalier de la Touche, capitaine de housards. Un exempt de police se transporta chez lui, l'interrogea. Il avoua qu'elle était ivre quand elle l'avait quitté, et qu'elle était allée chercher un fiacre; il ajouta que probablement elle était morte d'un coup de sang. Un commissaire succéda à l'exempt, il fit avouer au capitaine que la femme avait expiré chez lui, que la nuit il l'avait transportée dans la rue pour éviter les tracasseries de la justice. Sur cet aveu, on l'a conduit en prison. On assure qu'on a trouvé trente louis dans le bureau et qu'une reconnaissance du mont de piété prouve qu'il avait des habits en gage. Une demoiselle assez jolie qui vivait avec lui s'est trouvée compromise dans cette affaire atroce, qui s'est terminée par un plus amplement informé.

Most *chroniques scandaleuses* were made up of a string of stories like this one: each story was a self-contained unit of a paragraph or two, and each was recounted in a gossipy spirit, as if the author had uncovered a spectacular secret. Many were fictitious—outright "canards," or journalistic hoaxes, which had gone through several incarnations. One anecdote of *La Chronique scandaleuse* dated from 1618 and reappeared recently in *Le Malentendu* and *L'Etranger* by Camus.[113] Other episodes concerned the intrigues of notorious roués, filles d'Opéra, and courtiers. They seemed to be written according to the principle that names make news, and indeed they provided news for a public that was denied it.

The Old Regime did not permit the publication of news as we know it. Its journals were heavily censored and appeared by virtue of *privilèges* granted by the *grâce* of the king. They could not afford to publish anything that would give offence in Versailles; and since Versailles regarded government as its exclusive preserve, they could not discuss politics at all. Foreign journals could be less discreet about French affairs, but they were only allowed to circulate in

France by special permission from the king, who could make their distribution almost impossible by excluding them from the post and by persecuting them through the police. The French therefore got their news from rumors, and the flow of rumors was directed to a great extent by specialists called *nouvellistes*. These primitive journalists swapped stories in cafés, salons, and certain corners of the Palais Royal and the Luxembourg and Tuileries gardens. Having stocked up on *nouvelles,* they sometimes reduced them to writing and circulated them secretly in manuscripts known as *nouvelles à la main* or *gazettes à la main*. The *chroniques scandaleuses* were printed versions of these manuscript news sheets. They stood half way in the evolutionary process by which archaic rumor mongering developed into popular journalism.[114]

The most famous and influential of these printed *nouvelles à la main* was the *Mémoires secrets* of Bachaumont, which grew out of the gossip of *nouvellistes* who met in the salon of Mme Doublet de Persan. One of the group, Pidansat de Mairobert, also produced his own news sheet, *L'Observateur anglois, ou correspondance secrète entre milord All'eye et milord All'ear,* commonly known as *L'Espion anglois*. Two related works, *Suite de l'Espion anglois* and *Anecdotes du dix-huitième siècle,* were compiled from later volumes of the *Mémoires secrets*. All these publications were imitated, plagiarized, reprinted, abridged, and expanded in many ways. When taken as a group, they seem remarkably similar, though their tone and content varies. So Mauvelain's *chroniques scandaleuses* belonged to one rather homogeneous family.

This genre of underground journalism, so characteristic of the Old Regime and so forgotten today, shows up strikingly in the graphs drawn from Mauvelain's orders. He sent for more *chroniques scandaleuses* than for any of the other kinds of books represented by the subdivisions of the graphs. His clients seem to have been starved for news. Like all provincials, they were cut off from the nerve centers of gossip in Paris. They could not sample the *on-dits* of the Palais Royal or buy a manuscript from a waiter at the Café du Caveau. So they asked Mauvelain to procure *L'Espion anglois:* that is the most likely explanation of the surprisingly strong percentage of *chroniques scandaleuses* in his orders.

Just as they showed a penchant for news, Mauvelain's orders generally favored whatever was newest on the market. From the beginning, Mauvelain gave the STN a blank order to supply him with one copy of every *nouveauté* that came its way, and his letters constantly called for "toute sorte de nouveautés."[115] *Nouveautés* were not *nouvelles;* they were the latest, hottest thing being published. But they often made news themselves: the *chroniques scandaleuses* devoted a great deal of space to the most recent, most talked-about books. An underground dealer could not afford to be slow in stocking the works of Mirabeau and Linguet, because such books sold only as long as they were topical or enjoyed a *succès de scandale*. Their selling power also ebbed quickly if several pirate publishers brought out editions of them and if rival booksellers flooded the market. Thus Mauvelain's worries about Mallet and his complaints that Mirabeau's *Le Libertin de qualité* and Linguet's *Mémoires sur la Bastille* had saturated his territory long before the arrival of the STN's shipments of them: "Si vous ne nous fournissez que les livres qui se trouvent partout et que nous n'ayions pas les nouveautés les premiers et à leur aurore, il est inutile que nous courrions les risques de la saisie."[116] Judging from other letters to the STN, this emphasis on newness seems to have been characteristic of clandestine bookdealers. Although underground literature had some "classics" (mainly pornographic books like *Margot la ravaudeuse* and some irreligious works like *Les Trois Imposteurs*), it tended to be topical and present-oriented. It lacked the ageless best sellers—the Caesars, the Ciceros and the lives of the saints—that gave some stability to the commerce of legal dealers. Many of Mauvelain's books—*La Chronique scandaleuse, L'Errotika biblion, Le Vicomte de Barjac*—had been published during the same year that he ordered them. He ordered *Les Fastes de Louis XV* on 29 January 1783, less than four months after the first report of its appearance in Rotterdam.[117] He sent for *Des Lettres de cachet* and *La Vie privée . . . de Mgr. le duc de Chartres* within three months of the time that they first began to circulate under the cloak in Paris, according to the *Mémoires secrets,* which reported on everything that caused a sensation among the Parisian avant-garde.[118] Mauvelain was even quicker off the mark in ordering *L'Espion dévalisé:* he sent for it only a month after the correspondents of the *Mémoires secrets* were able to get their hands on it.[119] And in the case of one pamphlet, *Le Diable dans un bénitier,* he placed his order almost four months before the *Mémoires secrets* announced that it "perce depuis quelques temps, quoiqu' avec beaucoup de peine."[120] One would have to be deeply initiated in the secrets of the literary underground to snatch so quickly at these books, which were far too dangerous to be advertised or displayed openly. Clandestine publishers and booksellers kept each other informed through their own system of communication (they relied mainly on letter writing and sometimes used codes to hide book titles).[121] Mauvelain, who did a side business in supplying publishers with illicit manuscripts, must have been well connected and well informed by contacts throughout the clandestine circuits of the book trade. Of course he would order older books if his customers wanted them or if he thought they would sell. He asked for 24 copies of *L'Art de rendre les femmes fidèles,* which first appeared in 1717, and put in one order for the *Galanteries des rois de France,* which dated from 1694. But the majority of his books were very recent. He may have specialized in avant-garde literature, but more likely the contemporary bias of his orders corresponded to their emphasis on *chroniques scandaleuses.* Mauvelain was an agent in Troyes for everything new and newsworthy; he kept his provincials informed about the latest happenings in Paris just as he supplied them with the latest literature. So his *nouvelles* and his *nouveautés* were related; in fact they sometimes amounted to the same thing, because pamphlets about politics were often newsworthy in themselves and were discussed at length in the *chroniques scandaleuses.*

There must have been *nouvelliste*-booksellers like Mauvelain all over France, and they must have played an important role in politicizing the provinces. If as he claimed, Mauvelain frequented "ce qu'il y a de mieux dans la ville,"[122] he could have astounded his notable friends with tales taken from his contacts in Paris and his *chroniques scandaleuses*. He certainly used his correspondence to stock up on gossip, and he seems to have been a rumor-mongerer himself: thus his remarks about Mercier dying, Raynal marrying, the Garde des Sceaux dying, and the Lake of Geneva boiling. He even had a collection of "anecdotes rares manuscrites venant d'un homme en place sur la cour,"[123] which he planned to print as a *chonique scandaleuse* of his own. One can only conjecture about what the lawyers, manufacturers, and merchants of Troyes heard when they stopped by Mauvelain's apartment or while they thumbed through a book that he offered them as he made his rounds. If his sales pitch resembled his letters, it must have been spicy. One can barely glimpse the bookseller's role as a distributor of news, but it could have been important; for news was forbidden fruit, and during the last years of the Old Regime the reading public was hungry for it.

Mauvelain's *chroniques scandaleuses* varied in the extent of their political coverage. The mildest of them, *Le Journal des gens du monde* and *La Chronique scandaleuse*, contained only a collection of *faits divers*, which had no implications for politics, although they sometimes reflected badly on the aristocracy and clergy. A two-sentence vignette from *La Chronique scandaleuse*, for example, has some of the antiaristocratic flavor of Mauvelain's pornographic works: "M. de Duc de *** surprit un jour sa chère moitié dans les bras du précepteur de son fils. Cette digne femme lui dit avec une impudence ducale: 'Que n'étiez-vous là, Monsieur? Quand je n'ai pas mon écuyer, je prends le bras de mon laquais.'"[124] But other episodes showed respect for the aristocracy, and the king and his ministers received nothing but praise.[125] The *Mèmoires secrets* contained several barbed anecdotes about political affairs, which it discussed openly and critically, especially during the parlementary crises and the Diamond Necklace Affair. But the *Mémoires secrets* concentrated on events in the Republic of Letters; *L'Espion anglois* was more political and more outspoken. It dwelt on themes like the abuse of *lettres de cachet*, the decadence of the court, and the incompetence of certain ministers; and it expressed them in the form of extended essays, which included political analysis as well as reportage. In a typical passage of a well-informed account of the restoration of the parlements in 1774, the "spy," Pidansat de Mairobert, commented on the situation in Pau:[126] "Le discours du premier président, le moteur de tous les troubles de la Compagnie par le despotisme qu'il a voulu y introduire, n'est pas moins singulier que le précédent, en ce que, malgré la mortification que lui cause le retour des anciens magistrats, qu'il a traversé le plus qu'il a pu, il fait bonne contenance et semble se féliciter de l'événement comme s'il l'eût désiré avec ardeur." The tone indicates Mairobert's bias in favor of the parlements and his tendency to editorialize from a fairly radical point of view. He denounced "despotism" in everything he wrote, including libelous pamphlets, like the *Anecdotes sur Madame DuBarry*, which he plugged throughout *L'Espion anglois*.[127] But *L'Espion anglois* did not defend any consistent political "line": sometimes it criticized Turgot, for example, and sometimes it praised him.[128] Mairobert's radical remarks cropped up only occasionally, and they were incidental to the function of communicating news. So even the most political of the *chroniques scandaleuses* should be understood as underground journalism rather than as radical propaganda. The distinction may seem arbitrary, because the *chroniques* reviewed and printed long excerpts from the political pamphlets and libels, which were often written by the same men. Certainly *L'Espion anglois* and the *Mémoires secrets* helped spread discontent with the government. But their tone differs completely from that of the political tracts, as contemporaries noted. Thus the "spy" promised his readers that he would discuss "la politique, la finance, et la magistrature," but he especially stressed his inside knowledge of "faits particuliers . . . les anecdotes, aventures, historiettes de la cour ou de la ville, et les notices concernant les arts, les sciences, et la littérature."[129] And the continuator of *L'Espion anglois* disassociated himself from the "libellistes" who wrote pamphlets like *L'Espion dévalisé:* the public should not be taken in by the similarity of the titles, he warned. "Il ['l'espion anglois"] n'a ni ne veut avoir rien de commun avec ces confrères de trop mauvaise et trop dangereuse compagnie."[130] But how dangerous was this other genre? That question brings us to the last and largest category of Mauvelain's books.

The political works ordered by Mauvelain also indicate a strong demand for news, but not the ideologically neutral kind of *nouvelles* that prevailed in the *chroniques scandaleuses*. They concerned affairs of state, ministerial intrigues, and abuses of governmental power. Some treated rather remote topics—Pombal's reforms in Portugal and the partitioning of Poland—but most hammered at the themes of decadence and despotism so insistently as to make the weak rule of Louis XVI seem like the autocracy of an oriental potentate.

Linguet's *Mémoires sur la Bastille* and Mirabeau's *Lettres de cachet* typify this tendency. Each writer had a genius for presenting his personal misfortunes as a parable of French misgovernment, and each was instrumental in creating a political mythology that made many Frenchmen feel they were slaves—even though in reality the Bastille was almost empty by 1789 and even though *lettres de cachet* were frequently used as a kind of family discipline in cases where a scandal could dishonor a noble name. Linguet made his account of his *embastillement* sound like a revelation of the deepest, darkest secrets of state. Now that he was safe in England, he would tell all, he announced to his readers, and he proceeded to take them on a tour of the fortress, revealing all the horrors of its hidden workings. He recounted how new prisoners were frisked, thrown into fetid cells, cut off from all contact with the outside world, and denied the right not only to be tried but even to know what they had been accused of. His own innocence demonstrated the defenselessness of any Frenchman who might fall victim to the machinations of Versailles, he argued. And he drove the point home in a muckraking manner, by seizing on lurid details: the wormeaten mattresses, the thick, clammy walls, the villainous turnkeys, the repulsive food, and so on. All this inside information came with rhetorical outbursts against the unlimited power of "them," the unseen men at the top of the government who could reach into the life of any man, no matter how innocent, and bury him forever in an impenetrable *cachot*. It was a powerful pamphlet and one of Mauvelain's best sellers. Mauvelain placed seven orders for a total of thirty copies, despite his complaints that his area was already saturated with it. He also showed a strong interest in Mirabeau's *Lettres de cachet* (5 orders for 21 copies), which resembled the *Mémoires sur la Bastille*, as Linguet himself recognized.[131] Mirabeau provided the same spectacular details about his imprisonment in the dungeon of Vincennes as Linguet did about the Bastille. The humiliation of the frisking, the lack of light, the revolting food, the difficulties of getting exercise, everything suggested that France had degenerated into a prison state. But unlike Linguet, Mirabeau subordinated these details to some abstract considerations of political theory. His book began with a long discourse on the nature of government, which argued that all legitimate power derived from the people and that governments existed to protect the very natural rights that were violated by imprisonment through *lettre de cachet*. The journalistic revelations and philosophic declamations combined to give a very damaging view of French government.[132]

But the most effective and most violent propaganda belonged to the genre of political pamphlets called libels (*libelles*). These were violent attacks on individuals who commanded positions of prestige and power as ministers, courtiers, or members of the royal family. *Libellistes* like *nouvellistes* dealt in scandal, but they specialized in personal defamation, even in blackmail. Morande held up several courtiers for ransom by threatening to reveal the decadence of their private lives in pamphlets like *Vie privée . . . de Mgr. le duc de Chartres*. This typical libel presented the duke's life as a rake's progress or a contest between the competing vices of lust and greed. Thus, Morande explained, the duke only made love to his wife when he found prostitutes too expensive; he preferred the cheapest, vilest girls—streetwalkers who had been expelled from whorehouses because of misconduct; and he often dumped them where he found them without paying. This maneuver failed him on a grand tour of Italy's brothels, when a girl forced him to pay by summoning some thugs:[133] "Il crut apaiser cette furie en lui disant avec un sourire gracieux: 'mais dis donc, l'enfant, n'as-tu pas été bien payée de m'avoir possédé dans tes bras, moi, duc de Ch . . . s, moi, Prince du sang des Bourb . . . ?' 'Je ne me soucie guère de ce que tu es,' lui répliqua-t-elle. 'Je t'ai reçu comme j'aurais reçu ton laquais: chez nous autres, princes, valets, cardinaux, capucins, magistrats, et savetiers sont également bien venus et fêtés, mais tous, avant de sortir, doivent payer d'une manière ou d'autre.' " Morande continued in this vein for 134 pages, heaping up anecdotes about the duke's bestiality, cupidity, ignorance, cowardice, and egotism. Slander on such a scale might seem to destroy its own credibility, but the *Mémoires secrets* reported that the book was being read and talked about everywhere, "avec fureur."[134] Although he wrote it for money, Morande claimed that he spoke as a voice in the desert, crying "Princes soyez justes et pratiquez les vertus."[135] The real moral to his story, of course, was that princes were unjust and vicious—a point that could be made more effectively by sensational details than by abstract argument.

The libels therefore resembled *chroniques scandaleuses* in that they strung together anecdotes about "les grands" and "les gens en place"—the eighteenth-century counterparts to the famous and glamorous persons who occupy the popular press today. But they had political "bite." They probed the sensitive area where private decadence became a public issue, and by slandering eminent individuals, they desecrated the whole regime. *L'Espion dévalisé*, for example, sounded like *L'Espion anglois* and the *Portefeuille de Madame Gourdan* because it pretended to be the correspondance of a spy which had been discovered in a portfolio lying in the street. It contained journalistic accounts of unrelated events, including an essay on bullfighting in Spain and a report on Madame Gourdan's establishment. But most of the book treated politics, much of it in the form of court gossip—thus chapter 8: "Anecdote donnée par le marquis d'A * * * à la cour, dont il est ministre, et communiquée par le cousin du secrétaire d'ambassade." The spy gave a detailed account of the Guerre des Farines, which made the regime seem incompetent and insensitive to the desperate condition of the common people. He commented at length on ministerial intrigues, making Versailles look like a lottery for the benefit of undeserving aristocrats at the expense of the starving masses. And he maligned the most eminent figures of the government, notably Maurepas, whom he portrayed as the archetypical courtier—corrupt, blasé, and decadent, the embodiment of an elite that seemed incapable of facing social problems, much less of doing anything about them. The spy criticized the entire administration in this manner, naming names and prying out scandals. He even surveyed all the intendants and *maîtres des requêtes,* producing thumbnail portraits like the following:[136] "Le Laboullouse à Auch vivait avec la Pélin, était le jouet de Guimare; il ne sait pas lire. Il a une des plus belles intendances de France." The intrigues might appear trivial and the personalities despicable, but the spy presented them as if they were symptoms of a deep disease. The people of France were living like slaves, he said, and he seemed to summon them to revolt. He filled a chapter on the American Revolution with violent language about liberty, natural law, popular sovereignty, and the right to revolt. It was actually a reprint of a pamphlet by Mirabeau, which appealed to the Hessians to join the American rebels, but it sounded as though it were addressed to the French:[137] "Laissez à d'infâmes courtisans, à d'impies blasphémateurs le soin de vanter la prérogative royale et ses droits illimitées; mais n'oubliez pas que TOUS ne furent pas fait pour UN. . . ."

Two of Mauvelain's tracts libeled the monarchy itself. The *Vie privée de Louis XV* and *Les Fastes de Louis XV* treated the life of Louis XV as a *chronique scandaleuse,* a series of seductions, perversions, and despotic acts that made the Bourbons look like the source of everything rotten in the state. Louis had died before the libels appeared; but, they stressed, he had left behind a legacy, which made the story of his life particularly relevant to the reign of Louis XVI. Louis' agents had procured girls for his "harem" from the farthest corners of the kingdom, they explained. He had consumed two a week, pensioning them off after they ceased to arouse his jaded appetite. That came to a thousand girls in ten years and a total cost of a billion livres, "une des sources principales de la déprédation des finances."[138] The calculations were the same in both pamphlets, because *Les Fastes de Louis XV* lifted most of its material from the *Vie privée:* libels plagiarized one another as freely as *chroniques scandaleuses,* and in fact *Les Fastes* tried to pass itself off as a continuation of the earlier work. By spreading the same message, the two books reinforced one another; and so an analysis of *Les Fastes de Louis XV* should be doubly revealing, especially as there was far more demand for it than for any other book in Mauvelain's repertory. Mauvelain ordered 84 copies of it, almost twice as many as in the case of his next best sellers, and he ordered it eleven times, more often than any other work (he put in ten orders for *L'Espion dévalisé* and six for the *Vie privée de Louis XV*).

Striking a sage, objective tone, *Les Fastes de Louis XV* presented itself as an historical essay. It did in fact provide a two-volume narrative of political history from 1748 to 1774; so it should not be dismissed as a scandal sheet. But it used scandal to spice up the story, and it slanted all the details along the same bias. In discussing Madame DuBarry, for example, it was forever "tearing the veil" or "pulling back the curtain" to show her in some extravagant pose: caressing her Negro servant boy Zamore, flagellating a lady-in-waiting, mocking the Dauphin for his impotence, making a fool of the king while seducing his ministers behind his back, and all the while milking the treasury of millions—18 million, according to the libeler's best estimate. Depravity on this scale was a national disaster:[139] "La nation était au cri. On mourait de faim dans les provinces: les travaux étaient suspendus dans la capitale; l'image de l'indigence se présentait d'un bout du royaume à l'autre, et le Contrôleur-général faisait faire banqueroute. . . . Tandis que tous les états étaient dans la consternation, que la misère poignait la classe la plus indigente du peuple, tous les roués étalaient un luxe, faisaient parade d'une prodigalité effrayable." As if the reader could not reach his own conclusions, the text placed the blame directly on the king:[140] "Louis XV était toujours le même; c'est à dire qu'il restait toujours plongé dans la crapule et dans les voluptés. Malgré la misère des peuples et les calamités publiques, sa maîtresse allait tellement croissant en prodigalités et en déprédations, qu'elle eût, en peu d'années, englouti le royaume, si la mort du Sultan n'y eût mis un terme."

Political libel of this sort combined pornography, defamation of august persons, and radical political comment. The libeler smeared the entire regime, using every weapon at his command, but he especially sought to desanctify the symbols and to deflate the myths that made the monarchy appear legitimate in the eyes of its subjects. To turn this trick required rhetorical skill, not mere mudslinging. Consider this passage:[141] "Le sceptre de Louis XV, tour à tour le jouet de l'amour, de l'ambition, de l'avarice, était devenue entre les mains de la Comtesse [DuBarry] la marotte de la folie. Quelle extravagance en effet que de voir la Sultane sortir toute nue de son lit, se faire donner une de ses pantoufles par le Nonce du Pape et la seconde par le Grand-Aumônier, et les deux prélats s'estimer trop dédommagés de ce vil et ridicule emploi, en jettant un coup d'oeil fugitif sur les charmes secrets d'une pareille beauté!" The writer slipped in the dirty details without spoiling his tone of righteous indignation. He posed his characters as if he were constructing a tableau vivant. And he created an atmosphere that would appeal to an eighteenth-century audience: Madame DuBarry is a sultana, her boudoir a harem . . . and the king's scepter a jester's bauble. As in so many plays and novels of the period, the air is heavy with oriental exoticism and with irony; for the only person in command of the situation is the naked concubine; the lascivious prelates hardly dare look at her, and the action takes place behind the back of the king.[142] At the end of the book, the true despot of France turns out to be Madame DuBarry, whose career in brothels and gaming dens had been recounted carefully at the beginning, and the real cause of the king's death is traced to her role as his procuress. Having ceased to arouse Louis' exhausted sexual appetite, the DuBarry sweeps the streets in search of a "vrai morceau de roi" and comes upon a peasant girl, who is suffering from an undetected case of smallpox. The girl's father protests and is removed by *lettre de cachet*. Then the girl submits to her royal master, dies soon afterward, and the king follows her to the grave, having lived out his life according to the words of a doggerel that appeared earlier in the book:[143]

> Tu n'es plus qu'un tyran débile
> Qu'un vil automate imbécile
> Esclave de la Du Barry:
> Du Gange jusqu'à la Tamise
> On te honnit, on te méprise

Perhaps the most important and unexpected conclusion to be drawn from this analysis of Mauvelain's orders is not that he called for a fair number of irreligious and obscene books but that the great bulk of his orders went for political material—not Enlightenment treatises but hard-hitting underground journalism. The graph of political works towers above the others,[144] and its dominance is strengthened by the fact that the pamphlets, libels, and *chroniques scandaleuses* all fulfilled the same function of communicating news. Far from being neutral, this news made the regime look rotten. It served as radical propaganda, even in the *chroniques*, where political matters took second place to crime and sex. Of course "radical" does not mean revolutionary. The political tracts worked a dozen variations on a single theme: the monarchy had degenerated into a despotism. They did not call for a revolution or foresee 1789 or even provide much discussion of the deeper social and political issues that were to make the destruction of the monarchy possible. Inadvertently, however, they prepared for that event, because they sullied the aura of sanctity surrounding the crown. The government sensed this danger. Indeed the motive for the order of 12 June 1783, which had so badly disrupted communications between Neuchâtel and Troyes, was the need to suppress "la multitude des libelles imprimés dans l'étranger et introduits dans le royaume."[145]

Most of the books Mauvelain ordered were written anonymously by Grub-Street characters: Morande, Imbert, Manuel, Luchet, Buffonidor, Mayeur de Saint-Paul, Baudouin de Guémadeuc, Mouffle d'Angerville, Pidansat de Mairobert. Everything one can learn about their obscure lives suggests that they were marginal characters, who would put anything in print for a few sous—and perhaps also to vent their frustrations at living down-and-out in Paris, beyond the pale of respectability.[146] Mauvelain had sunken into this milieu himself, while covering up his indigence with talk about patrons and prominent friends. Although he may have lived for a while in the salon society of Troyes, he died in the poorhouse, or something very like it. His inside information about the latest libels, his offers of clandestine manuscripts to print, his contacts with hack writers like Brissot all suggest that he functioned as a liaison man between the literary underground and the polite society of the provinces. But this role could have made him favor libelous literature. Do his orders in fact reflect his personal situation and his personal taste rather than the general character of the underground book trade?

That question cannot be answered until the whole trade has been studied and analyzed statistically. But preliminary exploration of the vast correspondence of the STN shows that there were men like Mauvelain all over France and that they all wanted the same sort of books. Malherbe in Loudun, Chevrier in Poitiers, Lair in Blois, Caldesaigues in Marseilles, Sombert in Châlons-sur-Marne, Manoury in Caen, Machuel in Rouen, Le Lièvre in Belfort, Laisney in Beauvais, Resplandy in Toulouse, Guichard in Avignon, Desbordes in La Rochelle, Bonnard in Auxerre—all clamored for the same *livres philosophiques*. And what little can be known about the trade of the other booksellers in Troyes indicates that they ordered what Mauvelain ordered. All of them wanted to make money by satisfying their customers. Mauvelain was no different. His letters show a special interest in Mercier and Raynal and attitudes that might be associated with the Enlightenment or perhaps with underground journalism, but like everyone who lived from the book trade, he transmitted literary demand as he perceived it through contact with his customers.

Society and Culture in Troyes

How to identify those customers is the final problem in the analysis of Mauvelain's business, and unfortunately it cannot be resolved. At first he claimed to order only books for his friends:[147] "Voici une liste de livres que je vous serai obligé de m'envoyer. . . . C'est pour mon compte particulier pour des amis qui m'ont prié de leur procurer les articles suivants." But he dropped that pretense when he began to order large shipments. In one of his last letters,[148] he reported the disappearance of an *ami* to whom he had sent 130 volumes—behavior that suggests a book peddlar (*colporteur* or *marchand forain*) rather than the refined society that Mauvelain said he frequented. Troyes was one of the greatest centers of *colportage* in the country. Peddlars came there from all over northern France to stock up on the manufactures that made it famous: textiles and the primitive paperback books known as the *bibliothèque bleue*. It is difficult to believe that Mauvelain did not supply them with the works that he got from the STN, especially as his letters sometimes stressed the need for shipments to arrive in time for the fairs, where peddlars did their provisioning. In his very first order, which he placed in Bouvet's name, Mauvelain prescribed that the books arrive "pour la foire du 15 mars à Troyes qui, en y amenant beaucoup de monde lui procure un gros débit."[149] He may have tried to exploit the same market after he cut Bouvet out of the STN's trade. If so, his orders reflect literary demand in a wide area and not merely in Troyes. He certainly wanted to extend his business throughout Champagne, and some of his books must have traveled much farther.

Nonetheless, he probably concentrated on the local market. Unlike the *grossistes* of the wholesale trade who ordered dozens, even hundreds, of copies per title and sold them to small-town bookdealers throughout several provinces, Mauvelain ordered relatively small lots of books and retailed them on a small scale. His entire stock apparently did not amount to more than a few thousand volumes, which he kept in an attic and parceled out when "friends" stopped by or when he went on his rounds. But his letters do not tell how he sold his wares or who bought them. Although they refer to local customers in a general way, they mention only one group of clients: army officers who were stationed in Troyes for brief tours of duty. Thus Mauvelain specified that his order of 31 December 1784 needed to arrive by March, because it was "pour les gardes et officiers qui viennent faire leur service pour ce temps-là et qui m'ont fait demander tous les articles."[150] A later letter extended the deadline by a month, "parce qu'y en ayant une partie [*sic*] pour les gardes qui n'ont que trois mois de résidence, il faut que cela arrive les premiers jours d'avril au plus tard."[151]

The prices of the books would have put them beyond the purchasing power of the working classes but not of the bourgeoisie of Troyes. Although the STN's prices varied (see the first chart), it usually charged from one to two livres for a single-volume work. Mirabeau's *Errotika biblion,* one volume, is a typical example; it cost one livre 10 sous. The paper and labor that went into multivolume works made them more expensive: *L'Espion anglois* contained four volumes and cost four livres 10 sous. Mauvelain said that transportation, insurance, and other costs came to another 10 sous per volume[152] and that he needed a 33 percent profit to make his business worthwhile.[153] So he probably sold most of his books for about 2 livres 15 sous. Since the standard, four-pound loaf of rye bread normally cost about 8 sous, the *Errotika biblion* was worth almost half a week's supply of bread for a working-class family with three children. It also cost the equivalent of almost a day's wages of a carpenter, who would make about 15 livres in a good week. So even if the skilled and unskilled laborers of Troyes could read *livres philosophiques,* they could not buy them. But the books would have fit easily into the budgets of the magistrates in the bailliage court of Troyes, who made 2,000 to 3,000 livres a year, and they could have been bought by the other professional men, merchants, and manufacturers of the town whose income was over 1,500 livres.[154]

One can imagine Mauvelain's books passing from under his cloak to a middle-class clientele and probably also to some local noblemen. But that, alas, is mere speculation, because one cannot see past Mauvelain's orders to his customers. It is possible, however, to place him in the setting of prerevolutionary

Troyes.[155] While he lodged with Bouvet on rue Notre Dame, he lived in the heart of the old city, near a cluster of churches and market places, only a few steps from the Hôtel de Ville to the north and, just beyond it, the Oratorian college. When he moved to the Place du Marché au Blé in the summer of 1783, he shifted to the western edge of the town near the gate that opened toward Paris— a good place in which to receive contraband goods. Although it could boast about being the capital of Champagne, eighteenth-century Troyes had declined to the third rank of provincial cities and seems to have been less important than the rival champenois towns of Châlons and Reims. It had a population of about 22,000 in the 1780's—more than in the dark days of the seventeenth century but perhaps only half as many as in the sixteenth. The town's economic life depended on the trade and manufacturing of textiles. It had 360 master weavers in Mauvelain's time, and it produced a great variety of woolen and cotton goods, hosiery and calicoes in particular. Its large artisan population also manufactured pins, paper, and leather goods. Troyes contained a great many clergymen, because it had a dozen monasteries and convents and was the see of a bishopric. And its bailliage and présidial courts made it something of a legal center, although the courts contained only fifteen magistrates in the 1780's. Its cultural life seems to have been quiet in comparison with Châlons, which had an active provincial academy. But Troyes had a theater, which shared a troupe of actors with Châlons and Langres; an important library, thanks to a benefaction of 1650; and a masonic lodge. By 1780 its educational institutions included four primary schools run by the *frères de la doctrine chrétienne,* a seminary, an Oratorian college with 300 to 400 students, and schools devoted to design, midwifery, and surgery. There were four legally established booksellers, two of whom also functioned as printers, in 1764. That number represents a decline from the late seventeenth century, when Troyes had "onze imprimeurs et marchands libraires, trois boutiques, et deux ou trois maîtres qui travaillent comme compagnons," and it makes Troyes look weak in comparison with Châlons, which had eight booksellers in 1764, and Reims, which had nine.[156] The rate of literacy also seems to have been relatively low (for northern France) in the area around Troyes, where only 40 to 49 percent of the adults could sign their names on marriage certificates.[157] So in general, Troyes probably epitomized what the Parisians meant by "provincial": it was a cultural backwater.

If that were the case, the story of Mauvelain's book business takes on considerable importance, for one would not expect to see such a strong demand for radical literature in a small and sleepy corner of the provinces. Perhaps there was a hidden current of ideological ferment in the homeland of the archaic *bibliothèque bleue.* But the backwardness of Troyes should not be exaggerated. True, the town's historian found no evidence of any effervescence in its intellectual life during the eighteenth century. But Troyes could claim to have at least one, very minor philosophe, P.-J. Grosley, the "Voltaire Champenois." Not only did it harbor some freemasons, but its college contained "beaucoup d'impies," according to Daniel Mornet.[158] Religious skepticism apparently followed in the wake of a particularly violent local version of the Jansenist-Jesuit struggle. And one local authority asserts that "la bourgeoisie commerçante et la noblesse de robe, parmi lesquelles se recrutaient les administrateurs de la cité, étaient en générale acquises aux idées nouvelles [of the philosophes]."[159] Certainly the general cahier of the Third Estate in the balliage of Troyes expressed a militant, enlightened spirit. It demanded that the Estates General become the regular legislature of France, levying taxes and passing laws in the name of the nation, without regard to distinctions of estate. It called for an end to the tax privileges of the nobility and the favored treatment of the upper clergy. And it was especially insistent on the need to protect the natural rights of the individual against the government's tendency to violate them. The Troyens demanded that *lettres de cachet* be abolished, that no Frenchman be imprisoned without proper legal procedure, and that the arbitrary power of ministers be limited by making them responsible to the Estates General.[160] These ideas may only have been "in the air," or they could have traveled up the Seine from Paris. But some of them must have passed through the back rooms of Mauvelain's apartment in the Place du Marché à Blé.

CONCLUSION

The charts and graphs of Mauvelain's business do not do justice to the human element in it, which emerges only if one follows his affairs stage by stage as they evolved in his correspondence. If his account of his background is correct, he probably began his career with great expectations about his future as a man of the robe and a man of letters. But by 1781, when he had reached the age of forty-one and began to do business with the STN, his life had taken several wrong turns: a violent quarrel had put an end to his legal career and had made him a fugitive from justice; he had left a wife in Paris; he apparently suffered from a horrible case of venereal disease; and although he probably had written some pamphlets, his literary activities served mainly to camouflage his role as a small-town distributor of prohibited books. He presented himself as a gentleman author in order to capture the confidence of the Swiss publishers. While dangling proposals for the printing of his own works, he slipped in his first orders for books; and while acting as the STN's agent in its dealings with the other booksellers of Troyes, he won its good will and cut his competitors out of its business, all the time piling order on order and speculating in swindles on the side. Eventually he dropped the mask and began to order large quantities of the most extreme *livres philosophiques*, haggling like a veteran of the underground book trade. When his confidence game collapsed, he disappeared into an obscure corner of Paris and died, penniless, disease ridden, and determined to fight off creditors "until the Resurrection." It is an extraordinary story, but it does not differ in essentials from other histories of downward mobility and marginality in the republic of letters. Mauvelain's life ran parallel, on an obscure level, to the lives of the hack writers whose books he peddled. Indeed, there was an affinity between authors and book distributors at the bottom of the literary underworld: they undermined the Old Regime together in their common struggle to survive. And there were more of them than has been realized, although they usually disappeared into the fathomless depths of history, leaving behind only a signature on a police report, an entry in the registers of the Bastille, or nothing at all. What makes Mauvelain's case so fascinating is the fact that it can be known in enormous detail. To open his dossier is to come into contact with a colorful cross section of vanished humanity, to enjoy the first, close-up view of a world in which men's business was to stay invisible.

That world had its own organization, and the supporting cast of characters in Mauvelain's life reveals the operations of the literary underground at several points along the circuits that supplied Frenchmen with prohibited books. Mallet's activities show how clandestine manuscripts were produced, published, marketed, and policed—a matter of some importance, in Mallet's case, since the author of the manuscripts was Mirabeau. Mauvelain's dealings with Faivre indicate how the smuggling industry operated—how it functioned as an "insurance" business, that is, and not as a romantic adventure. And Mauvelain's relations with the STN reveal how an under-the-cloak bookdealer in a small city coordinated his business with a major supplier in a foreign country.

Mauvelain's affairs with the STN also raise the possibility of attempting some modest market analysis—modest, because it cannot pretend to any general conclusions and only has the value of a case study. It is worth undertaking, however, because the actual content of underground literature has never been studied at all. We simply do not know what Frenchmen read in the eighteenth century. Some research has indicated the general character of their legal reading matter; but owing to the restrictive character of the censorship and the conservative guild system of publishing, the readers of the Old Regime relied heavily on the illegal book trade for a substantial portion of their literary diet. Those illegal books have slipped through every net cast by historians investigating literary history and the ideological origins of the Revolution. So Mauvelain is a big catch even though he was a small fish. By studying his orders, one can calculate the demand for prohibited books in an undistinguished provincial town. The business of other dealers in other towns may have been different, but the papers of the STN suggest that Mauvelain was a fairly representative example of his species. The pattern of his orders therefore provides the first reliable indication of what actually constituted the underground literature in France on the eve of the Revolution.

Although the orders contain few books by the most famous philosophes, they show a considerable demand for works of the extreme, Holbachean Enlightenment. They also indicate a strong but subsidiary market for pornographic and irreligious works. But most important, they demonstrate an interest in politics and in contemporary affairs. Above all, Mauvelain wanted political pamphlets, *chroniques scandaleuses,* and libels about leading personalities in the government and the court. Most of those works were anonymous tracts by obscure hacks, and most served to communicate news—but news of a crude and radical kind; they villified authority without providing any intelligent analysis of social and political issues.

Having failed to rise to the level of at least minor classics, most of Mauvelain's books have dropped out of French literature, just as Mauvelain himself dropped out of French history. No one reads or remembers them today, because by a process of cultural evolution they have become extinct; they do not live in the repertory of reading that constitutes literary culture in the present. Unfortunately, one cannot follow the evolutionary path backward in order to discover the culture of the past. Too much has fallen by the wayside, and it is too easy to assume that the French of the eighteenth century read what passes today for eighteenth-century French literature. But by studying the business of a clandestine book dealer in the 1780's, one can catch a glimpse of that literature as it actually existed, at its most explosive, in its real context. Mauvelain's books and his life reveal a lost world of literary experience, waiting to be explored.

Appendix 1: The Production and Distribution of Mirabeau's Prohibited Books

Mallet wrote the following confession, which is one of the most revealing accounts of an underground publishing operation in the eighteenth century, during his imprisonment in the Bastille. Its background has been explained sufficiently in the preceding essay, but it should be noted that Mallet made a slip in asserting that Mirabeau supplied Fauche fils aîné, Favre et Witel with copy from the Château de Joux. By that time Mirabeau was in the prison of Pontarlier, where he remained from February to August 1782, while conducting his judicial battle against the marquis de Monnier. He had been incarcerated in the nearby Château de Joux from May 1775 to January 1776, when he escaped, abducted Sophie Monnier, and began the adventures for which he was eventually imprisoned in Vincennes and tried in Pontarlier and Besançon. The trial ended in a compromise settlement, which left Mirabeau free to deal with his printers in Neuchâtel, as Mallet describes. The syntax, expressions, and somewhat disordered character of the confession (it has been transcribed without modifying the grammar) suggests that Mallet did in fact write it himself, in an agitated state of mind. It is in the Bibliothèque Nationale, fonds français, Ms 22046, under the title "Copie de la déclaration faite et écrite à la Bastille par le nommé Mallet."

"Je déclare que ce n'est qu'au 20 juillet 1782 que je suis entré en société avec les sieurs Fauche fils aîné et Witel. Notre premier ouvrage que nous avons mis sous presse a été *Des lettres de cachet et des prisons d'Etat* dont nous avons acheté le manuscrit du comte de Mirabeau fils pour la somme de 150 louis, dans lequel marché est entré un ancien compte d'un mémoire qu'ils avaient déjà imprimé pour le comte de Mirabeau. Les sieurs Fauche et Witel avaient un traité avec lui par lequel ils s'engageaient d'imprimer tous ses manuscrits dont on n'avait pas communiqué aux nouveaux associés avant de conclure l'association. Le comte de Mirabeau était alors au Château de Joux à Pontarlier et nous envoyait des feuillets de manuscrit à mesure qu'on lui renvoyait ceux qui étaient composés et corrigés, après quelques feuilles imprimées. Je voulus faire juger cet ouvrage par quelque personne en état, n'étant pas moi-même à portée d'en juger. Je communiquai les quatre premières feuilles déjà tirées à M. l'avocat Convert, aujourd'hui des Quatre Ministraux de Neuchâtel. Il me répondit que cet ouvrage ne paraissait pas mauvais, mais qu'il fallait prendre garde à ce qui suivrait. Il me conseilla de les porter chez le censeur, ce que je fis le même jour. Je les apportai à M. le Maire Ballot, conseiller d'état, qui me dit deux jours après les avoir lues que nous pouvions continuer. J'en fis autant à M. le Banneret Boyve qui est aussi censeur. Nous nous croyons bien rassurés à continuer l'impression de cet ouvrage. M. le Comte de Mirabeau arrive dans ces entrefaits-là à Neuchâtel et fut fêté par tout ce qu'il y avait de plus distingué dans le pays, se fait gloire de son ouvrage, et continuellement nous recevions à notre imprimerie les premiers magistrats, et chaque feuille qui était seulement composée, on faisait des épreuves au rouleau, et il en distribuait à ces Messieurs, c'est-à-dire à M.M. Boyve Chancelier et conseiller d'état, de Marval conseiller d'état, de Rougement Président, Duperon [i.e., Du Peyrou] qui lisait toutes les épreuves et faisait mêmes des changements à bien des chapitres; de Pierre [i.e., de Petitpierre?], procureur général; de Saint-Robert etc. etc. Ainsi personne dans la ville n'ignorait que nous imprimions cet ouvrage. M. le Comte a resté à Neuchâtel tout le temps qu'a duré l'impression du premier volume et moitié du second. Il n'en est parti que quand nous avons commencé les preuves et éclaircissements, dont il n'a pas lu les épreuves. C'est deux ou trois jours avant son départ que j'ai eu une dispute très sérieuse avec lui pour ne pas imprimer ses ouvrages, en lui faisant observer que ses manuscrits étaient trop dangereux et trop chers, que nous ne pourrions les imprimer sans courir de grands risques. J'ai sollicité mes associés de rompre avec lui, et ils ont consenti. Nous avons pris des arbitres pour nous arranger, et ils nous ont jugé à garder seulement *Ma Conversion* pour la somme de 1000 livres payable en livres à son choix dans notre catalogue, dont il se trouvait en avoir reçu beaucoup, comme aussi lé manuscrit de l'*Erotica Biblion* dont il nous avait promis de nous remettre quatre dissertations qu'il ne nous a jamais envoyées; en conséquence l'ouvrage est incomplet; un autre manuscrit intitulé *Elégie de Tibulle,* qui pourra faire environ quatre volumes in 8°, qui est entre les mains de M. Duperon. Je n'ai jamais vu le manuscrit *Ma Conversion*. Je ne sais pas si c'est l'auteur ou M. Duperon qui le tient. Il nous a laissé seulement le sujet des figures dont nos associés ont fait graver deux à ce qu'ils m'ont marqué et envoyé pour les montrer aux libraires de Paris ou autres. Le comte de Mirabeau avant de nous remettre son manuscrit de l'*Erotica*, qui était cacheté, n'a pas voulu que nous le voyons qu'il n'eût de nous nos effets. Ainsi nous ne savions pas seulement de quel genre il traitait. Il tient de nous encore pour 200 louis d'or de nos propres effets pour sûreté de ses manuscrits. Nous avons imprimé avec les *Lettres de cachet*, l'*Erotica Biblion*, *Le Tableau des maladies aigues* et *Le Tableau de Paris grande et petite édition*. Voilà tous les ouvrages que nous avons imprimés jusqu'à ce jour depuis notre association. Nous avons fait notre catalogue sur celui de Fauche père et celui de la Société Typographique nos voisins qui nous ont fourni tous les ouvrages qu'on dit prohibés et que j'ai vendus dans mon voyage, qui a commencé au mois de décembre dernier. Nous n'avons échangé de nos *Lettres de cachet* qu'à Bâle contre des *Fastes* [i.e., *Fastes de Louis XV*], mais très peu, environ 50; je ne m'en rappelle pas, parce que cela n'est pas ma partie. C'est notre sieur Witel qui tient la correspondance. Ce dernier avait encore dans son magasin, quand nous nous sommes associés, quelques ouvrages prohibés, comme les *Lauriers ecclésiastiques*, des *Réductions* [*de Paris*], des *Verités rendues sensibles* [*à Louis XVI*]—je ne sais pas si ce dernier est prohibé—environ 20 à 25 *Espion dévalisé*. C'est tout ce que je puis me rappeler. Observez, Monseigneur, qu'il n'avait pas imprimé tous ces ouvrages. C'était des changes qu'il avait fait, soit à Lyon, à Genève, à Avignon, etc. etc. Dans tout mon voyage, qui a commencé au mois de décembre, je n'ai point fait de change contre mes articles, parce que je ne connaissais pas assez le commerce de la librairie. A Lausanne j'ai vendu à M. Mourer des *Lettres de cachet*. Celui-ci les avait sous presse quand j'ai été chez lui. Il me serait impossible de pouvoir vous donner un récit exact du nombre et des articles que chaque libraire m'a demandé: Je vous citerai seulement tous les ouvrages dont je me rappelle avoir proposé, qui n'étaient pourtant pas dans mon catalogue, comme l'*Espion anglois* (les quatre premiers volumes), l'*Espion dévalisé*, les *Fastes*, les *Lauriers ecclésiastiques*, des *Réductions de Paris*, des *Lettres de cachet* etc., etc., etc. Voici les noms des nos correspondants que j'ai vus dans mon voyage. A Lausanne, MM. La Combe, Heubach et Compagnie, Grasset, Des Combes, Pott; je n'ai vendu à ces Messieurs que quelques *Lettres de cachet* [par]ce qu'ils impriment tous les ouvrages prohibés qui ont cours. A Genève, MM. Cailler, Chirol, Bardin, Bassompierre; je n'ai point reçu beaucoup de demandes pour tous ces ouvrages, pas même des *Lettres de cachet*. A Lyon, MM. Jacquenet, Rosset, Grabit, Los Rios, Barret, LeRoy, Bernuset et Compagnie. J'ai vendu des *Lettres de Cachet* et des *Espion dévalisé* à presque tous ces messieurs. Il ne leur a pas été difficile de les faire entrer, parce qu'ils sont presque tous de la Chambre syndicale. Je suis venu en droiture à Paris. A Paris, Hardouin, Desauges, Desenne, Jobart. Ces deux derniers n'achètent point de prohibé ou du moins très peu. J'ai reçu des demandes de tous ces messieurs, et ma maison leur a expédié; mais les balles ne sont pas parvenues. Elles ont été saisies à Besançon. A Versailles MM. Poinçot, Blaisot; je n'ai vendu qu'à Poinçot du prohibé. A Dijon, Mailly; je n'ai rien fait avec lui, et je ne l'ai vu que cette seule fois. A Dôle, Chamboz; je lui ai vendu très peu de chose. C'est la maison de Fauche père qui lui fournit. A Besançon, MM. L'Epagnez cadet, Protade, Veuve Charmet. Je suis obligé de dire à Monseigneur que c'est ici qu'il faut que je lui donne des preuves de ma franchise. *C'est M. L'Epagnez comme l'un des syndics de la Chambre qui nous a favorisé le passage de nos balles sur les frontières et les remettais après à M. Renaud Du Creux* pour être expédiées à leur destination. A Pontarlier, M. Faivre; je lui ai vendu beaucoup de *Lettres de cachet.*

"De retour à Neuchâtel, je ne fus pas longtemps à me reposer. Mes associés m'obligèrent à repartir tout de suite pour Paris pour venir négocier des billets et pour faire des payements en passant à Besançon. Je fus voir·M. L'Epagnez cadet et le priai de faire tout son possible pour faire passer tous nos *Tableaux de Paris.* Toutes les demandes que les libraires m'avaient faites dans mon premier voyage, qui étaient expédiées au risque de MM. les libraires, passées Besançon furent saisies à l'exception d'une seule qu'on sauva et que l'on m'a expédiée. Elle contenait environ 150 *Lettres de cachet,* 6 ou 4 *Fastes,* 6 *Espion anglois,* 21 *Espion dévalisé,* 200 *Erotica.* Voilà tout ce qu'elle contenait de prohibé, et je· ferai serment que je n'ai point vendu de *Fastes* et d'*Espion anglois* davantage dans Paris, ni d'*Espion dévalisé:* ces trois articles ont été saisis entièrement. D'ailleurs le nombre que nous en avions n'était pas considérable, parce que de tous les articles de mon catalogue, je n'aurais pas été à même d'en fournir à un correspondant 25, à l'exception de ceux que nous avons imprimés. Il m'est arrivé il y a environ trois semaines ou un mois douze balles dont j'en ai disposé comme il suit: quatre balles dont il y en a deux du *Tableau de Paris* et les deux autres d'assortissement, qui sont celles que j'ai addressées à Monseigneur, et six autres qui avaient des destinations soit pour Emslet, Le Roy etc.; les deux autres petits sont entrés dans Paris. C'est moi-même qui les ai passés par petits paquets dans des voitures publiques, c'est à dire ces voitures que l'on prend rue Vaugirard pour aller au Bourg-la-Reine. Elles contenaient des *Mémoires de la Bastille* que mes associés m'ont fait expédier depuis Lausanne où on en a fait une contrefacon. Le nombre était d'environ deux cent soixante-dix que j'ai distribué sur le champ à deux libraires de Paris. Il y avait dans cette même balle 50 *Histoire de Suzon* pour Desauges père sans figures, parce qu'elles ne valent rien, 13 *Comte d'Estaing,* dont six que j'ai vendus au sieur Chambon ainsi que les *Bastille* et quelques *Lettres de cachet.* Voilà un aveu qui m'est bien sensible et qui ne peut me causer que de chagrin et une longue détention, mais j'ai promis à Monseigneur de tout dire.

"A l'égard des soupçons que l'on a sur moi d'avoir eu intention de faire imprimer la collection de tous ces mauvais ouvrages qui ont paru contre le Parlement, je n'ai rien à craindre de ce côté là. Monseigneur m'a fait l'honneur de me dire qu'il y avait quatre personnes qui déposaient contre moi. Il suffirait seulement d'une, si Monseigneur voulait me faire la grâce de la faire paraître devant moi, pour me justifier ou pour me convaincre; mais je répète encore une fois que je ne crains rien et que je suis innocent. Le manuscrit *Sauveur,* copie qui m'a été adressée, a été brûlé, dont je suis bien fâché, car quand il serait à 200 lieues d'ici, je serais toujours à même de le remettre à Monseigneur. Je voudrais cependant donner quelques preuves à Monseigneur, et je ne sais comment m'y prendre. Voice une idée que Monseigneur pourrait trouver peut-être bonne pour me justifier. Je vais écrire à mes associés, sans leur faire mention de la moindre chose que je suis arrêté. Il est très sûr qu'ils ne le soupçonnent même pas, car je leur ai écrit que j'avais été très bien reçu de vous Monseigneur, et que vous m'aviez pardonné d'avoir vendu tous ces ouvrages philosophiques sous la condition que je ne récidiverais pas. Je vais supposer ma lettre comme si je leur avais envoyé la copie de ce maudit ouvrage. Vous verrez ce qu'ils me répondront. Ils seront surpris de ce que je leur parlerai et me répondront en conséquence. Je ferai adresser la lettre où Monseigneur voudra, sans cependant leur donner aucun soupçon; ou bien si Monseigneur voulait faire faire une visite dans notre comptoir, et faire examiner toute ma correspondance, on n'en trouvera pas une qui fasse mention de cet ouvrage. Je ne leur en ai jamais parlé, et je ne puis pas comprendre comment on peut avoir des soupçons sur moi. Je puis peut-être bien en avoir parlé chez quelque marchand comme on parle de tant d'autres ouvrages; mais cela n'a jamais été mon intention de le faire imprimer.

"Je supplie très humblement Monseigneur de ne pas me perdre. Tout ce que j'ai fait dans le commerce de la librairie, je n'en connaissais pas les dangers; c'est plutôt par ignorance que par intérêt ou méchanceté. Tous les livres que j'ai vendus, je ne les ai jamais lus. Je suis extrêmement borné dans ce genre de commerce. Daignez, Monseigneur, avoir quelques égards pour ma petite famille: au nom de l'Etre Suprême, ne me perdez pas. Je fais serment que je ne ferai jamais plus le commerce de librairie ni en France ni dans l'étranger. Je ne m'inquiète plus de mes balles du *Tableau de Paris*. Elles sont à la disposition de Monseigneur. Notre maison est entièrement ruinée et discréditée par les pertes considérables que nous avons essuyées cette année et le retard de faire mes payements que me cause ma détention. Toutes les traites que l'on m'envoie seront protestées et renvoyées. Ce sera pour nous des frais très conséquents.

Ce juillet 1783"

Appendix 2: A Shipment to Mauvelain as Entered in the STN's Account Books

The above analysis of Mauvelain's orders fails to show what he actually received. It also excludes the nonprohibited books that he ordered, and it lacks complete information on the prices of the books. The following entry from an account book of the STN, dated 26 July 1784, compensates for some of those shortcomings, because it lists all the books, with their prices, in one of the largest shipments to Mauvelain. The accounts are not complete for the full period of Mauvelain's dealings with the STN; and in any case they do not provide an accurate reflection of the demand among his customers, because the STN sent him a smaller proportion of prohibited books than he ordered. But they do help to put his requests for *livres philosophiques* in the context of his overall trade. The entry is copied just as it appears in the account book, which is entitled "Journal C," except that words that were abbreviated have been written out in full.

Du Dit [26 July, 1784]

Bruzard de Mauvelain doit aux Suivants

	livres
à *Bonnet de Nuit*, exemplaires 12	36 [livres]
à Marchandises Générales,	
exemplaires 6 *Histoire philosophique*	162
1 *Oeuvres de Bonnet*, 8°, 18 volumes	45
2 *Catalogues de Genève*	3
12 *Homme sauvage*	18
6 *Mort de Louis XI*	4–10
6 *Destruction de la Ligue*	7–10
6 *Hommes de ma connoissance*	3
6 *Demande imprévue*	3
6 *Le gentillâtre*	3
6 *Tombeaux de Vérone*	4–10
6 *Zoë*	4–10
6 *Habitant de la Guadeloupe*	4–10
2 *Portraits des rois de France*	10
6 *Philadelphien à Genève*	9
6 *Taureau blanc*	3
6 *Essais sur les Turcs*	7–10
3 *Dernier voyage de Cook*	4–10
1 *Essais sur la santé des filles*	–15
2 *Oeuvres de Boulanger*	12
1 *Soins pour la bouche*	–15
6 *Train de Paris*	3
2 *Liaisons dangereuses*	5
6 *Histoire de Jésus-Christ*	9
2 *Elements d'orectologie*	2
6 *Inceste avoué*	9
6 *Les comédiens*	1–10
6 *Errotika biblion*	9
6 *Examen du christianisme*	7–10
6 *Catéchumène*	7–10
3 *Ciel ouvert*	3
6 *Oeuvres de Vargemont*	6
10 *Mémoires sur la Bastille*	7–10
10 *Oeuvres posthumes de Montesquieu*	10
2 *Voyage de Pages*	4–10
2 *Mémoires de Gibraltar*	–12
6 *Nuits champêtres*	6
6 *Dialogues des morts*	3
6 *Infortune de la Lande*	3
6 *Voyage de Genève à Londres*	3–12
1 *Christianisme dévoilé*	2
12 *Chronique scandaleuse*	15
2 *Vie privée de Louis XV*	12
4 *Intolérance ecclésiastique*	9
1 *Recueil de pièces galantes*	7–10
1 *Oeuvres de Virgile*	6
1 *Vie de Marsigli*	6
1 *Aventures de Robinson*	3–10
1 *Oeuvres d'Helvétius*	6
6 *Espion anglois*, tomes 1 à 4	27

12	*Apologie de la Bastille*	15
12	*Réflexions sur les Confessions*	9
6	*Lettres de Julie à Eulalie*	7–10
2	*Nouveau Robinson*	3–10
1	*Oeuvres de Lamettrie*	4–10
2	*Galathée*	1–4
1	*Femmes illustres*	3
1	*Histoire des diables*	1–10
6	*Fausseté des miracles*	7–10
12	*Bonhomme anglois*	9
2	*Profession de foi des théistes*	1
2	*Lettres sur la philosophie*	1
6	*Muses en belle humeur*	6
6	*Lettres d'Yorick à Elisa*	1–16
6	*Portraits d'Emilie*	1–16
4	*Correspondance de Gourdan*	6
6	*Histoire de Mlle. Morsan*	1–10
6	*Essais sur le préjugé*	1–10
12	*Mémoire sur la vie de Voltaire*	5
6	*Diable dans un bénitier*	6
13 pour 12	*Jardins potagers*	3
6	*Vicomte de Barjac*	7–10
1	*Aventures de Beauchëne*	3
1	*Contes des fées*	12
1	*Confessions de J.-J. Rousseau*	4
2	*Histoire de Cléveland*	18
1	*Idylles de Gessner*	1
1	*Contes et idylles de Gessner*	–15
1	*Henriette de Gerstenfeld*	3–10
1	*Oeuvres de Fielding*	15
6	*Montesquieu à Marseille*	4–10
1	*Oeuvres de Piron*	12
200	*Pontus de Thyard,* pour impression & brochage, 7 louis	168
400	idem pour *l'Histoire de Châlons*	36
		896–17

	896–17
A Dépenses Générales pour brochage de 578 volumes à 3 sous	86–14

	86–14
	1019–11

Notes

1. The best study is still J.-P. Belin, *Le Commerce des livres prohibés à Paris de 1750 à 1789* (Paris, 1913).

2. Mauvelain to STN, 14 April 1781, Bibliothèque de la Ville de Neuchâtel, papers of the Société typographique (cited henceforth as STN). The spelling and punctuation of the original French has been modernized throughout this essay. I should like to record my gratitude to the Bibliothèque de la Ville de Neuchâtel, not only for permission to publish its papers but also for serving as a friendly host to me for various periods over the last twelve years.

3. Mauvelain to STN, 8 May 1781. "Monsieur" meant F.-S. Ostervald, the director of the STN who handled most of its correspondence.

4. Mauvelain to STN, 5 June 1781.

5. Mauvelain to STN, 19 May 1782.

6. Mauvelain to STN, 10 January 1783.

7. Mauvelain to STN, 29 January 1783.

8. *Ibid.*

9. Mauvelain to STN, 4 February 1783.

10. This information has been pieced together from the STN's account books and the Livres de Commissions in which it recorded all orders and shipments. Unfortunately, the accounts are incomplete for the early stages of Mauvelain's dealings with the STN; so the total cost and weight of the first shipment cannot be known. The STN's copies of its replies to Mauvelain's letters are also missing for this period.

11. Mauvelain to STN, 9 April 1783.

12. Mauvelain to STN, 3 May 1783 and 7 June 1783.

13. Mauvelain to STN, 28 April 1783.

14. Mauvelain to STN, 7 June 1783.

15. Mauvelain to STN, 27 June 1783.

16. Mauvelain to STN, 7 June 1783.

17. Mauvelain to STN, 15 March 1784. Mauvelain's letters often contained gossip, which, as in this case, could be wildly wrong. On 28 July 1783 he asked the STN, "Est-il vrai que depuis le tremblement de terre de Bourgogne le lac de Genève bout?"

18. Mauvelain to STN, 23 January 1784.

19. Mauvelain to STN, 7 June 1783.

20. Mauvelain to STN, 16 April 1784. Although this work seems never to have appeared in print, it reached an advanced stage of preparation. The "Registres de la librairie" of the Parisian booksellers' guild show that Mauvelain received permission to open a subscription for a "Histoire ancienne et moderne de Châlons-sur-Marne" in January 1785: Bibliothèque Nationale, fonds français Ms 21866, entries for 12 and 15 January 1785.

21. Mauvelain to STN, 2 November 1783.

22. Mauvelain to STN, 31 May 1784.

23. Mauvelain to STN, 31 December 1784.

24. Mauvelain to STN, 16 June 1784.

25. Mauvelain to STN, 10 May 1784.

26. Mauvelain to STN, 16 June 1784.

27. For a fuller account of this crisis and the book trade in general, see Robert Darnton, "Reading, Writing, and Publishing in Eighteenth-Century France: A Case Study in the Sociology of Literature," *Daedalus* (winter 1971), pp. 214–56, and "Le livre français à la fin de l'Ancien Régime," *Annales: économies, sociétés, civilisations,* May–June 1973, pp. 735–44.

28. STN to abbé Mongez of Paris, 14 September 1784.

29. Mauvelain to STN, 21 July 1783.

30. Mauvelain to STN, 28 July 1783.

31. Mauvelain to STN, 6 August 1783.

32. STN to Saillant et Nyon of Paris, 17 January 1771. The information on Faivre comes from his dossier and other correspondence in the archives of the STN.

33. Mauvelain to STN, 1 September 1783.

34. Mauvelain to STN, 31 December 1783: "La maladie grave du Garde des Sceaux qui crache le pus et le conduit à la mort changera sûrement le régime de la librairie en France: tant mieux pour vous."

35. Faivre to STN, 4 October 1783.

36. Faivre to STN, 20 December 1783.

37. Mauvelain to STN, 16 April 1784.

38. Faivre to STN, 17 April 1784.

39. Faivre to STN, 22 April 1784. The eighteen crates came from at least three Swiss publishers and were intended for clandestine dealers all over France.

40. Faivre to STN, 26 April 1784. Shippers identified crates by the *marques* painted on them, which were cited in bills of lading and in commercial correspondence. "MT 183" meant "Mauvelain, Troyes," and it was the 183d crate shipped by the STN in 1783. "BM 13" referred to Bruzard de Mauvelain and the thirteenth crate shipped in 1784.

41. Mauvelain to STN, 17 May 1784.

42. *Ibid.*

43. Mauvelain to STN, 10 January 1783.

44. Mauvelain to STN, undated letter, received on 24 July 1784, according to a note by a clerk of the STN.

45. Mauvelain to STN, 3 August 1784.

46. Sainton to STN, 15 September 1776.

47. Mauvelain to STN, undated letter, received on 24 July 1784.

48. Mauvelain to STN, 13 September 1784.

49. Mauvelain to STN, 24 September 1784.

50. STN to Mauvelain, 26 September 1784.

51. Mauvelain to STN, undated letter, received on 24 July 1784.

52. *Ibid.*

53. Mauvelain to STN, undated letter, received 7 August 1784, according to a note by a clerk of the STN.

54. Mauvelain to STN, 9 August 1784.

55. For details on Mirabeau's extraordinary career, see the standard biographies: Alfred Stern, *La Vie de Mirabeau* (Paris, 1895), 2 vols., Lespès, Pasquet, and Péret trs., and Louis and Charles de Loménie, *Les Mirabeau: Nouvelles études sur la société Française au XVIIIe siècle d'après des documents inédits* (Paris, 1870–1891), 5 vols. Mallet's testimony contradicts the account by Stern and the Loménies, who maintain that Fauche fils aîné, Favre et Witel also published *L'Espion dévalisé*, and it tends to confirm Barbier's view that *L'Espion dévalisé* was written by Baudouin de Guémadeuc, Mirabeau's coprisoner in Vincennes, rather than by Mirabeau himself: see Stern, I, 186, Loménie, V, 462, and A.-A. Barbier, *Dictionnaire des ouvrages anonymes* (3d ed., Paris, 1874), II, 178. Mallet gave a somewhat inconsistent account of *Le Libertin de qualité*. At one point in his confession, he said that his firm received the book as a result of arbitration of its quarrel with Mirabeau in Neuchâtel. At another he claimed that he never saw the manuscript and that his company published only *Des Lettres de cachet* and *Errotika biblion*. Other evidence, cited below, proves that he helped distribute *Le Libertin de qualité* and was reprinting it a year later, when he met Mauvelain. So it seems reasonable to attribute the publication of all three of Mirabeau's works to Fauche fils aîné, Favre et Witel, or at least to the machinations of Mallet. *L'Errotika biblion* was spelled with two "r"s in its first three editions and with one in most of its later editions.

56. They actually paid more, because they also agreed to cancel a debt that Mirabeau owed them for the printing of a judicial *mémoire* for his trial. Mirabeau's bargaining may be appreciated by comparing his fees with those of Rousseau, who received about 2,000 livres for *La Nouvelle héloïse* and 1,000 for *Le Contrat social*.

57. Mallet's account of this transaction is somewhat confused, but it indicates that the total payments came to 6,000 livres in cash and 1,000 in books, which Mirabeau must have sold, perhaps to the STN. According to Mallet, Mirabeau was displeased with the settlement and therefore withheld four chapters of the *Errotika biblion*, which apparently have disappeared. Mallet's confession also indicates that Mirabeau left a manuscript "Elégie de Tibulle" with Pierre-Alexandre DuPeyrou. This could be a reference to *Elégies de Tibulle, traduction nouvelle avec des notes et les meilleurs imita-*

tions qui en ont été faites en vers françois (Paris, 1783), which Barbier attributes to the marquis E.-C.-J.-P. de Pastoret: *Dictionnaire des ouvrages anonymes*, II, 47.

58. Unsigned, undated memorandum, entitled only "Mémoire" in Bibliothèque Nationale, MS français, 21833, fo. 101. The memorandum showed no sympathy for the provincial booksellers' claim that the order of 12 June was ruining their business. Instead, it defended the order as "le moyen le plus capable d'empêcher l'introduction et distribution des mauvais livres qui se répandent partout. '. . . Doit-on sacrifier la tranquillité du gouvernement, le bien des moeurs, et le respect dû à la religion à des intérêts mercantils . . . ?"

59. Mauvelain to STN, 20 August 1784.

60. STN to Mauvelain, 29 August 1784.

61. Mauvelain to STN, 6 September 1784. Mauvelain was suggesting that he provide the copy for counterfeit editions of these highly illegal works.

62. STN to Mauvelain, 14 September 1784.

63. STN to Roland de la Platière, 2 November 1784. This information has been culled from the STN's extensive correspondence. See also Charly Guyot, *De Rousseau à Mirabeau: Pèlerins de Môtiers et prophètes de 89* (Neuchâtel, 1936), pp. 184–85.

64. Quandet de Lachenal to STN, 17 October 1782, and Raymond Birn, *Pierre Rousseau and the philosophes of Bouillon* in *Studies on Voltaire and the Eighteenth Century*, ed. Theodore Besterman (Geneva, 1964).

65. STN to Mauvelain, 24 October 1784.

66. Mauvelain to STN, 25 October 1784. Mauvelain added that Mallet also offered to supply *Le Diable dans un bénitier* and *Vie privée ou apologie de Mgr. le duc de Chartres.*

67. STN to Mauvelain, 16 November 1784.

68. Mauvelain to STN, 16 February 1785. Mauvelain believed that the STN had even informed Mallet of its shipments to Troyes, an absurd accusation, which the STN denied.

69. Mauvelain to STN, 21 March 1785.

70. Faivre to STN, 14 August 1784. On 23 August, Pion of Pontarlier reported to the STN, "Il y a quelque temps que [*sic*] cinq colporteurs furent arrêtés sortant des Verrières avec chacun un ballot de livres. Ils furent conduits au bureau de Frambourg. Là un Monsieur nommé pour Favre et Cie. nouvelle société les réclama sous prétexte qu'il les expédiait ainsi pour les faire présenter plus diligement au bureau, d'où il voulait les expédier à la Chambre syndicale de Paris. Au moyen de cette formalité ils ne peuvent être saisis, mais la conduite en a été assuré par un acquit à caution [i.e., the eventual confiscation in Paris could not be avoided]. On m'a assuré que les livres étaient mauvais, comme *Thérèse philosophe, Le Libertin parfait* [*sic*, for *de qualité*] etc." Thus Mallet's old firm was probably producing an edition of *Le Libertin de qualité* in Neuchâtel at the same time that he was printing one near Troyes.

71. Faivre to STN, 23 September 1784.

72. STN to Mauvelain, 29 August 1784.

73. Mauvelain to STN, 6 and 24 September 1784.

74. STN to Mauvelain, 3 October 1784. Of course the snows made the smugglers' work more difficult, but as Mauvelain remarked in his reply, dated 11 October 1784, "Voici les nuits longues et les froids. Les employés [des fermes] gagneront le coin du feu et l'on passera les paquets sans risque."

75. Faivre to STN, 8 November 1784.

76. Faivre to STN, 12 and 18 November 1784.

77. STN to Mauvelain, 24 October 1784.

78. STN to Mauvelain, 19 October 1784.

79. According to various entries in its account books, the STN charged Mauvelain 3 sous for the "brochure" of each volume. He presumably sold the books unbound, as was common at the time.

80. Faivre to STN, 18 November 1784. Reliable sources report that cigarette smuggling between Switzerland and Italy today operates almost exactly as book smuggling did in Faivre's time.

81. Mauvelain to STN, 13 December 1784.

82. STN to Mauvelain, 28 December 1784.

83. Mauvelain to STN, 31 December 1784.

84. Mauvelain to STN, 10 January 1785.

85. STN to Mauvelain, 18 January 1785.

86. Mauvelain to STN, 2 March 1785.

87. Mauvelain to STN, 12 March 1785. In a tiny, scribbled postscript, Mauvelain added, "Il y a autant d'inhumanité que de barbarie à persécuter un homme malade depuis cinq mois, qui a deux chirurgiens, un médecin et des veilleuses gardes, qui dépense des sommes étonnantes. . . ."

88. STN to Housset, 27 March 1785.

89. STN to Gérard, a lawyer in Troyes, 3 April 1785.

90. Thyard to STN, 7 March 1785. See also the other letters in Thyard's dossier and STN to Mauvelain, 13 March 1785.

91. Mauvelain to STN, 6 May 1785.

92. Gérard to STN, 6 June 1785.

93. Mauvelain to STN, 15 June 1785.

94. Mauvelain to STN, 22 July 1785. Mauvelain now wrote as though he had persuaded himself that his honor had remained intact. "Ce n'est point manque de probité . . . mais il est des occasions où le plus honnête homme, malgré lui et en rougissant se voit entraîné comme je l'ai été par une fatalité à faire des choses qui répugnent à son âme et à sa délicatesse."

95. Mauvelain to STN, 3 October 1785. The two variations on his name might have served Mauvelain as aliases. He used the first version in Auxerre and the second in Troyes. One or two others among the more disreputable debtors of the STN changed names as they changed residences, in order to escape their creditors. It has not been possible to find any reference to the brawl which put an end to Mauvelain's career in the law. As to his surgery, Mauvelain did not spare any details. "Ils [his doctors] décidèrent conjointement qu'il fallait commencer par me mettre une sonde dans la vessie, ce qu'ils firent, après quoi ils me dirent que dès qu'elle était entrée j'étais sauvé. Comme il s'était fait un épanchement dans les téguments du bas ventre, on me l'a ouvert. Ils m'y firent une plaie qui contenait tout le ventre. On y aurait caché un oeuf. Ils m'en ont fait deux autres au périnée pour donner l'écoulement aux humeurs."

96. STN to Brissot, 13 February 1787. Where Ostervald got this information is not clear, but he or his friends could have picked it up on one of their frequent trips to Paris. In his reply, dated February 1787, Brissot remarked, "Je ne sais où il est, ce qu'il fait, qui le protège. J'ai moi-même ainsi que d'autres personnes à me plaindre de lui—mais j'oublie tout cela—et je ne puis vous donner aucune lumière sur son compte."

97. The most important of these studies are in François Furet et al., *Livre et société dans la France du XVIIIe siècle* (Paris and The Hague, 1965 and 1970), 2 vols. For a perhaps excessively skeptical survey of the literature on this subject, see Robert Darnton, "Reading, Writing, and Publishing in Eighteenth-century France," *op cit.*

98. One of the few exceptions was Mirabeau's *Le Libertin de qualité*. Mauvelain ordered it only once, on 6 September 1784, but he ordered a dozen copies. As explained above, he wanted it badly and could have procured it from another supplier, possibly Mallet.

99. The *arrêt du conseil* of 30 August 1777, which lay down the basic laws for the book trade in Mauvelain's time, stressed the need to suppress all "livres ou estampes contraires à la religion, au bien et au repos de l'état, et à la pureté des moeurs, ou libelles diffamatoires contre l'honneur et la réputation de quelques uns des sujets de

S.M." Isambert, Decrusy, and Taillandier, *Recueil général des anciennes lois françaises depuis l'an 420 jusqu'à la Révolution de 1789* (Paris, 1826), XXV, 114. The importance of the additional category of "libelles diffamatoires" is discussed below. The three categories of offences against religion, the state, and morality appear constantly in the administrative documents concerning the book trade of the Old Regime. For another example, see the memorandum quoted in note 58 above.

100. Hans Wolpe, *Raynal et sa machine de guerre: L'Histoire des deux Indes et ses perfectionnements* (Stanford, 1957), traces the evolution of Raynal's text and associates it with a rhetorical tradition that had a strong influence on eighteenth-century taste in literature.

101. Jefferson's correspondence during his stay in France shows that he was concerned by the romantic view of the United States with which French *littérateurs* deluded themselves. For examples of his opinion of Raynal, who probably did more than anyone else to spread that view, see Julian P. Boyd, ed., *The Papers of Thomas Jefferson* (Princeton, 1950–), X, 3–65.

102. See especially chapter 38 in volume II (1786 ed.), a Rousseauistic account of the future political order, which operates according to the principles of equality and liberty and the dictate of the general will.

103. L. S. Mercier, *Tableau de Paris* (Hamburg, 1782), I, viii.

104. This list, like most charts and diagrams, has its own built-in bias. It eliminates authors who wrote only one of the books in Mauvelain's orders, even though that book could have been a spectacular success. Thus d'Holbach, who heads the list, really came in a poor second after Buffonidor, whose *Fastes de Louis XV* was ordered eleven times by Mauvelain for a total of 84 copies. As far as can be known, Buffonidor never published any other book, and in fact he took most of the material for his *Fastes* from the *Vie privée de Louis XV*. The *Mémoires secrets*, a collective, anonymous work, is a similar case. Mauvelain ordered it nine times for a total of 16 copies, but he also ordered the extracts from it that were printed separately as *Suite de l'Espion anglois* (5 orders, 16 copies) and as *Anecdotes du dix-huitième siècle* (3 orders, 18 copies), making a total of 50 copies ordered on 17 occasions. So in eliminating authors who wrote only one "best-selling" book, this list does not do justice to the fact that most of Mauvelain's books came from obscure hack writers, who have been forgotten today.

105. Jeroom Vercruysse's work on the editions of d'Holbach's writings tends to confirm this view. Vercruysse found thirteen editions of *Le Christianisme dévoilé* between 1756 and 1789 and eighty-one reeditions of d'Holbach's various works before the Revolution; see Vercruysse, *Bibliographie descriptive des écrits du Baron d'Holbach*. David Smith's bibliographical study of Helvétius, to be published soon, indicates the same tendency for extreme philosophic works to have a wide diffusion during the last decades of the Old Regime.

106. *Correspondance de Madame Gourdan dite la comtesse* (Paris, 1954), p. 41. This is a reprint of the second edition of Morande's book, which originally appeared as *Le Porte-feuille de Mme Gourdan dite la comtesse* (Spa, 1783).

107. Ibid., p. 84.

108. It does, however, contain some incidental social and political comment of a rather radical nature: see *Le Vicomte de Barjac* (Dublin, 1784), I, 158–69, and II, 63–81. The book apparently was based on some true incidents and in some cases included a key—which may account for its success, because it is a rather insipid novel. Considered as gossip, it could be classified as a *chronique scandaleuse*, and so it illustrates the impossibility of treating these categories as distinct and unrelated.

109. Mirabeau, *Le Libertin de qualité*, reprinted in Guillaume Apollinaire ed., *L'Oeuvre du Comte de Mirabeau* (Paris, 1910), p. 231.

110. For the political asides in the *Errotika biblion*, see *L'Oeuvre du Comte de Mirabeau*, pp. 75, 113, 121. Of course the *Lettres originales de Mirabeau, écrites du*

donjon de Vincennes . . . (Paris, 1792, Year II, and Year III), 4 vols., appeared after Mirabeau's death.

111. For more information and references on Morande as a libeler, see Robert Darnton, "The High Enlightenment and the Low-Life of Literature in Prerevolutionary France," *Past and Present*, no. 51 (1971), pp. 81–115.

112. *La Chronique scandaleuse* (Paris, 1783), pp. 64–65.

113. Ibid., p. 185. The son of an innkeeper of Cannes returns from the American wars. As a practical joke, he pretends to be a stranger and takes a room at the inn. His parents do not recognize him and kill him in his bed in order to get his money, which in fact he has brought for them. On the variations of this canard, see J.-P. Seguin, *Nouvelles à sensation: Canards du XIXe siècle* (Paris, 1959), pp. 187–90.

114. On early French journalism, see Claude Bellanger, Jacques Godechot, Pierre Guiral, and Fernand Terrou, *Histoire générale de la presse française* (Paris, 1969), vol. I, which has not entirely superseded Eugène Hatin, *Histoire politique et littéraire de la presse en France* (Paris, 1859–1861), 8 vols. On the *nouvellistes*, see Frantz Funck-Brentano and Paul d'Estrée, *Les Nouvellistes* (Paris, 1905) and the delightful essay by Mercier in *Tableau de Paris* (Amsterdam, 1783 ed.), II, 157–60.

115. Mauvelain to STN, 31 March 1783 and 10 May 1784.

116. Mauvelain to STN, 10 January 1785. See also Mauvelain to STN, 31 December 1784.

117. The report appeared in *Mémoires secrets pour servir à l'histoire de la république des lettres* (London, 1777–1789), 36 vols., entry for 8 September 1782.

118. Ibid., entries for 31 December 1782 and 9 January 1784.

119. Ibid., entry for 30 December 1782.

120. Ibid., entry for 10 October 1784. Mauvelain ordered the book on 16 June 1784.

121. The STN's vast correspondence kept it well informed, and it sometimes shared its shop talk with Mauvelain. For example, it wrote to him on 29 August 1784, "*Le Diable dans un bénitier* est la plus plate chose du monde, mais on dit que *Le Libertin de qualité* est bien écrit."

122. Mauvelain to STN, 27 May 1785.

123. Mauvelain to STN, 20 August 1784.

124. *La Chronique scandaleuse*, p. 38. There is a similar antiaristocratic tone to an anecdote about a merchant who was swindled by a nobleman and did not dare bring him to justice: "Il dévorait intérieurement son indignation, sachant trop bien qu'en vain il s'adresserait aux tribunaux, qu'en vain il y porterait sa réclamation, n'ayant que trop d'exemples récents qu'un grand parvient toujours non seulement à se justifier, mais encore à faire punir quiconque a légitimement suspecté sa bonne foi." Ibid., p. 22.

125. See for example pp. 35–36 and 64 on the chivalric spirit of the nobility; p. 253 on Necker; and pp. 180–81 on Louis XVI. The *Journal des gens du monde* was even more timid politically, but it was devoted mainly to literature and resembled a bona fide journal more than a *gazette à la main*.

126. *L'Observateur anglois ou correspondance secrète entre Milord All'eye et Milord All'ear* (London, 1777–1778), II, 279.

127. See for example, ibid., II, 275–76 and III, 33–44.

128. See for example, ibid., I, 301, and III, 358–87.

129. Ibid., I, 8.

130. Ibid., vol. V, "Avertissement," no pagination.

131. H.-S. Linguet, *Mémoires sur la Bastille* (London, 1783), p. 179.

132. Neither Linguet nor Mirabeau suggested that the monarchy was illegitimate; both spoke respectfully of Louis XVI, and Mirabeau actually dedicated his book to J.-C.-P. Lenoir, the lieutenant general of police. But the sensational character of their revelations made the regime look despotic.

133. *Vie privée ou apologie de très-sérénissime prince Monseigneur le duc de Chartres* . . . ("à cent lieues de la Bastille," 1784), p. 114. Like all libelers, Morande wrote anonymously. His affected reticence about printing the names Chartres and Bourbon in full was a stylistic convention used more to titillate the reader than to hide the names.

134. *Mémoires secrets,* entry for 9 January 1784. When the *Mémoires secrets* later reviewed the book, they criticized it for being thin and badly written: entry for 13 January 1784.

135. *Vie privée . . . de Monseigneur le duc de Chartres,* p. 131. Morande probably used the pamphlet to blackmail the duke, a common practice among his group of libelers, who were French expatriates in London. *Le Diable dans un bénitier,* another libel from this group, which Mauvelain also ordered, contains an interesting discussion of the operations of this smut factory and the French government's attempt to suppress it.

136. *L'Espion dévalisé* (London, 1782), p. 217.

137. Ibid., pp. 199–200, from Mirabeau's *Appel aux Hessois,* a typical case of "plagiarism," which has led to the probably erroneous conclusion that Mirabeau wrote *L'Espion dévalisé:* see note 55 above.

138. *Les Fastes de Louis XV* (Villefranche, 1782), II, 27. See the same passage in *Vie privée de Louis XV* (London, 1781), III, 14-15.

139. *Les Fastes de Louis XV,* II, 280–81.

140. Ibid., II, 296.

141. Ibid., II, 287.

142. A good deal could be said about the language of libels—expressions like "l'oeil fugitif" for example—but perhaps that subject should be left to a literary scholar who might be willing to leave "high" literature for a while.

143. Ibid., I, lxxxviii.

144. This is not so in the graphs based on the number of orders rather than the number of books ordered.

145. This is the text of the order as cited in a contemporary "Mémoire relativement à un ordre envoyé par MM. les fermiers généraux pour que tous les livres venant de l'étranger soient envoyés à la douane de Paris" by Périsse Du Luc, an eminent bookseller of Lyons, dated 29 July 1783: Bibliothèque Nationale, fonds français Ms 21833.

146. Pidansat de Mairobert, one of the most interesting of them, is believed to have written some of the most scurrilous works of the period, not only *L'Espion anglois* and a great deal of the *Mémoires secrets* but also *Maupeouana* and *Anecdotes secrétes sur Madame DuBarry.* He committed suicide by opening his veins in a bathtub, "parce qu'il se voyait accusé de ses relations avec la presse clandestine de Londres," according to Barbier: *Dictionnaire des ouvrages anonymes,* II, 175.

147. Mauvelain to STN, 29 January 1783.

148. Mauvelain to STN, 15 June 1785.

149. Mauvelain to STN, 10 January 1783. Troyes had two fairs a year: one began on 1 September, the other on the second Monday of Lent. They had declined greatly since their heyday during the late Middle Ages.

150. Mauvelain to STN, 31 December 1784. As mentioned above, Mauvelain also referred to some Parisian customers who spent part of the summer in Troyes.

151. Mauvelain to STN, 2 March 1785.

152. Mauvelain to STN, 31 December 1784.

153. Mauvelain to STN, 10 January 1785.

154. For information on incomes, see Henri Sée, *La France économique et sociale au XVIIIe siècle* (Paris, 1933); George Rudé, *The Crowd in the French Revolution* (Oxford, 1959); and, for the income of bailliage magistrates, Philip Dawson, *Provincial Magistrates and Revolutionary Politics in France, 1789–1795* (Cambridge, Mass., 1972), chap. 3.

155. For background information on Troyes, see T. Boutiot, *Histoire de la ville de Troyes et de la Champagne méridionale* (Troyes and Paris, 1874), 4 vols., an excellent, old-fashioned study, typical of the local history that flourished during the Third Republic. By contrast, Jacques Paton's *Corps de ville de Troyes (1470–1790)* (Troyes, 1939) seems superficial.

156. Bibliothèque Nationale, fonds français Ms 22126, "Libraires et imprimeurs des différentes villes rangées par généralités: Champagne."

157. Michel Fleury and Pierre Valmary, "Les Progrès de l'instruction élémentaire de Louis XIV à Napoléon III d'après l'enquête de Louis Maggiolo (1877–1879)," *Population*, no. 1 (1957), p. 81. The area is in the present department of the Aube, which was one of the departments where Maggiolo's researchers were most thorough.

158. Daniel Mornet, *Les Origines intellectuelles de la Révolution française 1715–1787*, 5th ed. (Paris, 1954), p. 184. Mornet did not cite the evidence from which he made this judgment. Boutiot considered the intellectual life of Troyes to have been rather inactive in the eighteenth century: *Histoire de la ville de Troyes,* IV, 588.

159. Paton, *Le Corps de ville de Troyes,* p. 177. Paton cites no evidence for his statement.

160. The cahier of the Third Estate of the bailliage of Troyes is printed in J. Madival and E. Laurent, *Archives parlementaires de 1787 à 1860* (Paris, 1870), VI, 80–87.

The Relish for Reading in Provincial England

Two Centuries Ago

Roy McKeen Wiles

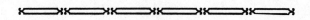

When Samuel Johnson observed that "he who is tired of London is tired of life"[1] he was only saying what most Londoners believed, for the capital city was then, as it still is, the cultural center of England. It had the largest concentration of people, it was the seat of government for the nation, it was a seaport, it offered the most dazzling variety of entertainment in drama, music, and other diversions, it had St. Paul's and a great number of other Wren churches, it had hundreds of coffeeshops, and from its printing presses came most of the books and periodicals whose titles now crowd the columns of *The New Cambridge Bibliography of English Literature*. But though Johnson loved London, he was not a Londoner. Like Fielding and Crabbe, he was born in the provinces, and he spent the first twenty-seven years of his life in country towns;[2] like multitudes of others Johnson made his way to the metropolis because that was where opportunity and recognition lay. Most English people two centuries ago lived not in London but in cities, towns, villages, and hamlets all over the land, where all together—it is easy to forget—there were more shops, theaters, schools, churches, inns, newspapers, and concerts than in London. The question concerning the reading habits of English people who were contemporaries of Johnson is too broad to be dealt with satisfactorily if it attempts to take in every person in the nation who had learned to read, and generalizations are dangerous. Because evidence concerning the reading habits of people living in the country has not been adequately explored, I should like to bring forward some specific details which show that intellectual activities were not confined to polite society in London. I shall have nothing to say about such manifestations of cultural interest as the theaters in York and Bath, the Three-Choirs festival in Hereford, Gloucester, and Worcester, the annual concerts of music in Winchester and Salisbury, the Literary and Philosophical Society of Newcastle, the amateur theatricals in Lymington, the programs of study in the two universities, the professional training in law, and the deliberations of the Royal Society (which had members from outside London). Our theme is "reading," and that is the aspect of literacy with which I propose to deal in this essay.[3]

Although the term "provincial" as applied to cultural matters commonly implies some degree of inferiority, one must not assume that readers living in the country were not quite so intelligent as those living in London, or that provincial readers generally were satisfied with second-rate publications. That there were differences in their reading habits is suggested in one of Samuel Richardson's letters, written when all of London was raving over Laurence Sterne. Richardson, writing to Bishop Hildesley of Sodor and Man early in 1761, quoted or pretended to quote a young lady's comments addressed to her friend in the country. "Happy are you in your retirement," she wrote, "where you read what books you choose, either for instruction or entertainment, but in this foolish town, we are obliged to read every foolish book that fashion renders prevalent in conversation; and I am horribly out of humour with the present taste, which makes people ashamed to own they have not read, what if fashion did not authorise, they would with more reason blush to say they had read!"[4] That sounds like Richardsonian squeamishness, but if it can be assumed that this unfavorable opinion of *Tristram Shandy* could be applied to many another book currently in vogue in London, perhaps the eighteenth-century's relish for reading is more accurately registered in what provincial readers *chose* to read than in books which Londoners looked upon as required reading because they were "prevalent in conversation."[5]

Recognizing that evidence on the reading habits of both Londoners and people living in the provinces can at best be fragmentary and therefore statistically inconclusive, I should like to examine a few phenomena which remove some of the uncertainty surroundng the question of literacy in eighteenth-century England. Taken together, these eight or ten specific manifestations of an interest in reading disprove, in my view, the belief that the proportion of nonreaders compared to the total population in provincial England was high. So many towns had local newspapers with extensive circulation, so many books and pamphlets and magazines were offered for sale,[6] so many lending libraries sprang up and flourished, that it would be denying the obvious to insist that the century which began with *A Tale of a Tub* (1704) and ended with *Lyrical Ballads* (1798) was a period when illiteracy predominated.

For reasons which will presently emerge, I turn first to the newspaper. It is easy to state explicitly how many local newspapers were appearing in any one year of the eighteenth century, for although from time to time a reference turns up to an unrecorded paper,[7] such fly-by-night ventures soon expired and cannot have had any significant effect on the firm figures that can be derived from the listings in the second volume of *The New Cambridge Bibliography of English Literature*. Even after the Stamp Tax was imposed in 1712, ten years after the first provincial newspaper appeared,[8] there were nine newspapers in seven different towns. And when the Stamp Tax was reimposed in 1725 there were twenty-five papers in twenty towns. Most of those twenty-five papers continued to appear regularly for many years, a few of them—the *Northampton Mercury*, the *Gloucester Journal*, and the *Worcester Postman* (under various titles)— continuing to the end of the century and beyond. Other long-lasting local papers beginning later were the *Derby Mercury* (established 1732), *Howgrave's Stamford Mercury* (1732), the *Salisbury Journal* (1736), the *Ipswich Journal* (1739), *Aris's Birmingham Gazette* (1741), and *Boddeley's Bath Journal* (1744). One can say quite definitely that in 1760, even after the Stamp Tax had been increased by a halfpenny in 1757, there were local papers in thirty English towns. In the 1770's several very successful new local papers were established, and by 1780 the number of towns having their own papers was thirty-seven. All this time London newspapers were being sent to readers in the provinces, as is clear from advertisements in local papers. In the 1770's Ann London, William Coqu, and William Taylor, all of London, frequently advertised in several papers that they would send London papers regularly by post to readers in the country at considerable savings. They even persuaded the printers of the local papers to take orders for the London newspapers. And it was not only London papers that came into towns which had their own newspapers. Thomas Wood, printer of the *Shrewsbury Chronicle,* indicated in the issue of 18 June 1774 that his town was "regularly supplied with other Country News-papers."

Granting that locally printed newspapers were available to readers in most regions of England, we must ask the next obvious questions: how many copies were printed, and how widely were they distributed? Exact figures of circulation are hard to find. Elsewhere I have shown that in 1739 Isaac Thompson said he had nearly two thousand regular purchasers of his *Newcastle Journal;*[9] and Dr. Cranfield cites a reference in *Whitworth's Manchester Magazine* of 30 December 1755 to the printing of twelve hundred copies of that paper.[10] Later in the century Christopher Etherington, printer of the *York Chronicle,* actually printed in numbers 183 (14 June 1776) and 184 (21 June 1776) the names, from Armstrong to Zouch, of 2,260 regular subscribers to his paper. Earlier that same year Thomas Wood, in his annual expression of thanks to readers of his *Shrewsbury Chronicle,* declared in number 157 (6 January 1776) that "from the increasing sale of this Paper, upon a moderate computation they are read by TEN THOUSAND PERSONS." Without the firm figures that only office records could provide, the frequent claims of increased circulation of particular newspapers are not very helpful, though there is probably some significance in the explanation by the printer of the *Reading Mercury* number 738 (4 March 1776) that delivery of that issue was delayed because "the great and increasing number printed" kept the presses running longer.[11] Increasing demand sometimes forced the printer to run off extra copies after the normal quantity had gone through the presses. Something can also be made of the fact that additional news carriers were required because of increasing areas to be served. "Some industrious Men, of good character, who have clear and audible Voices, are wanted to distribute this Paper in different Country Circuits." So declared the printer of *R. Cruttwell's Bath and Bristol Chronicle* in number 549 (25 April 1771), and two weeks after the *Shrewsbury Chronicle* began to appear the printer gave some prominence in his number 3 (5 December 1772) to a notice that he wanted "Two or Three more Men to distribute this Chronicle in the Country."

Once a local paper had become well established, the printer often testified to the wide scope of its circulation by indicating in which counties his subscribers lived, or by naming the towns and villages to which it was regularly taken by his newsmen, or by naming the numerous distributors in the area, and sometimes by stating, "Those persons who live at a Distance from such Places as the Newsmen go through, may have the Paper left where they shall please to appoint." Under the title of the *Berkshire Chronicle* in 1771, for instance, one reads, "This Paper is circulated with the utmost Expedition thro' Berkshire, Buckinghamshire, Hampshire, Oxfordshire, Surry, Sussex, Wiltshire, Part of Gloucestershire, Hertfordshire, Northamptonshire, and Middlesex." In 1777, R. Bowen, printer of *Jopson's Coventry Mercury,* gave a list of thirty-nine places to which he said his paper was dispatched "with the utmost expedition," adding that his newsmen left papers at "all the intermediate Hamlets." In 1775 the proprietors of the *Hampshire Chronicle* not only named the counties to which their paper went by road; they boasted that they had bought a yacht to take copies of their paper to the Isle of Wight every Sunday.[12] That the yacht did actually sail is indicated in the *Hampshire Chronicle,* number 133 (6 March 1775), in which it is stated that the *Duchess of Gloucester* was back in service after having been damaged in a storm. Christopher Etherington did not deliver his *York Chronicle* by sailing ship, but in that same year (1775) he sent his paper to eighty-eight towns, with their adjoining villages, in a "Circuit comprehending about FIVE HUNDRED MILES in circumference"; and in his paper on 10 May 1776 he actually named the 88 distributors of his paper in 85 places. Ten years earlier Isaac Thompson in his *Newcastle Journal* on 21 June 1766 listed 188 communities to which his newsmen went every week, using italics to distinguish the places in which he said no other Newcastle newspaper was vended, and adding, "Besides the abovesaid Places and many un-named Environs of most of the Market Towns, a great Number of Papers are sent per Post to York, Leeds, Lancaster, Liverpool, Norwich, London, &c. &c."

One equally convincing kind of evidence of the extent of the territory to which a single paper was carried is the statement by the printer that his newsmen could, for a suitable fee, deliver small parcels in the towns and villages to which they went every week. If specific places are named, one can be reasonably sure that the newsmen did actually go there on their regular runs. In the *Shrewsbury Chronicle* on 29 April 1775, Thomas Wood said quite explicitly, "As the circulation of this Paper is now become very extensive, small Parcels may be conveyed by the News-Men to the following Places, viz. Ellesmere, Overton, Wrexham, Chester, Namptwich, Tarpoley, Wem, Whitchurch, Drayton, Newport, Wellington, Shifnal, Wolverhampton, Bridgnorth, Wenlock, Brosely, Coalbrookdale, Madely, Stretton, Ludlow, Westbury, Worthing, Chirbury, Poole, Montgomery, Newton, Llansillan, Llangollen, Llanymynach, Oswestry, Chirk, and most other Towns and Villages in North-Wales, as also to Gentlemens Houses on the different Roads." Spotted on a map these thirty-one places in the West Midlands and northern Wales are spread over an area more than forty miles wide from east to west and over sixty miles from north to south. The "different Roads" led out of Shrewsbury in a dozen directions, and the newsman who delivered papers on the road running north-northwest to Ellesmere, Overton, and Wrexham traveled about as far as the carrier who went south to Church Stretton and on to Ludlow, nearly thirty miles each way. The road north to Wem, Whitchurch, and Chester is about forty miles long, but did the newsman on that route return to Shrewsbury by the same road or did he circle over to Tarporley and on to Nantwich? That and similar questions about the other roads from Shrewsbury cannot be answered, but it is obvious that by 1775 readers in a large area received Thomas Wood's lively paper fifty-two times a year.

There is, in other words, plenty of evidence that every week of the year newsmen from many centers all over England carried thousands of local papers to thousands of customers. Would those customers have continued to take the papers if they did not read them? That extensive readership is in itself a significant fact, for even readers of newspapers have at least some capability in reading; we should not call them illiterate merely because their relish for reading may seem to have been limited to what Thomas De Quincey later called "literature of knowledge" as distinct from "literature of power."[13]

Now what was in those newspapers in addition to a week's accumulation of news and current prices and an assortment of advertisements? There were in most of the local papers contributions of prose and verse, about which I shall have something to say presently. At this point I should like to draw attention to the fact that the advertisements in those newspapers can reveal much about reading in the provinces. Although most of the advertisements have to do with miracle-working medicines, strayed or stolen mares, absconded servants and wives, stage plays, farms for sale or to be let, musical performances, oculists and dentists, coaching services, fresh supplies of tea or rum or hats or timber, and so on, there were advertisements of books published in London, advertisements of circulating libraries, advertisements of book auctions, advertisements of current magazines, advertisements of schools in which English was taught—all of these having to do with an interest in reading. There was even an eighteenth-century equivalent to the *American Book Publishing Record*. When J. Bell, a London bookseller, announced in the *Reading Mercury*, number 574 (11 January 1773), and other papers that he would in a few days publish the title page for the twelve sixpenny monthly numbers of his *Universal Catalogue* issued in 1772, he said that the volume just completed contained "an exact List of every Tract (not one excepted) Volume or Pamphlet, printed in the Year 1772, either in England, Scotland, or Ireland," and that subsequent issues would serve as "a useful Directory to the Trade, pointing out instantly the Size, Number of Sheets, Price, Publisher, and other Particulars of every new Publication." What makes this advertisement significant for my purpose is that Bell said customers in the country might receive the *Universal Catalogue* regularly from Bell's own shop near Exeter Exchange in the Strand, London, or from the country booksellers.

That vast quantities of substantial reading matter were to be found in the country is clear from the numerous advertisements for sales of used books, either at prices marked in catalogues or by auction. Advertisements in the *York Courant* in 1751 show that Joseph Lord, a Wakefield bookseller, offered 15,000 volumes in a sale which began on 30 August of that year, and that John Hildyard of York had for sale about 30,000 volumes in "all Branches of Literature, Arts, and Sciences, and in most Languages . . . at Cheap Prices, for Ready Money only." It was at such a sale in 1761 that Laurence Sterne acquired 700 books "cheap— and many good."[14] Similar book sales were advertised in many other places, a few examples being John Burdon's of Winchester in 1773 (10,000 volumes), T. Burroughs' in Devizes that same year (5,000 volumes, "priced remarkably low"), and J. Eddowes' of Shrewsbury in 1778 (7,000 volumes). That last sale, adver- tised in several papers, among them *Adams's Weekly Courant* in Chester on 10 March 1778, included "the Libraries of the late Godolphin Edwards Esq. of Frodesley; Dr. Berington of Shrewsbury; John Paynter, Esq. of Hafod; Rev. Mr. Martin of Kidderminster; and several other Parcels of valuable and useful Books, lately purchased, in good condition, and many of them in very neat and elegant Bindings." In addition to these continuing sales of used books at marked prices there were many book auctions, thousands of works on various subjects being listed in catalogues issued in advance. There is a twofold significance in those sales: when a dealer announced that he was offering some thousands of volumes from libraries of deceased persons it is clear that the original owners had been quite ready to spend money buying books; and it is equally clear that the dealer expected to get back the money he had invested in acquiring the books, plus the cost of having the catalogue printed and the fees paid for advertising the sale.

Local newspapers in the eighteenth century often printed lists of recent publication by London booksellers, much like the monthly lists in the *Gentleman's Magazine*. Such a "List of New Books" is in the *Berkshire Chronicle* of 18 March 1771, which gives the titles of thirty-four publications, with prices and publishers. The *Shrewsbury Chronicle*, number 180 (15 June 1776), carried this notice: "The printer hereof is much obliged to the gentleman who, (in order to render this paper the more valuable) has recommended him to insert a catalogue of all the publications which are taken notice of in the different reviews. They will in future appear monthly, together with the price affixed to each." Thereafter those booklists appeared in one issue each month; and the lists were followed by the announcement that "Any of the above Books may be had of T. Wood, Printer of this Paper, by giving a few Days Notice."

The readiness of the printers of local papers to order books from London and have their distributors deliver them to their customers is well attested throughout the century. Back in 1724, George Ayscough, printer of the *Weekly Courant* in Nottingham, customarily printed on the verso of the title page of that twelve-page paper a "Catalogue of Books published at London since our last," and added—in number 30 of volume XII (5 March 1723/1724), for example—"Note, Gentlemen by sending their Orders to the Printer hereof, may have any of the abovesaid Books." Ayscough's catalogue was selective. He must have enjoyed listing among more serious publications a pamphlet alluringly entitled *The Church Rambler, or Sermon Taster. Being a merry and diverting Description of the Nature and Character of those who straggle from Church to Church to hear Sermons.* He continued to print a list of recent publications even after the reimposed Stamp Tax severely reduced the space available for the weekly issue of the paper. Like Ayscough, the printers of other local newspapers believed their readers would be pleased to know what the rest of the world was reading. William Dicey, printer of the long established *Northampton Mercury*, gave nearly a full column on 16 March 1752 to listing "Books, &c. published in February, 1752," classifying them as Theological and Moral, Law and Politics, History, and so on, with prices ranging from sixpence for *A Sure Guide to Heaven* to six shillings for the two pocket volumes of *Leisure Hours Amusements for Town and Country*. What is more, Dicey said that the books in his list might be "had of the Printer hereof, and of the Men that carry this News; also of Mr. Clay, in Daventry, Mr. Ratten, in Market-Harborough; Mr. Ratten, and Mr. Brookes, in Coventry; Mr. Seeley, in Buckingham; Mr. Stevens, in Bicester; Mr. Cattling, in

Chesham, Bookbinder, or at his Shop in Hempstead on Thursdays; and of Mr. Ellington, in St. Ives, St. Neots, and Huntington."

In addition to named agents in various towns there were apparently itinerant sellers of books, who visited fairs and showed up on market days, hoping for business. In the form of news rather than of a paid advertisement there is in the *Shrewsbury Chronicle*, number 228 (17 May 1777), an announcement that *A True and Faithful Narrative of the Life of Edward Williams, the celebrated Cooper*, was then in the press and would be published the following Monday evening; and after further details came this note: "N.B. A Person will attend Ellesmere Fair, on Tuesday, and Oswestry Market, on Wednesday, to supply the Flying-Stationers."[15]

The existence of numerous book lists published on the initiative of the printers of local newspapers as a service to their readers is illuminating. Perhaps even more significant are the lists of recent publications sent in as advertisements—and paid for—by individual London publishers who had come to some arrangement with the local printers and booksellers to handle their books. Andrew Millar, in the Strand, London, advertised in the *Norwich Mercury* on 16 June 1750 that thirty-three books published by him were sold by W. Chase, a local bookseller who was also the printer of the *Mercury*. His list included works by James Thomson, Henry Fielding, Tobias Smollett, and David Hume. Evidence of the eagerness of London publishers to profit from sales in the country is supplied by the advertisements of Henry Woodgate and Samuel Brooks, at the Golden Ball in Paternoster Row, London. In the *York Courant*, number 1862 (30 June 1761), they listed twenty-one "New Editions" of little one-shilling books written by W. H. Dilworth, M.A., and published by them "For the Improvement and Entertainment of the British Youth of both Sexes." That advertisement in the *York Courant* gave the names of booksellers in twelve Yorkshire towns, among them C. Etherington, bookseller in Coney Street, York. Two statements at the end of the advertisement are worth noting: "As a Proof of the extraordinary Reception" these books enjoyed the publishers asserted that "upwards of Thirty Thousand of them have been sold in a Year"; and they announced that "Large Allowance is made to Country Booksellers, Shopkeepers, &c. who buy a Parcel of their entertaining Histories."

During the last quarter of the century the London publishers advertised long lists of inexpensive books in the local newspapers, for they obviously found the country trade lucrative. In the *Chester Chronicle*, number 581 (7 July 1786), and other provincial papers, for example, Joseph Wenman of 144 Fleet Street listed thirty-eight of his "neat pocket volumes" at prices as low as ninepence for Goldsmith's poems and as high as six shillings for Sterne's sermons. In 1793 the advertisements which Wenman and his partner, Hodgson, placed in local papers gave the titles of fifty-six of their "cheap editions," each item with three prices, one for copies "Elegantly bound & gilt on the back," one for those "Neatly bound, and lettered on the back," and the cheapest "Sewed in marble paper." The prices were really low: *Rasselas* was offered at two shillings, one shilling and sixpence, and ninepence; the same prices would buy Sterne's *Sentimental Journey*, Rochefoucault's *Maxims,* or Fielding's *Voyage to Lisbon;* for sixpence more one could get *Gulliver's Travels, Hudibras, The Castle of Otranto,* or Young's *Night Thoughts.* The most expensive books offered by Wenman and Hodgson were three-volume editions of *Tom Jones* and *Peregrine Pickle* at seven shillings and sixpence, six shillings, and four shillings and sixpence. A name that stands out in the English book trade is that of James Lackington for his enormous sales of remainders. His advertisements in local papers in the spring of 1793, for example, were headed "Books Extremely Cheap," and they listed twenty-three titles at prices which he said were "much less than half the publication prices." But most of his remainder copies were substantial works, among them "Dr. Johnson's English Dictionary, folio, well bound in calf, and lettered, 1£. 17s.—in boards, 1£. 9s. 6d," "Cook's Three Voyages, complete, in 80 sixpenny numbers, with 160 plates, 17s.—or six vols. bound and lettered, 1£. 4s. 6d," and "Bishop Newton's Works, three vols. royal 4to. in boards, 1£. 12s. 6d." The cheapest works in that particular list were "Dr. Gregory's Life of T. Chatterton, boards, 2s. 6d.," and "Ireland's Life of Henderson, 8vo. in boards, 2s." Lackington's printed catalogue, available at his shop in Chiswell Street, London, listed ninety thousand volumes, and readers in the country could obtain any of his books through the local booksellers.[16]

    Lackington apparently gave no discount to local booksellers for handling his remainders. Even if a London publisher did make some allowance, the margin of profit to the local bookseller or to the printer of the local newspaper cannot have amounted to much when prices were low. But there is no doubt that some of the country dealers prospered. I read in *Boddely's Bath Journal* dated Monday, 22 June 1772, that on the preceding Saturday Mrs. Sarah Chaulklin, an eminent bookseller of Taunton, died "worth upwards of 10,000£."

    I find more positive evidence of an interest in acquiring books in the fact that the London booksellers bought much column space in local newspapers to advertise individual books which they had just published or were about to publish. Throughout the century there were thousands of such books advertised in provincial newspapers; and if anyone ever compiles a list of the books set in type by provincial printers it will provide further substantial evidence that there was a reading public of considerable dimensions in the country. An impressive body of precise information about the buyers of books is now being accumulated by F. J. G. Robinson and P. J. Wallis of Newcastle. Their enormous and exciting project—already well advanced and progressing rapidly—is to compile and analyze the lists of persons whose names were printed as subscribers to the books published by subscription, whether in London or in the provinces. Enough work has thus far been done by Robinson and Wallis and others to establish the fact that large numbers of the subscribers lived in the country. An example is the list of named persons in seventy-one provincial towns—there were other subscribers in Edinburgh and Glasgow—given by Mr. Wallis in Appendix 1 to the revised form of his lecture to the Bibliographical Society on 21 November 1972. The persons named were those out of a total of 836 who had subscribed for more than one copy of the edition of Shakespeare's plays published in five volumes by J. Bell in

1774. Most of those multiple subscribers were booksellers or printers, several of whom took twelve or eighteen or twenty-five copies for their country customers. This kind of evidence confirms my contention that the reading public in the provinces provided a substantial market for books. The London publishers realized that advertising their books in the country newspapers could expand their trade considerably.

The cost of advertising a new book or the current issue of a magazine varied with the length of the newspaper notice, but after 5 July 1757, when the government tax on an advertisement was raised from one shilling to two shillings per insertion,[17] the normal charge for a short notice was three shillings and sixpence, larger ones in proportion. Typical are the rates given in the *Shrewsbury Chronicle*, number 68 (23 April 1774): three shillings and sixpence plus a penny per line over twenty lines. The majority of book advertisements were longer than twenty lines of fine print, often filling half or three quarters of a column. It is understandable that some readers of newspapers thought that too much space was given to notices of new books. But when the printer of the *Shrewsbury Chronicle* received such a protest he explained in number 41 (16 October 1773) that he allowed so many advertisements in his paper because they were a source of income for him. Publishers, he said, know that it is profitable for them to give plenty of details in announcing new publications to potential buyers, whether those publications were cheap or expensive.

Certainly there were inexpensive books to be bought, and they did not have to be used books or abridgments. Complete works could be obtained for as little as fourpence halfpenny or sixpence. Just as in the 1730's Tonson and Feales and Walker had all offered once a week the complete text of a play for threepence or fourpence or sixpence,[18] so in the 1770's several publishers, not all of them in London, offered a complete play every Saturday for sixpence or less. One such series came from a provincial printing shop. In 1771, Nicholas Boden of Birmingham brought out an "Elegant Edition of Shakespeare's Plays and Sonnets," issuing one play each week for fourpence halfpenny. In his advertisement in *Felix Farley's Bristol Journal* on 20 July 1771 he announced the tenth play in the series, listed the titles of the preceding nine, and said there would be thirty-eight weekly numbers in all, the last two containing the sonnets and a life of Shakespeare.[19]

Obviously some of the London publishers of books in numbers[20] had their eye on the provincial market, for during the next few years they widely advertised in the country newspapers no fewer than four series of weekly playbooks and two series of weekly booklets of nondramatic poetry. Naturally there was the strongest rivalry. Most vigorous in his protests against competitors was John Bell, who began in 1775 to print one of Shakespeare's plays every week.[21] When he had finished issuing the Shakespeare plays he announced in the *Reading Mercury*, number 745 (22 April 1776), and other country papers that the sixpenny numbers of his *British Theatre* would begin on the following Saturday with Aaron Hill's *Zara* and would continue weekly until one hundred numbers had appeared. In that initial sixty-four-line advertisement he offered "as an encouragement to the Country Trade" a discount of 25 percent to any who would regularly dispose of a dozen or more copies of each weekly number. In subsequent advertisements in various newspapers he listed the titles that had already appeared,[22] but warned customers to be careful to ask for *Bell's British Theatre*, "least a false copy should be obtruded on the purchaser," for, he said, "several other booksellers, envious of the success of this work, are meanly attempting to take advantage of their general influence with their correspondents in the country, and endeavouring, by every other undue means, to foist their own futile productions, when this is particularly wanted."

Those other booksellers were both numerous and influential. They included J. Rivington and Sons, T. Davies, J. Dodsley, T. Longman, and several others. Their weekly sixpenny numbers of *The New English Theatre* began in July 1776 with Mrs. Centlivre's *The Busy Body*, and the series was carried on for over a year.[23] Meanwhile two other attempts were made to induce readers in the country to buy plays in sixpenny installments. Under the title *The French Theatre* a collection of French plays, "printed for T. Bell, No. 26, Bell yard, near Temple Bar," was announced in the *Reading Mercury*, number 745 (22 April 1776), as to begin on Saturday, 27 April 1776, and there were to be one hundred octavo numbers ("the overplus will be given gratis"). The other collection of plays, beginning later that year, bore the title *The Theatrical Magazine; Or, Gentlemen and Lady's Dramatic Library*.[24] It was "Printed for J. Wenman, No. 144 Fleet-street; and sold by all Booksellers, Stationers, and Newscarriers, in Great-Britain and Ireland." Unlike the other sixpenny playbooks the *Theatrical Magazine* contained three plays in each issue and came out once a month instead of weekly. It was to continue only "till the Whole is finished," which means that notwithstanding its title the *Theatrical Magazine* was a collective work of predetermined length, not what is normally understood by the term "magazine."

Readers of provincial newspapers in 1777 were made aware of two sets of weekly volumes which London publishers promised would bring within their reach the texts of English nondramatic poems, with lives of the poets and critical remarks. The enterprising John Bell announced in local papers—one of them was the *Hampshire Chronicle*, number 243 (14 April 1777)—the first of the proposed one hundred little volumes of *The Poets of Great Britain*, "comprising all the British Poets from Chaucer to Churchill." It was not long before Bell felt compelled to publish in several local newspapers a statement headed "To the Country Booksellers" drawing attention to the strong opposition to his *Poets of Great Britain* by a large body of London booksellers who, refusing to fill provincial booksellers' orders for the work, were themselves "attempting an edition of their own on a similar scale." That rival edition was advertised prominently in the *Shrewsbury Chronicle*, number 227 (10 May 1777), and other local papers as already "In the Press." What makes the announcement especially interesting is that after the twenty-one names "&c" of authors to be included in *The English Poets* came the statement that each author's works was to have "a Preface, Biographical and Critical . . . By Samuel Johnson, L.L.D." Stating that the series would not exceed forty volumes and that specimens of the paper, print, and copper plates might be seen at the booksellers', the advertisers said that the work was "Printed for J. Rivington, L. Davis, T. Davis, S. Crowder, B. Law, R. Baldwin, T. Longman, J. Dodsley, E. and C. Dilly, T. Cadell, C. Robinson, W. Davis, T. Evans, and the rest of the Proprietors." They went so far (in the *Shrewsbury Chronicle* announcement) as to add, "sold by T. Wood, Shrewsbury, and D. Salmon Pool." As everybody knows, this was the tremendously important *Lives of the English Poets,* not actually published until two years later. Meanwhile, John Bell continued to publish volume after volume week after week, at one shilling and sixpence, beginning with four volumes of Milton, four of Dryden, three of Butler, three of Prior, and one of Pope, Thomson, Gay, Young. And, said Bell, "Should any difficulty in getting this edition arise to individuals either in town or country they are desired to apply to the publisher who has appointed agents for distribution in all the principal towns in the kingdom." Now why would he say that if there were no relish for reading in the country?

Something of the same frenzied effort to obtain and to keep a share of the provincial trade shows up in the large advertisements printed in various local papers early in 1771 and frequently in the following years by John Wheble in a persistent attempt to persuade country readers that they should purchase *his* publication, the *Lady's Magazine, or entertaining Companion for the Fair Sex,* rather than a work of precisely the same title published by Robinson and Roberts. The dispute continued for several years, with a lawsuit and much shouting in the newspapers.

Magazines published in London were advertised in local papers all over England, often with a detailed list of the contents of the current issue. This is true not only of the long-established *Gentleman's Magazine* and of the *Critical Review* but of the many new monthlies, some of which did not win enough readers either in London or in the country to keep going more than a year or two. But it is to be noted that projectors of new magazines usually made a point of announcing their first issue in the country newspapers as well as in the London ones, and the announcements usually indicated that the current issues could be obtained from local booksellers or from the printers and distributors of the local newspapers. Thus in addition to regular notices, with full details, of the successive issues of the *Town and Country Magazine,* which ran from the beginning of 1769 to the end of 1796, the local papers had hopeful announcements of number 1 of such publications as *Every Man's Magazine; or the Monthly Repository of Science, Instruction and Amusement,* the *Classical Magazine; or Monthly Repository for Persons of Real Taste,* and the *General Magazine; or, complete Repository of Arts, Sciences, Politics, and Literature.* Although these and several other monthlies soon folded, there were some which country readers could continue to see year after year, among them the *Westminister Magazine; or the Pantheon of Taste* (1773–1785) and the *London Review of English and Foreign Literature* (January 1775–December 1780).

Certainly efforts were made by the publisher of the *London Magazine* to increase the circulation in the provinces. The transcript of Charles Ackers' printing shop records shows that in 1739, when seven or eight thousand copies of the

London Magazine were printed every month, Ackers also printed "1000 Titles for Gloucester" in March and a year later "2000 Titles for Gloucester" and "2000 Titles for Salisbury."[25] I cannot be sure what those figures mean, but perhaps Ackers was paid to produce separate title pages of the current issue of the *London Magazine* to be sent to booksellers in the two towns mentioned, perhaps to be sent to the printers of the *Gloucester Journal* and the *Salisbury Journal* for distribution with the newspapers.

A special effort to accommodate country readers is to be seen in the announcement early in 1776 that the *Monthly Miscellany; or Gentleman and Lady's Compleat Magazine,* hitherto published on the fifteenth of the month, would thereafter be issued on the first, "owing to the Difficulty those residing in the Country have had to obtain it in due Time (most of the Country Booksellers sending their Orders once only in the Month, and that in the latter end)."

And it was not only London magazines that provided something for country people to read. Many of the magazines printed on provincial presses did not last long, but the list of such miscellanies is impressive.[26] One of the best of these was the *Newcastle General Magazine* (1747–1760).[27]

The one mode of book publishing that strikes the eye more forcibly than any other as one reads the columns of eighteenth-century newspapers is the issuing of a large book, a few sheets at a time. These were stitched in blue paper covers and sold for a few pennies a week. The trade began in the seventeenth century, developed enormously from 1730 onward, and was immensely popular in succeeding decades as a means of persuading persons of moderate means to acquire expensive books piecemeal by paying a little for each weekly "number."[28] Most of those "number books" or "subscription books," as they were called, were printed in London, but they were undoubtedly extremely popular in the provincial towns and cities. Several printers of local newspapers had a direct financial interest in those printed in London, and some of the number books were in fact printed locally.[29] Normally only the first number was advertised, with full details of when the series would begin, authorship, format, Royal license (if any), publisher or printer (or both, if not the same), frequency, number of sheets in each weekly part, total expected number of parts, price per number, plates (if any), and usually the names of booksellers in the area who had copies of the proposals or of the first number. The two points to be emphasized here are (1) the fact that so many large books published in this way were advertised in the provincial press, and (2) that in most instances the weekly numbers were available regularly without extra charge from the men who distributed local newspapers.[30] The proprietors of a number book were quite ready to pay for advertisements in a dozen or more newspapers in expectation that those advertisements would induce readers in the country to put their names down as regular subscribers; they hoped that out of the thousands of readers who saw the advertisements in their local papers there would be a number who would welcome the opportunity to acquire substantial reading matter with no effort at all and with only a small weekly payment.

If one's main interest is in the fact that *something* was read, no matter what its subject or quality, the number-book trade must figure largely in any study of the reading habits of our ancestors in England. Certainly the range of subjects was broad. As might be expected, travel books, state trials, biography, history, geography, descriptions of England and Wales, commentaries on the Bible were frequently offered, but there were many departures from the conventional. In the 1740's, for example, there was the *Harleian Miscellany*, which Samuel Johnson assisted William Oldys in preparing for the press; and the two hundred others that appeared in the decade from 1740 onward included George Whitefield's *Sermons*, Robert James's *Medicinal Dictionary*, and Torbuck's *Compleat Collection of Debates in the Parliament of England*. In the following decade the many books issued in weekly parts included Robert Walker's second piratical edition of Milton's *Paradise Lost*, in sixteen threepenny weekly numbers (30 October 1751 to 12 February 1752), *The Lives of the Poets of Great Britain and Ireland*, published by Ralph Griffiths in twenty-five duodecimo weekly numbers in 1753, Johnson's *Dictionary*, reissued in numbers shortly after the original folio volumes appeared on 15 April 1755,[31] and Tobias Smollett's enormously popular *History of England*.[32]

To support my assertion that books issued in weekly numbers must be reckoned a substantial part of the reading matter available to English people living in the provinces two centuries ago, I could list all those that were advertised in local newspapers during any one decade. I shall not do that, but I shall pick out a few to show that in the 1770's country readers were offered not only some of the old familiar things, such as the works of Flavius Josephus, which had first appeared in weekly numbers back in 1732, and the full text of the Bible, many times issued in fascicles, but a remarkable variety of books which came from the presses of J. Cooke, G. Kearsley, T. Vallance, Alexander Hogg, and other aggressive London booksellers. A very popular work was *England's Bloody Tribunal; or Popish Cruelty Displayed*, by the Rev. Matthew Taylor, D.D., advertised to begin in June 1770, again in September 1772, again in May 1775, and yet again in July 1776. Appealing to the same relish for violence but not to quite the same religious prejudices was another gory work, *The Newgate Calendar; or Malefactors' Bloody Register*, which Cooke brought out in fifty numbers beginning in July 1772, "The whole tending," he said, "to guard young Minds from the Allurements of Vice, and the Paths that lead to Destruction." Expecting to sell a similar work in the country, Joseph Wenman of Fleet Street advertised *The Annals of Newgate; or, Malefactors Register*, "by Rev. Mr. Vilette, Ordinary of Newgate," to begin on 13 January 1776 and to make four large octavo volumes. But there were milder things, too, among them *The Complete English Peerage*, described as an "entire new work," by the Reverend Frederic Barlow, M.A., Vicar of Burton, beginning in October 1772, and two editions of *The Pilgrim's Progress* (in 1776 and again in 1778). There were editions of the *Spectator* (in 24 numbers beginning on 14 December 1776 and in sixteen numbers beginning at the end of August 1778); there were editions of Thomson's *Seasons* and Young's *Night Thoughts* (in 1777); there were the sixty quarto numbers of William Russel's *History of America, from Its Discovery by Columbus to the Conclusion of the late War,* beginning on 3 January 1778, followed a week later by the first of the folio numbers of another edition of the ever popular *Chambers' Cyclopaedia,* this time printed for W. Strahan and the thirty-four other members of the conger that had acquired the copy, a work which Samuel Johnson wished to have edited in 1774. And there was another work of the kind which Johnson might have enjoyed preparing, *British Biography; or, An accurate and impartial Account of the Lives and Writings of Eminent Persons, in Great-Britain and Ireland, from Wickliff . . . to this present Time,* advertised in 1766 as a new work, "Printed for R. Goadby" and offered again by Goadby in 1778.

All of these and dozens of others were advertised in the country newspapers between 1770 and 1780, sometimes with special emphasis on serving provincial customers. Thus in the *Chester Chronicle,* number 20 (11 September 1775), R. Snagg of Fleet Street printed a note that indicates a lively interest in a perennial favorite:

> Mr. Snagg having received several letters from the country, intimating that the TRIALS were not to be got, and the writers wishing to be informed how they might be procured; he takes this method to acquaint them, that some of the Numbers were THEN out of print, but are now *reprinted;*—the FIRST NUMBER, in particular having been THREE TIMES reprinted since its *first publication,* which is *only* seven weeks; any persons, therefore, may NOW be supplied with complete SETTS, as far as are published, by giving their orders to any bookseller in the town where they reside, or place adjacent.

To go on with the list of substantial works published in numbers in the remaining years of the eighteenth century and advertised extensively in the provincial newspapers would of course be intolerably tedious, but I should like to mention that a group of proprietors, including Thomas Longman, brought out an edition of Johnson's *Dictionary* in quarto numbers beginning on 1 November 1784 and another edition in eighty-four folio numbers beginning on 10 December 1785. Meanwhile Harrison and Company, at No. 18 Paternoster Row, had begun their folio edition in one hundred numbers on 22 October 1785. That is the same firm that in February of that year began to issue the weekly numbers of *Harrison's British Classics; or New Weekly Library of Celebrated Works by Eminent English Authors,* starting with Johnson's *Rambler* and continuing with *The Spectator, The Adventurer, The World,* and other standard periodical essays.

Thus far it has been my purpose to show that people all over England could easily obtain a wide variety of reading matter in the form of books and magazines advertised in their local papers. But we must not neglect the reading matter in the newspaper itself, for it provided not only several columns of news and advertisements but a variety of prose and verse. Four things can be said of the belles lettres occupying space in the regular columns of the local papers: First: there was a vast amount of it, some reprinted from London publications, some contributed by local readers of the paper,[33] for, as Samuel Johnson said facetiously in his second *Idler* essay, it was a time when the rage of writing had seized the old and the young, "when the cook warbles her lyrics in the kitchen, and the thrasher vociferates his heroics in the barn." Second: the reprinted matter cannot be dismissed as having been used merely to fill space when news was scarce. Third: proprietors launching a new paper often announced that in addition to news and advertisements they expected to include contributions in prose and verse, and they both invited and received such contributions from authors in the region. Fourth: editors often rejected contributed material, especially verse, as unacceptable because in bad taste, libelous, "not sufficiently finished for the public eye," or fraudulent.[34] On that last point it is refreshing to read this editorial note in the *Hampshire Chronicle,* number 239 (17 March 1777): *"We are infinitely obliged to our correspondent at Gosport, who signs himself* Verus Amator, *for the trouble he has been at in* copying *an Elegy, which appeared in this paper a few months since, and sending it to us as an* original."

Even without special contributions from correspondents there was no lack of prose and verse to satisfy those who looked for something less evanescent than current news and notices. Most editors printed the Poet Laureat's New Year and Birthday odes, and most country papers reprinted the satiric and polemic letters of "Junius," Wilkes, and John Horne Tooke, as well as, earlier in the century, the "Britannicus" and "Cato" letters from London newspapers, the "Inspector," the "Remembrancer," and the essays of Samuel Johnson.[35] Much space was given to current controversy, such as the Game laws, the bill governing the export of corn, the outbreaks of foot-and-mouth disease in cattle, articles attacking or defending inoculation, detailed accounts of the trials of Mary Blandy, Jonathan Britain, Dr. Dodd, Admiral Keppel, and others.

There was a good deal of original matter, too. Contributed prose did not appear in every issue of the country papers, but it would not be difficult to assemble a volume of quite readable pieces, including such things as the numerous articles in defense of the Americans, the essay on "the different Methods of celebrating . . . Christmas" in *Berrow's Worcester Journal,* number 4004 (27 December 1770), and Edward Rigby's 2,500-word account of James Deeker's ascent in a balloon from Norwich on 1 June 1785.[36] It was doubtless that sort of matter that led a correspondent in the *Shrewsbury Chronicle,* number 212 (25 January), to commend newspapers for having "encouraged and disseminated a general taste for letters amongst the middling and inferior ranks of people."

Much of the contributed verse is conventional or worse, and though there are some reasonably good lyrics, "Sabrina" was somewhat extravagant in praising the printer of the *Shrewsbury Chronicle* when she exclaimed:

> To grace your Work the sacred Nine inspire,
> And every Genius tunes the warbling Lyre.

If genius seldom shines through the thousands of verses in the "Poets Corner" of provincial newspapers it is nevertheless possible to find a few sprightly ditties that may have given almost as much pleasure to their first readers as to their authors. Here, for example, are the first two of the sixteen stanzas of "A Bowling-Green Song" by "J.J." of Christchurch, in the *Hampshire Chronicle,* number .119 (28 November 1744):

> I sing of no ancient achievements of might,
> No Trojan, or Grecian, so sturdy in fight;
> These Trojans, and Grecians, and Romans I ween,
> Were naught when compar'd with the *Sons of the Green.*
> > *Derry down.*
>
> Let others the praises of *cricket* rehearse,
> Or sing of mad contests in the derry-down verse,
> Tho' manly their game, tho' dauntless their souls,
> Yet what heroes can vie with my heroes at bowls?

There is a less bouncy rhythm in the verses by "Juvenis" of Cockermouth in the *Cumberland Pacquet,* number 10 (22 December 1774). Like many of the very competent verses printed in that paper under the regular heading, "Literary Articles," this one, entitled "On Dreams: An Imitation from Petronius Arbiter," was especially written "For the Cumberland Packet." It begins:

> Whence come these Dreams! this busy, idle train
> Of airy forms that flutter round the brain!
> Sure, not from Heav'n descend these trifling guests.
> No.—These are creatures form'd within our breasts.

The piece is good enough to make it seem perfectly reasonable for the editor to add, "We shall be obliged to this Gentleman for a continuance of his Favours."

I hesitate to reproduce the shapely but sentimental heroic couplets in *Felix Farley's Bristol Journal* on 10 November 1770, but the title of the piece, written by a Bristol reader, is worth quoting: "To a Robin, which has lately taken up his Residence in the Cathedral, and accompanies the Organ with his Singing." The piece that follows in the same column is a trifle more down-to-earth: "Written by a Brewer's Daughter, on her Father's discharging his Coachman for getting in Liquor." The stretched-out lines with atrocious rhymes show a certain inventiveness, but one must not look for true poetic fire. It begins:

> Honest William, an easy and good-natur'd Fellow,
> Wou'd a little too oft get a little too mellow;
> Body Coachman was he to an eminent Brewer,
> No better e'er sat on a Box to be sure;
> His Coach he kept clean,—no Mother or Nurses
> Took more Care of their Babes than he took of his Horses.

The piece ends brightly enough: after the brewer has replaced his tipsy coachman with a teetotaler he tells the offender that if he had been a water drinker he would still have his place:

> Drink Water! quoth William,—had all Men done so,
> You ne'er wou'd have wanted a Coachman, I trow;
> For 'tis *Soakers* like me, whom you load with Reproaches
> That enables you *Brewers* to ride in your coaches.

If many another set of verses printed in a provincial newspaper shows more effort than inspiration, it is still a fact that young Tom Chatterton first appeared in *Felix Farley's Bristol Journal*.[37] It is also a fact that when the editor of the *Warwickshire Journal* gave readers of the paper on 14 September 1769 David Garrick's "Ode upon dedicating a Building and erecting a Statue, to Shakespeare, at Stratford-upon-Avon," he had to print it again the following week because of the "sudden and extraordinary Demand for the *Warwickshire Journal* on Thursday last, on Account of Mr. Garrick's Ode."

Much of what has been said thus far in this essay has to do with books and other forms of reading matter that could be acquired by purchase, whether the price was twopence or six guineas. But there is another kind of evidence of a relish for reading among English people in the eighteenth century. It is a plain fact that in towns all over England there were libraries where books could be borrowed for a small fee. The very existence of such a collection of books in a community made it easy for people who could read to obtain books. The presence of a commercial lending library can be taken as evidence that a demand for reading matter was recognized by men who were ready to invest hundreds of pounds in expectation of substantial returns in the form of fees paid by borrowers.

In many towns the printer of the local newspaper was also a bookseller, who not only sold books but lent them. That was true of J. Wilkes of Winchester after he became the printer and publisher of the *Hampshire Chronicle* in June 1778. But long before that he had announced in the *Reading Mercury*, number 513 (11 November 1771), and other papers that he had just then opened a large circulating library "at the Printing Office in Winchester," and that it consisted of "upwards of a Thousand Volumes of the most entertaining Histories, Voyages, Travels, Romances, Novels, Plays, Magazines, and all other diverting Pamphlets; together with some select Novels in the French language." He issued a catalogue for sixpence. And Wilkes was not the only man who had a circulating library in Winchester at this time. In the *Hampshire Chronicle* on 2 and 9 November 1772 is an advertisement by one Greenville, "Bookseller, Stationer, and Printer, at his Circulating Library, No. 42, In High-Street, Winchester," where magazines and reviews were "delivered the first Day of the Month, and all new Publications procured at the shortest Notice.—Weekly Numbers taken in by Subscription, and all new and entertaining Books and Novels are added to his Circulating Library, as soon as published." Perhaps Winchester readers did not provide enough patronage to support both Wilkes and Greenville in the early 1770's, but during the next few years the number of interested readers must have increased, for Wilkes printed a large advertisement in the *Hampshire Chronicle* in 1779 announcing "A New Music Shop and Circulating Library," to be opened on 29 September. The circulating library, he said, would consist of "a selection of the most useful and entertaining English and French Books in every Department of Polite Literature," and would "be increased by the addition of every new publication to be procured regularly every week."

All the new Plays, Pamphlets, Magazines, &c. &c. will be included in the
Library; a Catalogue of which, with Terms of Subscription, will be
delivered gratis the 26th instant. The London newspapers will be taken in
every day for the use of subscribers to the Library.
N.B. Ladies and Gentlemen at any distance may be supplied from this
Library, on their paying the carriage of the books.

In the advertisement which Wilkes printed in his *Hampshire Chronicle* on 4
October 1779 he said that the catalogue could be obtained at the library or from
the thirty-five booksellers and others named at the bottom of the fourth page of
the paper, as well as from the newsmen who delivered the *Hampshire Chronicle.*

Thomas Wood, printer of the *Shrewsbury Chronicle,* also had a lending
library, as is clear from his announcements in that newspaper and from some
verses entitled "A Poor Man's Wish" on the back page of number 128 (17 June
1775). The writer said that, "being fond of books," if he had about five hundred
pounds a year he would acquire "A thousand volumes, may be more," including
"History, Milton, Young, or Gay," and that if his own books proved unsatisfying
for himself and his friend he'd

> send to Wood, who keeps to hire,
> Not doubting ev'ry thoughtful mind
> In books may entertainment find.

A little later that same year Joseph Knight, "Bookseller and Stationer, at his
Circulating Library, in Fisher-Row," Reading, advertised that he had taken over
the shop of Mr. John Samman, who had given up his business, and that he had
in stock "A great Choice of Books, in History, Divinity, Voyages, Travels, Novels,
Poetry, &c. which are lent to read either by the Year, Quarter, Month, or single
Volume; Catalogues of which may be had as above."

The extent to which readers in provincial towns found entertainment in
books borrowed from local libraries is suggested by the fact that Professor Paul
Kaufman has listed circulating libraries in 117 English towns outside of London,
as well as a number of what he prefers to call "subscription" libraries.[38] Advertisements in local newspapers enable me to add details about some libraries
mentioned by him and to provide information about others not in his list. For
example, the *Nottingham Weekly Courant* on 15 and 22 March 1750 indicates
that a collection presented by a local clergyman six years earlier is now to be
made available to qualified users:

The lending LIBRARY, founded by the Rev. Dr. WILLIAM STAND-
FAST Rector of Clifton near Nottingham, in the Charity School Chamber
in the Town and County of the Town of Nottingham, for the Use and
Benefit of the Clergy, Lawyers, and Physicians, and other Persons of a
liberal and learned Education, living and inhabiting in the said Town, or
with, or not above the Distance of eight computed Miles from it, will be
opened on the 26th Day of March 1750; and the Librarian will attend to
lend Books to all such Persons, as shall be intitled to the Use of them

according to the Rules of the said Library. N.B. A Catalogue of the Books, with the Rules to be observed by the Borrowers, may be had of Mr. Ayscough Printer in Nottingham, price Three pence.

That same newspaper a few months earlier (Thursday, 14 September 1749) carried the printer's announcement that on the following Saturday he would publish at fourpence *A Catalogue of the Library In the Charity School Chamber in Nottingham. With Rules To be observ'd by the Readers of the said Library.*

As Professor Kaufman indicates, there were book clubs, private societies which had their own libraries for use by members, cathedral libraries, parochial libraries, school libraries, and coffeehouse libraries, in addition to purely commercial libraries open to anyone who paid the usual fees—half a guinea per annum, three shillings per quarter, one shilling and sixpence per month, or threepence for a single volume. Those are the rates advertised in the *Berkshire Chronicle* in 1772 by Elizabeth Cruttwell, a bookseller and stationer in the Market Place, Wokingham. She issued a catalogue of her circulating library at threepence. The rates given by William Green, printer, stationer, bookseller, and bookbinder in Cook-Row, Bury St. Edmund's, in the *Bury Post, And Universal Advertiser* on 6 February 1783 and later issues for his circulating library, "containing many hundred Volumes of the newest publications, plays, &c. which are let out to read" were higher: twelve shillings per year, four shillings per quarter, one shilling and sixpence per month, sixpence per week, or a penny per night for a single book. Presumably no fee was charged by proprietors of coffeehouse libraries if the books were read on the premises; but I have come upon one advertisement which suggests that the books kept by the proprietor of a coffeehouse might be taken out. In *R. Cruttwell's Bath and Bristol Chronicle,* number 501 (24 May 1770) and again in number 505 (21 June 1770), is an announcement that Loggon's New Long-Room, Tavern, and Coffee-House at Hot-Wells, Bristol, had "opened for the Summer Session" and that the facilities included a "Circulating Library."

The distinctions between a "subscription" library, a Library Society with officers and a paid membership, and other lending libraries open to the public is somewhat obscured by the fact that the notice in the *Leeds Mercury,* number 139 (29 August), summoning the subscribers to the annual meeting in order to elect a new President and Committee is headed "The Circulating Library":

> On Monday next the 4th of September, the Annual and General Meeting of all Subscribers to the CIRCULATING LIBRARY in this Town, is appointed to be held at Mr. Myer's, the New-Inn, at Three O'Clock in the Afternoon. At this Meeting, a new Committee and President are to be chosen, and the annual Payment of Five Shillings is to be made. Those Persons, Therefore, who cannot be present, are desired not to fail to send their Subscriptions at the Time.
>
> This Library, though of only one Year's standing, already consists of upwards of SIX HUNDRED VOLUMES of valuable Books, calculated for the Instruction and Entertainment of every Class of Readers. Every Member is intitled to a printed Copy of the Laws of the Society, and a Catalogue of all the Books.

Immediately after this Meeting will be the Time for Subscribing to
the most Advantage. It is hoped, therefore, that all those Gentlemen and
Ladies, who are disposed to become Members, will take this Opportunity
of doing it. The Institution is such, as cannot fail to be greatly advantageous both to the Subscribers themselves, and to their Posterity; since
none of the Books are ever to be sold, and the whole Stock, it is hoped,
will be increased by the Addition of several Hundred Volumes every Year.

The commercial circulating libraries usually had many more than six hundred
volumes. Thomas Baker's advertisement in the *Hampshire Chronicle*, number 21
(11 January 1773), announced that, because the subscribers to his circulating
library were "daily encreasing" in number, he had made "a very great Addition
to it, so that the Catalogue, with the Appendix (which is just printed) contains
above 3000 Vols. . . . and Persons living at a Distance may be regularly supplied
with Books." There is no indication of how many volumes William Dawkins,
bookseller in North Street, Gosport, had, for when he advertised in the *Hampshire
Chronicle*, number 27 (22 February 1773), that he had "made great Additions
to his CIRCULATING LIBRARY" he did not say how many volumes of "History,
Travels, and Novels, &c." were in the collection.

Further reading of local newspapers will undoubtedly turn up evidence
of lending libraries in other provincial communities. Certainly any bookseller
who wished to start a lending library could do so by obtaining a supply of books
and advice from someone who had already succeeded in what William Lane of
Leadenhall Street, London, called "a profession at once genteel and profitable."
Lane advertised in various newspapers in 1785 that for "any Person, either in
Town or Country, desirous of commencing a Circulating Library" he always
had, ready bound, "several Thousand Volumes, in History, Voyages, Novels,
Plays, &c. suitable for that Purpose," and he added that he would be "happy in
instructing them in the Manner of keeping a Reading-Library." Two years later
Lane's advertisements were even more persuasive, and while some of his
enthusiasm must be set down to the usual zeal of the aggressive salesman it is
worth observing that in his view the relish for reading was by then quite general.
One of those advertisements begins, "At a period like the present, when a general
taste for READING and RECITATION so universally prevails, it will be found
entertaining and useful to establish PUBLIC LIBRARIES in every town though-
out the kingdom."

With vast amounts of reading matter available for purchase in books,
magazines, "numbers," and newspapers, plus the thousands of volumes that
could be borrowed from circulating and other libraries, anyone living in the
country who wished to read did not have to go without something for the mind.
But what evidence is there that children living in the country had an opportunity
to learn to read? Some boys, like the young Wesleys, had mothers who were
determined that learning to read should be part of their early education. Young
William Cobbett went without supper and spent his last threepence to buy a
copy of *A Tale of a Tub*, which he read eagerly and kept by him as a valued

possession until he lost it some years later when a box of his belongings fell over-
board in the Bay of Fundy. Where Cobbett had learned to read I do not know;
it does not appear to have been through formal instruction in a local school. The
point is that he could read and liked to read. I believe that was true of many
another English boy, and it must have been true of many English girls, too.
Otherwise why should Sir Anthony Absolute have vehemently condemned a
circulating library as "an evergreen tree of diabolical knowledge," and why
should a correspondent in the *Hampshire Chronicle* in 1774 have been so anxious
to "open the eyes of parents, that they may clearly perceive the impropriety of
permitting their daughters to destroy their time in the perusal of Novels"?

In the great "public" schools of Eton, Harrow, and Westminister, as in
the "grammar" schools, the emphasis was on classical studies. But the extent to
which English language and especially English literature were taught has only
recently begun to be studied. What attempts were made in the charity schools,
the dame schools, the nonclassical endowed schools, and the Sunday schools to
teach English children to read books in their own mother tongue? Well-documented studies by Richard S. Tompson[39] gather together much valuable information on the subject and show that the teaching of English was a matter of
great concern to many eighteenth-century educators besides Thomas Sheridan,
who argued in his *British Education: or the Source of the Disorders of Great
Britain* (1756) that an exclusively classical education was unsuitable for most
boys. Earlier in the century another Irishman, Richard Steele, had pointed out
the folly of trying to pound Latin syntax into the heads of boys who would have
profited more from other studies.[40] Because clergymen, printers, and others, both
men and women, all over England were free to open and operate schools and to
teach whatever subjects they felt competent to offer—or whatever subjects they
believed to be in demand—it is possible to obtain a great deal of quite specific
information from the advertisements they placed in the local newspapers,
especially in the issues of January and midsummer, when schools reopened after
a vacation period. There is no knowing how good or how bad the instruction
was. Oliver Goldsmith had no very high opinion of the teachers in boarding
schools. "Is any man unfit for any of the professions, he finds his last resource
in setting up a school. If any become bankrupt in trade, they still set up a
boarding-school, and drive a trade this way, when all others fail: nay," continued
Goldsmith in his short-lived periodical, the *Bee*, number 6 (10 November 1759),
"I have been told of butchers and barbers who have turned school-masters; and,
more surprising still, made fortunes in their new professions."

It is difficult to suppose the successful applicant for a post advertised in
the *Manchester Magazine*, number 737 (13 March 1750), made much of a
fortune, even if the stipend was ultimately increased:

Wanted at ROCHDALE,

A SCHOOL MASTER, properly qualified to teach English, the present
fix'd Salary (which is like to be improv'd) is Six Pounds per Annum: A
House and School Rent Free, (to enter upon at May-Day next) in

Consideration of the Master's teaching Twenty petty Scholars, the Master
at Liberty to take in what Number of Scholars he can teach over and
above the Twenty, for his own Benefit . . .

Goldsmith's disparaging remarks about teachers drawn from the ranks of trades-
people seem occasionally at least to have been justified. *Felix Farley's Bristol
Journal* on 16 June 1770 carried an announcement that Mrs. Lodge, "Many Years
a Milliner, in Corn-Street, Bristol; Having entirely quitted the Selling Part of
the Business, has taken a large and commodious House, in the open Part of
Cathay, facing the Fields, where she intends, on the 25th of this Instant opening
A BOARDING and DAY SCHOOL for young Ladies; to teach them all Sorts
of plain Work, and also to dress and make up either for themselves or Friends
every Thing in the Millenery Business." Mrs. Lodge may have been well qualified
to give instruction of that kind; but she added that she proposed to teach the
young ladies "to spell and read grammatically"; and after stating that her charge
would be "14£ a Year and 2£. 1s. Entrance" she said she would teach children
to read for sixpence a week!

Even schoolmasters capable of teaching English sometimes proved negli-
gent, if one may judge by William Relph's advertisement in the *York Courant*
on 28 January 1752. At his school in Spurrier Street, York, he said he would
"teach the ENGLISH, LATIN, and GREEK Languages, according to the Method
laid down by the late Eminent Mr. CLARKE . . . Also WRITING and VULGAR
ARITHMETICK." What makes Relph's advertisement worth mentioning is that
at the end he made an unusual admission:

I hope my former Inadvertences, which, by the good-natur'd and
generous Part of Mankind, may candidly be imputed to the Levity of
Youth, will not retard my future Success; as I determine, hereafter, to use
the utmost assiduous Application to instruct those committed to my Care.

Assurances of assiduous application were probably more trustworthy when they
appeared in such an advertisement as that by the Rev. Mr. Stopford in the
Manchester Mercury on the first day of January 1771, announcing that his school
in Ridge Field would reopen on the following Monday and that he would
"continue to use his utmost Endeavours to instruct his Pupils in the *English* and
Latin Classics, after the best and most expeditious Manner."

Those terms imply that the Reverend Mr. Stopford's pupils were really
introduced to some of the great works of English literature. There are scores of
other advertisements that listed reading as one of the subjects of instruction, and
often it is named first in the list. When Linden and Ward advertised their school
in Southampton in January 1774 the first subject mentioned was "Reading only,"
the fee being six shillings per quarter; but pupils taking "Reading, with Writing
and Arithmetic," had to pay seven shillings and sixpence. Every one of the other
subjects—Merchants Accompts, Navigation, Geography, Drawing, Mensuration,
and Land Surveying—cost more. The value placed on reading was even less in
Mr. Duncombe's Real Mercantile School at Nantwich in Cheshire, for his adver-

tisement in *Adams's Weekly Courant* on 10 March 1778 placed "Reading English only" at the bottom of the list, and the quarterly fee for that subject was only four shillings plus an entrance fee of one shilling. On the other hand there were schools in which English literature was a special feature. The ten masters and assistants who conducted the Academy at Heath, near Wakefield in Yorkshire, offered "a compleat Course of English Education," the first subject listed in the advertisement in the *York Courant* on 25 February 1752 being "a Course of English Classics." Even greater emphasis on instruction in reading was apparently placed by John Hathway at his school in Castle Green, Bristol, according to his advertisement in *Felix Farley's Bristol Journal* on 16 June 1770. Latin, handwriting, mathematics were offered, but at the head of the list was "Reading the English Language in all its Beauties and to its utmost Extent, whether it be calmly persuasive, humorous, and familiar Prose; or Poetry, waking the Soul to sensations of the Sublime, Tumultuous, Mourning, &c. with the peculiar Accent and Pathos the several Parts require." Hathway also offered instruction in English grammar, and made a point of assuring parents that "if any . . . intend that their Sons shall attain to an elegant Stile in Composition, and shall think proper to commit them to my Care, I will frequently exercise them therein by appointing them Themes at a convenient Time on various moral Subjects."

In that same issue of *Felix Farley's Bristol Journal* (16 June 1770) John Jones had a good deal to say about English as taught at his Academy at Cotham House on Kingsdown, near Bristol, where, he said, "Young Gentlemen are Boarded and Half-Boarded in the most genteel Manner, and carefully instructed by John Jones, And proper Assistants, To Speak, Read, and Write the English Language with the Propriety and Correctness, which is seldom observed in our modern Schools, notwithstanding it is the most interesting, and essential Branch of Education to Youth in general; but more especially to such whose After-Sphere in Life may chance to require a frequent Conversation with those of the highest Class of Individuals." Sixteen guineas was the charge per annum for such coaching in snobbery, plus two guineas entrance fee.

It is obvious from hundreds of other advertisements of schools in the provinces that instruction in English was often designed not so much to introduce young pupils to good literature or to encourage them to enjoy fine books as to develop their capabilities in writing and speaking. Over and over again one encounters the phrase "English taught grammatically." J. Malham at Long Preston, near Settle in Yorkshire, advertised in the *Leeds Mercury* early in 1769 that he gave instruction in ten branches of education, the first to be named being "English grammatically, after a Method most easy and familiar, whereby the Young Scholars may learn to write as true English as those who have attained a Classical Education." But it is not hard to find evidence that material in English for extracurricular reading was provided in some schools, sometimes at a separate charge. Mrs. Clarke at Mansfield in Nottinghamshire described in her advertisement in the *Manchester Mercury*, number 1042 (25 June 1771), the whole "plan of education" at her boarding school for young ladies, which showed that before breakfast the girls heard prayers, had lessons in French and English—

"spelling and pronouncing properly"—and from two to five in the afternoon worked at their needles and "read French or English Authors, as the History of England, Addison's Spectators, the Preceptor . . . &c." On Sundays, before and after worship, "the Boarders are engaged in reading or hearing the best Authors in Divinity, as Sherlock's and Fordyce's Sermons, Nelson's Festivals, Dodderidge's or Burkit's Exposition of the New Testament, Stackhouse's History of the Bible, &c." There was no extra charge for that opportunity to read.

At Nathaniel Cope's boarding school for young gentlemen at Somerset House, Cathay, according to advertisements in *Felix Farley's Bristol Journal* in 1771, the boys were taught to "speak, read, and write, with Propriety of Style," and "at so small a Gratuity as Half a Crown per Quarter" they had the opportunity to pursue "a Selection of Books, of the most esteemed Authors, upon the best Subjects." Cope named no authors and no books, but the list of subjects covered by them included history, religion, philosophy, politics, anatomy, "and many other useful and entertaining Subjects." John Jones, whom I have already mentioned as favoring instruction in English, was more explicit in describing the books which the boys in his school could have the privilege of reading, and his charge was lower than Cope's:

> For the more speedy Improvement of his Pupils in a correct Manner in reading every Branch of Lecture in the English Language, and to give them a Knowledge of History, sacred and Profane, Mr. Jones has procured, not only some hundred Volumes of interesting, entertaining, and improving Books (such as History, Travels, Memoirs; the Tatlers, Spectators, Guardians, Homer's Iliads, and Odyssey, the Works of Tillotson, Pope, Dryden, Young, &c. &c. in Prose and Verse) but also the several Translations of the Classicks, by the most eminent Translators; for the Use of which Books, the Pupil is only charged One Shilling and Six-pence per Quarter.

If the reading of such books was intended more to provide instruction or to develop skill in writing and speaking than to whet the youthful appetites for belles lettres, reading was quite definitely a part of the curriculum in many schools.

Corroborative evidence appears in several forms. The country newspapers often printed the advertisements of London booksellers who published little works written especially for children or youths to read. Sometimes there are long lists of moral treatises presumably intended for parents to dangle before their helpless youngsters, such as those advertised in *Felix Farley's Bristol Journal* on 14 December 1771 by T. Carnan at number 65 St. Paul's Churchyard London. Among the delectable offerings, which could be obtained from eleven different booksellers in Bristol as well as from "all other Booksellers in Town and Country," were *Juvenile Trials for robbing Orchards, telling Fibs, and other high Misdemeanours*, and *Hymns for the Amusement of Children*. Both of these had illustrations, and the price of each was sixpence. Quite obviously the publishers of books for young people were convinced that the primary requirement was to provide moral instruction, and they apparently made some effort to make that instruction palatable. Representative of such ostensible concern is *The Pleasing Instructor: Or, Entertaining Moralist,* a new edition of which was advertised in various country papers in 1777 by G. Robinson of Paternoster Row and T. Slack in Newcastle. This three-shilling book, consisting of "select Essays, Relations, Visions, and Allegories, collected from the most celebrated English Authors," was "Designed for the Use of Schools, as well as a valuable Parlour Book; with a View to form the rising Minds of the Youth of both Sexes to Virtue, and to destroy in the Bud those Vices and Frailties which Mankind, and Youth in particular, are addicted to."

It is impossible to estimate how many English boys and girls living in the country enjoyed having their wicked propensities destroyed in the bud by reading *The Pleasing Instructor,* whether in school or in the parlor. But many a schoolmaster must certainly have kept his pupils hard at work learning *how* to read. Consider this fact: Charles Ackers of London in 1733 printed ten thousand copies of the nineteenth edition of Thomas Dyche's *Guide to the English Tongue;* by February 1748 he had brought out thirty-two more separate printings, making a total of 275,000 copies.[41] In 1778 the fifty-ninth edition was published, and by the end of the century there had been at least fourteen more printings. Add to these the editions that preceded the nineteenth, including the tenth edition, published by Burbage and Stretton of Nottingham in 1709, and it is obvious that in the eighteenth century hundreds of thousands of boys—and who knows how many girls?—studied the English tongue with the help of Thomas Dyche's *Guide.*

Now, what was the ultimate effect of such exercises in school? One result may have been that some of the children ultimately not only wrote well but spoke well. When "W.H." of Whitwell in the Isle of Wight began the series of eleven letters on education, which were printed in the Hampshire Chronicle in 1776 and 1777, he declared, "Reading is the foundation stone of the whole literary fabric." But he had in mind not the developing of a sensitive delight in great books; his emphasis was on rhetorical effectiveness. "Youth ought not only to be grammatically instructed in their native language," he insisted, "but be taught to read with ease, grace, and eloquence, to give each syllable its proper accent, each word its proper emphasis, and frequently every sentence a variation in sound according to the subject, be it with energy, extasy, gravity, or feintness." That rather Churchillian striving for oratorical subtlety is just the sort of skill such schoolmasters as John Jones and Nathaniel Cope were trying to induce in their pupils; they hoped to turn them into eloquent public speakers. It is amusing to find publishers catering to the ambitions of youthful persons eager to impress audiences with studied eloquence by furnishing them—as J. Roson of London did in 1773 with such a manual as *The British Spouter; Or, Stage Assistant*[42]— the kind of textbook that appealed to the amateur thespians whom Dickens later ridiculed so delightfully. It may be a regrettable fact that many a proud parent stood his precocious young spouter on a table to bore relatives and long-suffering neighbors with a recitation, for it will be remembered that when

William Lane offered to help with the establishing of new circulating libraries he said it was a time when "a general taste for reading and *recitation*" universally prevailed. Some of those juvenile elocutionists may have grown up to be actors or lawyers or parsons; but the point is that they and many others learned to read in school and kept on reading, even if there were some who never achieved a higher degree of literacy than the ability to sign their names.

I offer as my contribution to the subject of literacy in England in the eighteenth century the contention that the local newspapers, which I have been using as my main source, provide abundant evidence that people living in the provinces not only could read but were sufficiently interested to buy or borrow books on every conceivable subject. Some notices to support that contention appeared in only one paper as items of local news, as when the *Manchester Mercury* at the end of October 1771 announced that on the following Thursday the topic to be debated by the Conversation Society of Manchester would be "Whether has Commerce or Literature been more advantageous to Mankind?" and a week later reported that the question "was determined Literature." Advertisements of local schools were normally inserted only in the newspapers which covered the region in which the schools were situated; and the same is true of announcements of book auctions and of circulating libraries. But books and magazines published in London were invariably advertised in a large number of local newspapers, for the whole country was looked on as a potential market. Undoubtedly great quantities of books were sold, and while it is arguable that not everyone who buys a book necessarily reads it, one cannot really suppose that so many books were bought and bound only to be stacked on shelves as ornaments. And the newspapers themselves furnished reading matter to increasing numbers of English people of all classes. There is no possibility of demonstrating statistically what proportion of the population in eighteenth-century England both could and did read. But even without the unchallengeable facts in the form of printers' records, frequent reprintings, lists of subscribers, and sheer numbers of titles, there is sufficient testimony in the newspapers alone that increasingly in successive decades multitudes of English people developed and enjoyed a relish in reading.

NOTES

1. This is one of Johnson's many indications of his fondness for London. See *Boswell's Life of Johnson*, ed. G. B. Hill, rev. L. F. Powell (Oxford, 1934–1950), III, 178, and cf. the references in the Index (VI, 244–45).

2. Ibid., III, 450.

3. In "Literacy and Education in England 1640–1900," *Past & Present*, no. 62, (1969), pp. 69–139, Laurence Stone limits the term "literacy" to the ability to sign one's name, though at one point he observes that in the eighteenth century most of the semiliterate lower middle class moved into the ranks of the fully literate, who could read as well as write.

4. *Selected Letters of Samuel Richardson*, ed. John Carroll (Oxford, 1964), p. 341.

5. The compulsion to read whatever was currently popular led Samuel Johnson, in

a conversation with Allan Ramsay on 29 April 1778, to declare, "We must read what the world reads at the moment." Yet he added, "But it must be considered, that we have now more knowledge generally diffused; all our ladies read now, which is a great extension."

6. The eighteenth century was aware of the vast numbers of books that were printed. "One of the peculiarities which distinguish the present age is the multiplication of books," wrote Johnson in the *Idler*, no. 85 (1 December 1759); and soon afterward Goldsmith's Letter XXIX in the *Public Ledger* on 14 April 1760 began, "Were we to estimate the learning of the English by the number of their books that are every day published among them, perhaps no country, not even China itself, could equal them in this particular." Later in the century Vicesimus Knox wrote an essay "On the Multiplication of Books" in his *Essays, Moral and Literary* (1782).

7. For example, the *Hampshire Chronicle*, no. 318 (21 September 1778), refers to a rival paper printed locally; and in the same paper, no. 362 (27 [= 26] July 1779), Mr. Peadle, bookseller and printer at Arundel, warned all quarterly subscribers to the *Sussex Gazette* not to pay any money into the hands of George Palmer, one of Peadle's newsmen. The *Sussex Gazette* is not otherwise known.

8. The first provincial newspaper in England appears to have been the *Norwich Post* (circa November 1701). See G. A. Cranfield, *The Development of the Provincial Newspaper 1700–1760* (Oxford: Clarendon Press, 1962), pp. 13 f., and R. M. Wiles, *Freshest Advices: Early Provincial Newspapers in England* (Columbus, O. [1965]), pp. 15 f.

9. *Freshest Advices*, p. 97.

10. Op. cit., p. 172.

11. Notwithstanding the new increase in the Stamp Tax from a penny to three halfpence per copy on 5 July 1776 the *Hampshire Chronicle* testified just one month later that "the great increase in the demand for this paper" made it necessary to go to press "some hours sooner."

12. The *Hampshire Chronicle* was regularly dated as published on Monday, but there are several references to its being delivered on the preceding day, for example, in no. 170 (20 November 1775).

13. The distinction was made by De Quincey in an article on Alexander Pope contributed to the *North British Review* in August 1848.

14. Letter of 28 July 1761 from Coxwould to John Hall-Stevenson, reprinted in *Letters of Laurence Sterne*, ed. Lewis Perry Curtis (Oxford, 1935). Hinxman's advertisement is in the *York Courant*, no. 1864 (14 July 1761).

15. Such traveling book salesmen were not always welcome. The *Chester Chronicle*, no. 652 (16 November 1787), printed a warning to the "flying booksellers" who were said to be "generally the harbingers of Christmas" not to appear in the Chester area.

16. Lackington tells his own success story in *Memoirs of the First Forty-five Years of the Life of James Lackington, The present Bookseller in Chiswell-street, Moorfields, London. Written by Himself. In a Series of Letters to a Friend* (London, [1791]).

17. 30 Geo. 2, c. 19.

18. R. M. Wiles, *Serial Publication in England before 1750* (Cambridge, 1957), pp. 16–21.

19. Boden had advertised the proposals for his edition of Shakespeare in *Felix Farley's Bristol Journal* on 2 March 1771 and in other papers issued about the same time.

20. These series of weekly booklets were called "numbers" because they were numbered consecutively, but they are not to be confused with installments of large works published piecemeal in fascicles, to be considered hereafter.

21. Bell had already published by subscription in 1774 twenty-four of Shakespeare's plays in five volumes. The series in numbers was announced in the *Hampshire*

Chronicle, no. 167 (30 October 1775), and other papers. In the *Chester Chronicle,* no. 515 (6 May 1785), Bell announced that he was once more publishing the plays of Shakespeare in weekly numbers, "complete and correct from the TEXTS of SAMUEL JOHNSON and GEORGE STEVENS" at sixpence on ordinary paper, one shilling and sixpence "on a superfine *silky* paper," and "to gratify some noble personages, and others of exquisite taste . . . a few . . . on very large paper" at five shillings.

22. In the *Hampshire Chronicle,* no. 211 (2 September 1776), for example, the list goes as far as no. 17, Mrs. Centlivre's *The Wonder! A Woman keeps a Secret;* and in the *Reading Mercury,* no. 819 (22 September 1777), he gave the titles of nos. 65 to 71, already published up to that time, assuring country readers that the weekly numbers would proceed regularly. Eighty-one titles are printed in *Adams's Weekly Courant* (Chester), no. 2360 (13 January 1778).

23. No. 51 of *The New English Theatre* was advertised in the *Shrewsbury Chronicle,* no. 238 (26 July 1777), and in other country newspapers of approximately the same date.

24. No. VIII was advertised in the *Shrewsbury Chronicle,* no. 230 (31 May 1777), and in other newspapers as to be published on 1 June.

25. D. F. McKenzie and J. C. Ross, eds., *A Ledger of Charles Ackers Printer of the London Magazine,* for the Oxford Bibliographical Society (Oxford, 1968), p. 273.

26. See *NCBEL,* II, cols. 1349–52.

27. For other periodicals published before 1760 see my "Early Georgian Provincial Magazines," *The Library,* ser. 5, 19 (1964, published 1968), 187–95.

28. My study of the earlier phases of this mode of publication, *Serial Publication in England before 1750,* listed over 350 different works so published in the period covered. Subsequent research has added nearly a hundred more titles.

29. Nicholas Boden, mentioned above, brought out a set of weekly numbers of the *Compleat Family Bible* at 2½ d. per number, disposing of them through agents in various towns. According to *Felix Farley's Bristol Journal* on 2 March 1771, Boden's agent in the Bristol area, John Amos, proved "remiss" and had to be replaced. Thomas Wood of Shrewsbury likewise published a complete *Family Bible,* in weekly quarto numbers, announcing it in advance in his *Shrewsbury Chronicle,* no. 114 (11 March 1775), giving full details in no. 118 (8 April 1775), and announcing the last part in no. 283 (30 May 1778).

30. Circumstances beyond the control of the printer sometimes interrupted the regular distribution of the weekly numbers in the country. When that happened the printer took special pains to account for the delay. In January 1740, for instance, Robert Walker, who had been issuing *The Beauties of the English Stage* since 7 December 1738, explained to readers of his *Warwick and Staffordshire Journal* in no. 129 (31 January 1740) that "Customers to the Collection of Plays from the best Dramatick Authors, are desired to excuse the Delay in publishing it, the Weather being so extremely cold that my Workmen were not able to perform their usual Business; but I promise, that the Number which has been thus delayed, shall, without fail, be sent down with the next Weekly Return of these Books, and to be continued till this Volume is finished."

31. *Serial Publication in England,* pp. 7, 244.

32. Ibid., pp. 5–7.

33. *Freshest Advices,* p. 312.

34. Ibid., pp. 274–76.

35. For example, *Rambler* papers were reprinted in the *Bristol Weekly Intelligencer,* the *Bath Journal,* the *Leeds Mercury, Aris's Birmingham Gazette, Whitworth's Manchester Mercury,* the *Western Flying Post,* the *Salisbury Journal* and the *Portsmouth and Gosport Gazette.*

36. There is an advance notice of the flight in the *Bury Post,* 27 April 1785, headed "The Royal Baloon." An advertisement to the "Nobility, gentry, etc.," advising

them of the coming "Aerostatic Experiment" appears in the same paper for 1 June, and the full account appears on 8 June. Young Miss Weller, a girl of the "most astonishing intrepidity," had been intended passenger, but the combined weight of Miss Weller and Mr. Deeker was too great—after a false start, he ascended by himself.

37. See "Note on Some Pieces in *Felix Farley*, 1763–1768," in E. H. W. Meyerstein, *A Life of Thomas Chatterton* (London, 1930), pp. 125–28.

38. Paul Kaufman, *Libraries and Their Users: Collected Papers in Library History* (London, 1969).

39. For example, *Classics or Charity?* (Manchester, 1971), and his "English and English Education in the Eighteenth Century," a paper presented as part of the symposium on "Popular Education in the Age of Improvement" at the 1973 Annual Meeting of the American Society for Eighteenth-Century Studies.

40. *Spectator*, no. 157 (30 August 1711).

41. *A Ledger of Charles Ackers*, pp. 18–19.

42. This piece, and a handful of similar works (see *CBEL*, II, 393) used as basic texts for the "spouter"—the prologues and epilogues of the contemporary theater—a rich vein of eloquence, wit, and bombast.

English Books and
Their Eighteenth-Century German Readers

Bernhard Fabian

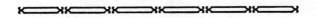

In the long history of intellectual exchanges between England and Germany the eighteenth century stands out as a period of special significance. It was a period in which Germany assimilated the contemporary literature of England to an extent and with an intensity that has few parallels in the relations between two national cultures. The flow of ideas began in the last decades of the seventeenth century and continued uninterrupted throughout the eighteenth into the early part of the nineteenth. It extended beyond the realm of belles-lettres and reached many other, if not all, fields of contemporary knowledge.

Some aspects of this process are familiar. It is well known that the presence in Germany of a large body of English literature was a powerful incentive to literary development and a major factor in precipitating that outburst of literary activity which brought forth, in the later decades of the century, the literature of Storm and Stress and of early German Classicism.[1] It is also known, though not yet adequately documented, that with the spread of English culture England became an important force in the political and social thinking of Germany.[2] In a country that was notoriously given to the admiration of foreign nations an ever-growing number of Anglophiles vied with the established Francophiles in their enthusiasm for the right kind of enlightenment and the right model of social grace. The ceremonious imitation of what was regarded as a superior English style produced distinctive patterns of thought and behavior, traces of which can still be observed today.

I shall here be concerned with aspects that have hitherto not been given the attention that they properly deserve. My point of departure is the simple fact that the medium of the assimilation of English thought and English culture was primarily, and in many cases exclusively, the printed page. Regardless of what England ultimately meant—a reservoir of ideas, a well of inspiration, an ideal, a mirage—the source of knowledge was a book or a journal in the original language or in a translation.

This fact is easily stated, but its implications are many and far reaching. The dissemination of British authors in eighteenth-century Germany has not yet been analyzed as a whole, and hardly any attempt has been made to identify the mechanisms at work. Understandably so: the evidence is widely scattered and generally uncharted. Except for small parts the territory is not only unexplored but also, because of the postwar disruption of the German library system, difficult of access. Thus I cannot hope to present more than a contour map—in the expectation that further details will be supplied by those bibliographers and historians of ideas and of literature who share my view that this phase in Anglo-German relations can in many ways be studied as a model process.

Bibliographical Problems

When the study of the influence of eighteenth-century English authors on contemporary German poets, novelists, and playwrights was initiated in the late nineteenth century,[3] little attention was given to relations other than those in belles-lettres. Apart from certain philosophical and theological connections, such relations, if not ignored, were treated as incidental to the literary ties between the two countries. Later scholars retained this outlook, and with minor modifications it is still widely accepted today. As a result, the bibliographical approach to the reception of British writers in eighteenth-century Germany has to a large extent been determined by purely literary considerations, and the available information is far from complete.

There are only two checklists dealing with the publication of English works in Germany, both compiled by Mary Bell and Lawrence Marsden Price: *The Publication of English Literature in Germany in the Eighteenth Century*, published in 1934, and *The Publication of English Humaniora in Germany in the Eighteenth Century*, published as a sequel in 1955. Both are based throughout on secondary sources: on the standard bibliographies for the period, on contemporary review journals, and on the catalogues of selected libraries. The first bibliography is devoted to literature in the narrowest possible sense—"novels or works of a quasi-fictional character, dramas, poetry . . . , and essays . . . of a literary character" (p. 2). The second takes *humaniora* as a generic term to cover disciplines from philosophy to geography and from criticism to cultural anthropology.[4] The borderline is not drawn between humanistic and scientific disciplines but, for instance, between items of medico-literary interest and purely medical interest. Titles not meeting the humanistic criterion are disregarded.

I do not intend to disparage these indispensable pioneer works, but I find it difficult to accept their bibliographical rationale. In restricting themselves to what is of actual or potential interest to the literary historian, they proceed on a kind of degressive principle and produce a concentric arrangement of the evidence. A highly important body of scholarly, scientific, and technical writings is relegated to fringe areas, if not omitted entirely. At any rate, the distinction the Prices made between central and marginal material appears to be unsuitable for any attempt to ascertain which texts of British origin were actually accessible in eighteenth-century Germany.

If the evidence is to be properly established, a fresh survey will have to be made from at least two points of view: language and subject matter. The importance of the second is self-evident. The relevance of the first might be questioned. My reason for proposing it is that it brings into perspective certain phenomena and certain kinds of material which we ought not to disregard in trying to establish a relationship between the German reader and his English authors.

From the language point of view, the bulk of material consists, quite naturally, of translations from English into German. Leaving aside possible intermediate stages (such as German translations of translations into French) one can say that direct translations constitute the largest part of the texts of British authorship that were at the disposal of the German reader. If an author was made available in another way, for example in a translation into French or Latin, this translation was frequently, but by no means invariably, in addition to the translation into German.

It is difficult to form an adequate idea of the vast range of material that was translated. It appears that more than 300 authors cited in the belles-lettres volume and more than 750 in the *humaniora* were involved in the large-scale effort to render into German whatever was of genuine interest or of marketable value.[5] In view of these figures there is no need to point out in detail that nearly all of the major authors were translated and that a host of minor ones followed in the wake of the great. Not a few of the minor writers are so obscure that they cannot be traced even in the old or new *Cambridge Bibliography of English Literature*.

It has never been assessed how many works were in fact translated, and for the time being there seems to be no way of arriving at reliable statistics. The Prices list more than 1,000 translated titles in belles-lettres, and more than 1,400 in *humaniora*. But the checklists are incomplete and, moreover, they exclude important categories of books. The number of possible additions may be found to be large, if and when the checklists come to be revised. In any case, as the user is properly warned by the compilers, each item needs verification.[6]

In establishing the record, future bibliographers will have to go beyond the quasi-national bibliographies of Heinsius[7] and Kayser[8]—purportedly "vollständig" and often the envy of the English bibliographer working in this period. Both have been searched by Professor and Mrs. Price, but only recently has Heinsius been found to list no more than about 20 percent of the total book production of the eighteenth century, and Kayser no more than about one third of the production between 1750 and 1800.[9] Thus the lacunae are considerable, not only among ephemera and regional publications but also among major authors. The first edition of Johann Joachim Christoph Bode's translation of *Tristram Shandy*, for instance, is missing.

Much pertinent information appears to be contained in the book fair catalogues,[10] a bibliographical source that has never been systematically exploited in the study of the eighteenth-century German reception of British authors.[11] These catalogues were issued for the Frankfurt Book Fair (until about 1740) and for the Leipzig Book Fair (throughout the period). Though not complete and not reliable in listing the new publications twice a year,[12] they provide (at least until 1759) a subject arrangement of the titles, which should greatly facilitate the compilation of a master checklist and of much-needed sectional checklists. Moreover, various statistical data can be derived from them.[13] Reference to the fair catalogues will also enable the bibliographer to establish the relative importance of various kinds of literature and to trace, as in the case of belles-lettres in the last decades of the century, the ascendency of particular types. Finally, the section on forthcoming books, which was a regular feature of the catalogues throughout the century, is likely to yield a large amount of information on publishing schemes and literary activities for which no other evidence survives.[14]

A second group of books—smaller in number, though not inferior in importance—consists of English works in the original language. They were, for various reasons, distributed in Germany to meet the needs of those who had newly acquired a sufficient knowledge of the language to read their English authors in English. It is therefore not so much as a specimen of foreign-language publishing that these books deserve attention (though this aspect must not be neglected) but as an index to the taste and interests of a special section of the reading public.

This group falls into three categories. The first, and smallest, consists of parallel-text editions of translations of poetic works. Examples are furnished by Gottfried Ephraim Müller's rendering of the *Essay on Criticism* (*Versuch über die Critik aus dem Englischen des Herrn Pope*)[15] or by Johann Arnold Ebert's ambitious annotated edition of *Dr. Eduard Young's Klagen oder Nachtgedanken über Leben, Tod und Unsterblichkeit*.[16] The second comprises straightforward reprints of English books on a great variety of subjects. Friedrich Nicolai's *Verzeichniß einer Handbibliothek*,[17] compiled in response to requests he had received as a bookseller, gives some idea of the range of books that had been reproduced by the early 1780's. The section "Englische Bücher, die in Deutschland gedruckt sind" (pp. 281–86), reads like a standard canon of eighteenth-century authors: Addison, Fielding, Gay, Goldsmith, Johnson, Lady Mary Wortley Montagu, Ossian, Pope, Prior, Richardson, Sterne, Swift, Thomson, and Young, surrounded by such minor authors as Aikin and Glover (who was highly appreciated in Germany), Hawkesworth, and Edward Moore. In addition, he lists some moral works such as the Chesterfield-Trusler *Principles of Politeness* or Fordyce's *Sermons to Young Women*, as well as ten volumes of the *Philosophical Transactions of the Royal Society*.

These reprints have never been studied as a separate group, and a surprisingly large number do not seem to have found their way into the general and special bibliographies which the student of the reception of English writers in Germany is likely to consult. Among the unrecorded items announced in the catalogue of the Leipzig Easter Fair of the year 1800 are Coxe's *Memoirs of Sir Robert Walpole*, Farmer's *Essay on the Learning of Shakespeare*, Ferguson's *Institutes of Moral Philosophy*, two editions of Hayley's *Life of Milton*, Knox's *Essays Moral and Literary*, and Malone's *Historical Account of the Rise and Progress of the English Stage*.[18] Moreover, such reprints tend to be absent from the author bibliographies because the compilers appear to have been unaware of their existence.[19] In any case, they present a special bibliographical problem when seen in relation to the third category of English language books.

This last, and in many respects most interesting, category is composed of English books which seem to have been imported by German publishers and marketed by them as quasi-original publications.[20] As a rule, they can be traced only in the book fair catalogues, which purportedly list "Bücher, welche . . .

entweder ganz neu gedruckt oder sonst verbessert wieder aufgelegt worden sind."
A typical entry, in somewhat garbled English, reads "London, and to have by
Gleditsch [in Leipzig]." It appears in the autumn catalogue for the 1775 Leipzig
Fair (p. 949) and refers to C. J. Phipps's *Voyage to the North Pole*, published by
John Nourse in 1774. Can this be dismissed as a bookseller's import, when in
1767 Benjamin Hederich's *Graecvm Lexicon Manvale* appeared with the imprint
"Lipsiae in Bibliopolo Ioh. Frid. Gleditschii Prostat etiam Londini apvd I.
Nourse"? Another, and still more intriguing, entry is in the autumn catalogue for
1756 (p. 742): "Johnsons, Sam. Dictionary of the English Language, fol. and 8.
Leips. J. Wendler." Does it imply that Wendler merely imported the original
edition of 1755 and the abridgement, in octavo, of 1756? Or was there a separate
Leipzig edition?[21] I have not succeeded in tracing copies, but Johann Georg
Hamann in Königsberg appears to have owned a two-volume edition of the
Dictionary "Lips. 1756."[22]

The third group consists of French and Latin translations. French translations played an important part in acquainting the German reader with
British authors.[23] Many of these translations appear to have been bought
from France or from Holland. But a number were also published or republished in Germany. How large the production was and which authors were
involved is, again, a question to be answered by future bibliographers. Pope at
any rate figured prominently. Beginning in 1749, French translations of his collected works appeared with an Amsterdam and Leipzig imprint.[24] One of them
was reprinted in Vienna in an edition that was intended both for the domestic
and for the French market.[25] The point to be made here is that the French
translations precede both the first German translation of Pope's collected works,
which did not come out until 1758,[26] and the German reprint of the Warburton
edition, which was published between 1762 and 1764.[27] Thus those works of Pope
which had not previously been translated separately reached the German reader
first in French translations.

This was also the case with other authors. Bolingbroke's *Letters on the
Spirit of Patriotism* (1749) came out in French translation in London in 1750[28]
and was imported from Edinburgh to Leipzig in the same year.[29] The German
translation dates from 1764.[30] His *Letters on the Study and Use of History* (1752)
was published in French in Berlin in the same year,[31] to be followed by a German
translation six years later.[32] The problem of special editions for the German
market arises again. Is, for instance, the 1777 edition of Robertson's *Histoire de
l'Amérique* ("4 Voll. 12. Paris & à Dresde, chez G. C. Walther.")[33] a hasty import
to compete with the simultaneous German translation[34] or a joint venture of a
French and a German publisher? Similarly, was the 1771 French translation of
The Dunciad published only in London or also in Frankfurt?[35]

Translations of seventeenth- and eighteenth-century English poems into
Latin are generally seen in the tradition of Neo-Latin authorship. Often such
translations were virtuoso performances and had no function in transmitting a
text to the reading public. Latin translations of scholarly books served a different
purpose. In earlier periods the reception of English authors on the Continent

depended to a large extent on the availability of Latin translations, as many philosophical and theological works testify.[36] In the eighteenth century Latin translations served a much smaller but still sufficiently large public of scholars and educated readers. It was for these readers that, for instance, Anthony Black-wall's *Introduction to the Classics* was translated into Latin, to be published in Leipzig in 1735.[37] Another example is Colin Maclaurin's *Account of Sir Isaac Newton's Philosophical Discoveries* (1748). The book was never translated into German, but a French translation by Lavirotte appeared in 1749. This was in turn translated into Latin, including the French preface, by the Austrian Jesuit Gregor Falck and appeared in Vienna in 1761.[38] The number of these books is not large, but they should be studied as the last traces of a tradition whose fading away can be observed in the eighteenth century.

By suggesting a new subject approach to the bibliographical study of the reception of English authors in eighteenth-century Germany I want to propose an approach that is at once broad and specific. It should enable us on the one hand to avoid the limitations inherent in a purely or predominantly literary approach and on the other to produce a body of information that is more detailed and comprehensive than the one hitherto available. Instead of dividing the bibliographical evidence into literature, *humaniora,* and unspecific marginal material we should, more appropriately in view of what was actually translated and published, define an area that is constituted by scientific and technical books, another that comprises scholarly works in the humanities, and a third that includes literature in the strict sense and such related categories as travel books.

The first area is properly the province of the historian of science, and I cannot pay more than passing attention to the fact that many medical and technical works were translated into German.[39] The importance of this field is indicated by the appearance, in the second half of the century, of more than half a dozen journals devoted to the sole purpose of disseminating the results of medical research in Great Britain.[40] The second area, humanistic scholarship, extends into various disciplines, of which I want to mention only two. One is classical scholarship. Here the Germans were indebted to the English for profoundly stimulating works like Robert Wood's *Essay on the Original Genius and Writings of Homer* (translated into German from one of the few privately printed copies prior to its publication in England).[41] Moreover, wide use was made in Germany of the English editions of the classics. The significance of this branch of scholarly relations is best seen in what may, at first sight, appear as a curiosity: Ludwig Wilhelm Brüggemann's *View of the English Editions, Translations and Commentaries of the Ancient Greek and Latin Authors*—a book of 850 pages, written by a German in English and published in Germany.[42] The other is biblical scholarship, with the central figure of Johann David Michaelis, who promoted and annotated Lowth's *De sacra poesi Hebraeorum.*[43] The bibliographical context for the scholarly exchanges between Michaelis, Lowth, Benjamin Kennicott, and others remains to be established.[44]

The purely literary texts, which have been studied for nearly a century, are recorded more extensively than any other group. The fact that a checklist exists would seem to suggest that from the point of view of subject bibliography little remains to be done. But such an assumption is unwarranted—not only because of the additions which a search of the fair catalogues and other sources is likely to yield. In the eighteenth century, publication was no longer confined to separate publication in book form. With the rapid spread of the periodical (in Germany the proliferation was enormous),[45] a new medium of publication established itself, and the processes of extracting and anthologizing assumed, especially in the reception of a foreign literature, an importance which they had not previously had. Thus the field for investigation is broader than in any previous period and, given the peculiarities of literary translation, also more diversified than in the case of nonliterary texts.

Among the various modes of transmission, the republication of original English texts was the simplest, though not the most frequent. Many of the classical works of eighteenth-century English belles-lettres can be found in this category. Textually, the editions are on the same level as other unauthorized reprints (like those published in France or America). As I have suggested, the interest they have derives primarily from the fact that they were published and read in Germany. The commercial aspects have to be considered in another context, but I should like to draw attention to the range of material that still awaits investigation.

From one point of view, it extends from coarse reproduction to fairly high-class private press printing. The typographical (and other) depths of reprinting are still to be fathomed, but some of its heights are visible in Johann Heinrich Merck's reprints of *The Deserted Village* (printed in 1772 "for a friend of the Vicar," i.e., Goethe) and of Ossian (published between 1773 and 1776 in a private and a commercial four-volume edition with a vignette designed by Goethe).[46] From another, it extends from the single title to the omnibus anthology such as Johann Heinrich Emmert's *Collection of Maximes, Anecdotes, Fables, Tales, Allegories, Histories, Orations, Reflexions, Letters,*[47] or to the serial collection of choice new poems such as Eschenburg added to his *Brittisches Museum für die Deutschen.*[48] These and many other selections are a significant index to the German taste in English literature.

Translations into German present additional problems on account of the freedom generally tolerated in a literary translation. Straightforward translations and adaptions form two categories; a third is constituted by faked translations. Little need be said about the first, for here the translation can easily be referred to the original. The second may cause considerable difficulties, depending on the degree of closeness with which the original is followed. All kinds of imitative procedures can, and do indeed, occur. This applies to both novels and dramas. Sometimes it is difficult to draw the line between a translation and a full-scale imitation which attempts to be a literary work in its own right.[49] Accordingly, new titles were adopted not only to suit the German market but also to conceal the relation to the original text. The Price checklist contains several appendices of unidentified items. Scholars have disregarded them since 1934. The third category consists mostly of German novels which pretended to be translated to profit from the vogue of English novels in the second half of the century. Not all novelists were as candid and at the same time as clever as Johann Timotheus Hermes, whose *Geschichte der Miss Fanny Wilkes* (1766) has "so gut als aus dem Englischen übersetzt" on the title page.[50]

Thus many bibliographical lacunae remain to be filled. Next to a thorough revision of the existing checklists the most important desideratum is their continuation into the early decades of the nineteenth century. In Germany, as elsewhere, the year 1800 does not mark the end of the eighteenth century. Interest in the classical English authors apparently did not diminish. The production continued, not only of translations (Akenside, Thomson, and others were newly rendered into German just before or after the turn of the century) but also of original-language editions.[51] We should explore these later phases—even at the risk of witnessing the deterioration of great eighteenth-century writers into schoolbook authors.

Publishing

If we survey the eighteenth century from beginning to end, the flow of ideas from England to Germany was hardly more than a trickle during the early part of the period. In the first decades relatively few works of British authors were published in German. For nearly half of the century the publication of translations in belles-lettres and humanistic literature remained on the fairly low level of fewer than twenty and sometimes even fewer than ten titles per year (see Graphs 1 and 2).[52] Of course, these early translations included, as in the case of *Robinson Crusoe* and *Gulliver's Travels,* works that were widely read and highly appreciated.[53]

Shortly after the middle of the century the publication of translations began to form, in quantitative terms, an appreciable portion of the German book production. Their number in the two fields rose sharply and reached its first peak in 1753 with about fifty titles in belles-lettres and humanistic literature. From then on, years with a fairly high output alternated with years in which the number of published translations was only slightly larger than in the early decades. The various literary, political, social, and economic factors that brought about these oscillations remain to be identified. To generalize about them would be little more than guesswork, considering the limited amount of information that is at present available. At any rate, the trend was an upward one, and after the end of the Seven Years' War a new peak of nearly one hundred titles per year was reached in the early seventies. A fall in the curve of new translations occurred in the early eighties, but there was also another peak in the early nineties. Toward the end of the century the curve of humanistic literature shows a downward movement, that of belles-lettres a rising tendency. No statistics, however crude, can at present be made up for the early nineteenth century.

In the only available contemporary survey of German book production around 1770 (presented by Johann Christoph Gatterer in a lecture at the then

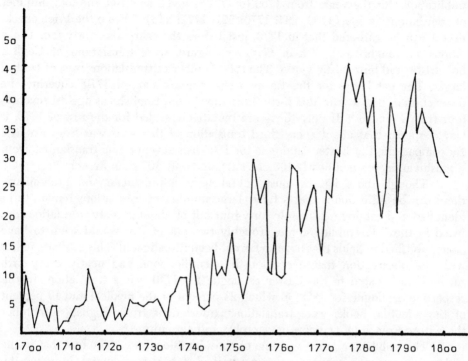

Graph 1. Translations of titles in humanistic literature, 1700–1800

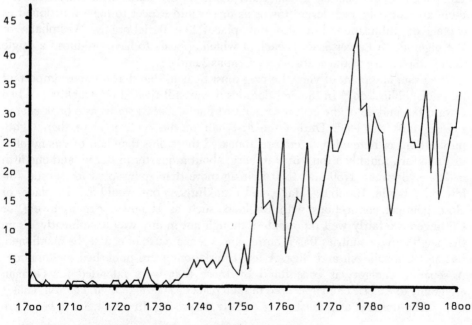

Graph 2. Translations of titles in *belles-lettres,* 1700–1800

new Historical Institute of the University of Göttingen)[54] the total number of publications for the years from 1769 to 1771 is given as 4,709, the total number of translations as 709 (1769: 234; 1770: 221; 1771: 246).[55] From the Price checklists it can be gathered that in 1770, just before the sharp rise, forty-four translations, or roughly one fifth of Gatterer's figure, were translations of English belletristic and humanistic works. The total number of translations was, of course, larger. The catalogue for the Easter Leipzig Book Fair of 1770, covering the production of half a year, lists forty translations from English (as against seventy-four from French).[56] If only thirty are tentatively added for the rest of 1770, it would appear that about every third translation of that year was from English. By comparison, the Easter catalogue for 1800 lists seventy-nine translations from English (an increase of nearly 100 percent), and only 102 from French.[57]

Though these figures must be taken as approximate and preliminary, there can be little doubt that a fairly large number of translations remain to be identified and catalogued. If only forty-four out of about seventy translations are listed in the Price bibliographies, roughly two out of five would seem to have been published in fields that have so far not been investigated. This estimate tallies with the observation that every fourth scientific book and nearly every fifth medical book listed in the Easter catalogue for 1770 was a translation. In the respective catalogue for 1800, in which 23 percent of the medical and 10 percent of the scientific books were translations, translations from English outnumber those from French in medicine, geography, and agriculture.[58]

The publishing scene was one of considerable variety. The fact that in the eighteenth century Germany was not a unified state with a capital, in which the intellectual life of the country was concentrated, accounts for the more than 110 places of publication in the translations of the humanistic works. Among them are not only such larger towns as one would expect to have functioned as centers of publication, but also tiny places like Berleburg in Westphalia or Wernigerode in Lower Saxony, each of which appears to have produced a single item in the course of the century (see Graphs 3 and 4).

From any point of view, Leipzig must be considered as the most important place of publication.[59] In the first decades it was still rivaled by Frankfurt. When toward the middle of the century Frankfurt finally lost its status as a book center, Leipzig took the lead. During the first half of the century more than eighty publications of humanistic literature appeared there, less than half of this number in Frankfurt, roughly a third in Hamburg, about a quarter in Berlin, and one fifth in Halle. Between 1750 and 1800 Leipzig more than quintupled its output, followed by Berlin, Hamburg, Halle, and Frankfurt. As one would expect, places of close political connections with England, such as Hanover, Braunschweig, or Göttingen are fairly well represented, though not in any way prominently. From the neighboring countries Basel, Zurich and Vienna must, of course, be mentioned, but also Copenhagen and Riga. A few translations were published in London.[60] A separate category is constituted by those that were intended for German emigrants to America and appeared in such places as Germantown, Pennsylvania.[61]

The number of publishers is equally surprising. In provincial towns there

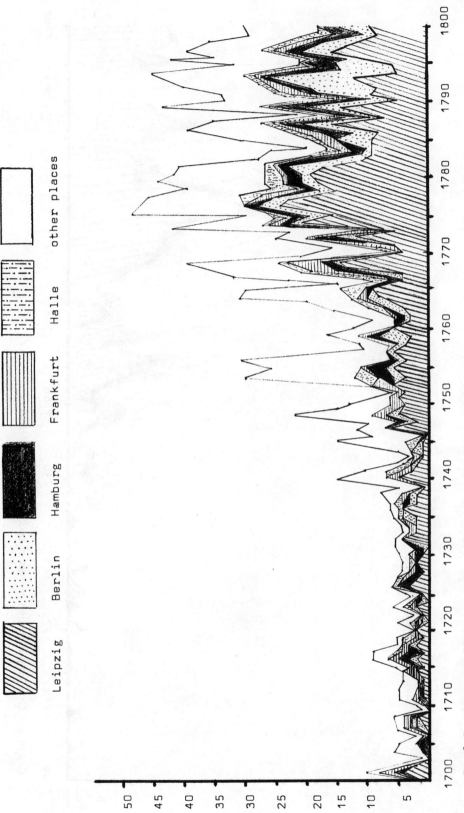

Graph 3. German publication centers of humanistic literature, 1700–1800.

Leipzig   Berlin   Hamburg   Frankfurt   Halle   other places

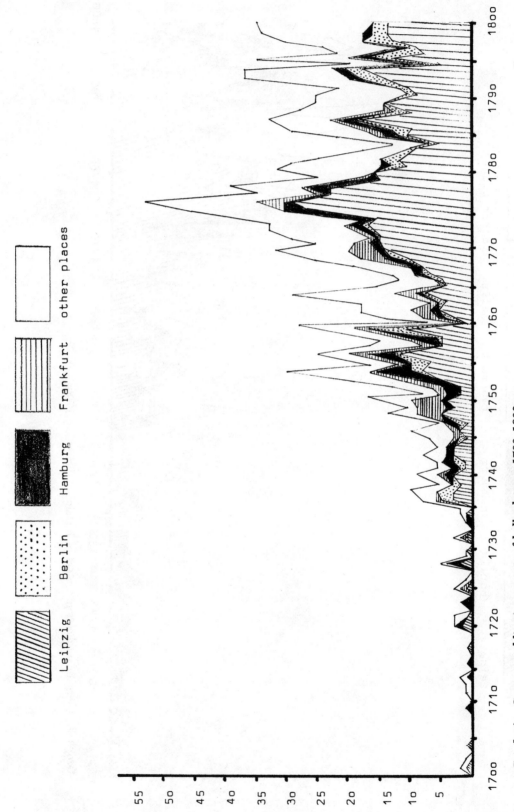

Graph 4. German publication centers of belles-lettres, 1700–1800

were, quite naturally, only one or two firms, but these were sometimes of high standing and their productivity gives these places a certain distinction on the list. In Altenburg in Saxony, for instance, the firm of Richter published a variety of translations and also reprints. Two of the first medical journals to be translated were brought out by Paul Emmanuel Richter.[62] Later, reprints of Sterne and other classics were issued by Gottlob Emmanuel Richter.[63] In Lemgo in West-phalia, to give another example, the well-reputed Meyersche Buchhandlung published translations of theological, historical, and medical writings.[64]

In the main publishing centers numerous publishers seem to have attempted to profit from the translation (and, later, also from the republication) of British writers. The Leipzig record of publishers of English humanistic literature is made up of more than seventy names.[65] In Berlin thirty can be traced, and from Hamburg twelve would seem to have contributed. Though the numbers are considerable (and greatly add to the difficulties of the bibliographer), the shares of the individual publishers were unequal. Some apparently took an early interest in English books and then discontinued these publishing activities, only to revive them when English letters later were in vogue. Others appear to have made continuous efforts to establish British authors, and still others joined in when, in the late sixties, a new field of publishing opened up.

Among the Leipzig publishers only six stand out for the number or the continuity of their publications: Weidmann, Weygand, Gleditsch, Dyk, Junius, and Schwickert.[66] In Berlin, Voss and Nicolai appear to have been the significant publishers of English works,[67] and in Hamburg, Bohn and Hoffmann.[68] A more extensive list would also have to include some leading publishers outside these towns, among them Vandenhoeck in Göttingen as well as Orell in Zurich.[69] Almost all of them belong to the front rank of the eighteenth-century German publishers. The exception is Schwickert, who began his career as a disreputable reprinter under the name of "J. Dodsley und Compagnie."[70]

With due reservations in view of many bibliographical uncertainties, it may be said that the more important British authors (including those that were then considered to be important) were published by the major German firms. Of course, this cannot be established as an invariable rule, and as a general statement it would seem to hold true chiefly for scientific and humanistic books. Scientific and particularly medical works were per se the domain of the large scholarly publisher, and the works of humanistic authors, especially the major philosophical and critical writers, tended to issue from the prominent firms. Belles-lettres present a somewhat different picture. The share of the major publishers appears to have been smaller. Among the novels, for instance, few of the first translations of the great works are associated with the great names in publishing. If at all, the chief publishers brought them out in second or third translations after their authors had become established with the German public.[71]

To set up the record for each individual publisher will prove difficult and in some cases impossible for lack of source material. The Price checklists often omit the name of the publisher and because of their self-imposed restriction yield only a limited amount of information. Even if the book fair catalogues and related lists are fully preserved, the publishers' own catalogues, against which they should be checked, were in some cases scarce even in the late nineteenth century,[72] and many are now no longer extant. Johann Friedrich Gleditsch's retrospective catalogue, however, survives from the early nineteenth century,[73] and here at least a tentative assessment can be made. Gleditsch appears to have published 88 translations of English works between 1732 and 1800, out of which 79 appeared after 1760 and 59 after 1770. Of the individual titles 24 can be considered as belles-lettres and 36 as humanistic literature,[74] while no fewer than 20 are medical books, and 8 are scientific and various technical works. Allowance must, of course, be made for incompleteness and inaccuracy, but even so, the impression that can be derived from the catalogue of the scope and relative importance of the various branches of literature can perhaps be taken as representative of the general publishing situation.

Since most of the publishers' archives are destroyed or inaccessible little can be ascertained about how the publishers promoted English authors in Germany. That they worked efficiently is obvious from many publication dates. Certain works, such as *Roderick Random* and *Tristram Shandy*, had to wait for their translation, if only a few years. Many others were translated almost instantly, as for example *Clarissa, The Vicar of Wakefield*, Hester Chapone's *Letters on the Improvement of the Mind*, Beattie's *Elements of Moral Science*, and Home's *Elements of Criticism*. If a publisher brought out between four and seven titles of English humanistic works in one year, as Weidmann or Weygand did in the late 1770's, the speed and precision of the publishing is indeed impressive. One must assume that they availed themselves of the best sources of information, and of fast and reliable translators.[75]

Certain details appear from published records of the firm of Weidmann, which under Philipp Erasmus Reich became the leading German publisher.[76] In the later decades of the eighteenth century Reich's business relations with England were so important that he had his own agents and correspondents in London.[77] On the one hand, they received orders for English books and had to arrange for them to be sent. On the other, they had to keep an eye on the London publishing scene in order to make recommendations for English books to be translated. One of the agents, Mr. Maty, who received £15 for his services, would seem to have been Paul Henry Maty (1745–1787), assistant librarian in the British Museum from 1776 onward and later editor of *The New Review*, a review organ for foreign publications.[78] He was succeeded by Johann Friedrich Schiller, a translator of some importance,[79] who lived in London before he became, in 1784, a Mainz bookseller.[80] As Reich's correspondent he was paid up to £52 per year, but unfortunately the precise nature of his services is not recorded. Rudolf Erich Raspe,[81] the well-known author of *Münchhausen*, also acted as Reich's correspondent.[82] He reported from London in November 1780 that John Moore's *View of Society and Manners in Italy* was in the press.[83] The book appeared in 1781, and in the same year Weidmann brought out a German translation. Likewise, Raspe recommended John Gillies' *History of Ancient Greece* (1786), and again Reich accepted his advice, so that the first volume of the translation appeared in the next year. Horace Walpole's *Essay on Modern Gardening*,[84] however, was a suggestion that did not materialize. Either Raspe could not obtain a copy of the Strawberry Hill printing, or the work was too short to make a profitable book for the German market.

Competition in the translation business was keen, especially in the absence of effective legal protection. Sometimes two translations of a book were projected or prepared at the same time or even appeared simultaneously.[85] Reich repeatedly corresponded with his publisher-friend Friedrich Nicolai in Berlin on the question of whether or not an entry in the Leipzig Register (*Bücherrolle*) could secure or protect rights of translation.[86] The firms of Weidmann and Weygand also quarreled about translations. Would it not be better, Weygand tried to persuade his colleague, if they mutually gave notice of their plans and communicated either the true English or the translated titles, so that the book fairs might hold no surprise? It would remove many inconveniences, and Weygand would be willing to enter into this kind of cooperation.[87]

Publishers had but few means of securing a translation for themselves. They could try to be the first on the market. This tactic may account, at least in part, for the fact that so many translations were produced so rapidly, and awareness of it may correct the widespread view that both the speed and the volume of translations must exclusively be attributed to a genuine intellectual curiosity on the part of the German reading public. They could also try to give their translations (and original-language reprints) advance publicity.[88] Some of the specimen translations that are to be found in the periodicals should probably be seen in this context.[89] Notices of forthcoming publications appeared frequently in journals,[90] and regularly in the fair catalogues, which had for a long time had a special section of books in preparation ("libri futuris nundinis prodituri").[91] Occasionally a warning tried to dissuade publishers from undertaking a translation because the book seemed untranslatable (as in the case of Erasmus Darwin's *Zoonomia*)[92] or was itself a translation from German.[93]

To what extent publishers cooperated would seem to be a question of some importance, but the bibliographical investigation of English authors in Germany has not reached a point at which one could hope for a satisfactory answer. There are many puzzling items. A translation of John Campbell's *Lives of the Admirals and Other Eminent British Seamen* (1742–1744) was published in Göttingen and Leipzig in the same year. To what extent was it a joint publication?[94] The translation of Hogarth's *Analysis of Beauty* (1753) appeared in the following year with a London and Hanover imprint.[95] The book was printed in London, and one would like to know the precise nature of the collaboration between the publishers and how business was transacted. Are second and third editions of the same translation to be regarded as pirated or as authorized editions, if brought out by another publisher?—an inevitable question in the case of such widely read authors as Edward Young.[96]

We have as yet no idea of who was, from the publisher's point of view, regarded as a best-selling English author in Germany. One could, of course, go by the number of editions, but this cannot with any degree of certainty be established from the available bibliographies and checklists. Even if it were possible, the absolute number of copies printed or sold would be difficult to estimate. The size of an "edition" varied considerably, and little precise information has been handed down.[97] A few figures, however, can be ascertained. The firm of Vandenhoeck sold more than 500 copies of the second edition of their translation of George Anson's *Voyage Round the World, in the Years MDCCXL, I, II, III, IV* (1748) during the Easter Book Fair of 1764—apparently a remarkable success. The house of Weidmann considered Richardson's *Aesop's Fables* as translated by Lessing a best seller. When *Sir Charles Grandison* (1754) came to be translated it was thought a highly seasonable book and consequently 2,500 copies were printed. William Guthrie's et al. *General History of the World* (1764–1767) was expected to sell 1,500 copies in translation, whereas 1,000 were regarded as sufficient for Richard Chandler's *Travels in Asia Minor* (1775).[98]

The Hamburg *Patriot,* one of the earliest and most important German imitations of the Moral Weeklies, disclosed that while 400 copies were originally expected to be sold, in fact nearly 6,000 had to be printed.[99] By any contemporary standards this would appear exceptional. Johann Arnold Ebert, the translator of *Night Thoughts,* reverently reported to England that "after several editions, there are now about 5,000 copies of it, and together with them the glory of the immortal poet, and the solid advantages rising from the poem, spread over all Germany."[100] This was written in 1761 after Ebert had published four editions of his translation within ten years.[101] Again, this should be seen as an outstanding success.

A peculiar index to the publishing success of a book is the interest which the ill-famed eighteenth-century reprinters took in it. They were particularly active during the peak period in the reception of English literature.[102] Though English authors were naturally less attractive to them than German authors, some translations were obviously considered as lucrative. As Jean Paul said: "Ein elender Ladenhüter wird so wenig auf einem Nachdruckerlager angetroffen, als unter den von Eichhörnchen gestohlenen Nüssen eine hohle."[103] The most disreputable German reprinter, Christian Gottlieb Schmieder in Karlsruhe, republished J. J. C. Bode's translation of *Tom Jones* and, more surprisingly, also that of Dodsley's *Economy of Human Life.*[104] In Vienna, Johann Thomas Edler von Trattner, another famous reprinter, found Pope and Lord Kames of interest.[105]

Perhaps the most noteworthy reprint item is the series known as "Mannheimer Sammlung der Werke ausländischer schöner Geister." It was the work of the controversial Mannheim Professor Anton von Klein, who founded in 1778 a "Gesellschaft der Herausgeber der alten klassischen Schriftsteller und ausländischen schönen Geister." This was a publishing house of dubious reputation, but Klein succeeded in bringing out an enormous collection of texts. Within four years, 20 volumes of Shakespeare appeared (in Eschenburg's translation), together with 8 volumes of Pope, 3 volumes of Young, another 3 of Ossian, and the *Sentimental Journey* in four parts. After seven years the collection comprised 68 volumes, of which between 4,000 and 5,000 copies were printed, so that in all some 300,000 copies of reprints had been made available.[106] Insofar as Klein made use of existing translations the series must be grouped with the piracies; insofar as it was a serious attempt to bring together, for the German reader, some standard authors of English literature, it should perhaps be seen as one of the numerous encyclopedic efforts of the period. At any rate, it must be assumed that these reprints (and numerous others, which need, as do Klein's books, the attention of the bibliographer) made a significant contribution to the spread of English literature in Germany.

The publication of original-language editions forms a separate chapter in the history of eighteenth-century German reprinting with interesting literary, legal, and commercial aspects. In the later decades an English-reading public emerged,[107] and it was for these readers that *literati* and reviewers encouraged publishers to bring out English-language editions. Thus in 1775 Johann Heinrich Merck suggested in the *Allgemeine deutsche Bibliothek*, the leading review journal of the day, that English authors should indeed be printed in Germany. Instead of translations of low achievement and mediocre German books forgotten six weeks after the book fair, the best foreign books should be made available in reprint editions. The catalogue he added includes works of Shaftesbury, Sterne, Hume, Richardson, Robertson (the Scottish historian), Shakespeare, Addison, and Prior.[108]

Merck's suggestion is indicative of the pragmatic considerations of the period. From England could be imported a body of literature which was superior to what was then produced in Germany and which could count on a public that was sufficiently large and sufficiently familiar with the language. The suggestion coincided with an observation which the agent of the Weidmannsche Verlagsbuchhandlung made in Paris and which he communicated a few years later to his brother-in-law Reich. "French literature has been dreadfully barren for the past five or six years; there have been many novelties, but such miserable productions that you would think ill of my taste, if I sent them to you."[109] Such, in short, was the situation which made the publication of English books in Germany both possible and desirable.

There were few qualms about the illegality of reprints. There was no general copyright protection. In 1773, Saxony became the first part of Germany in which an act against reprints was passed (Prussia followed in 1794),[110] but Württemberg continued to consider them as legal, and the different handling of the matter accounts for the flourishing reprint trade in southwest Germany. Treaties between England and Prussia, and England and Hanover, protecting literary property were not signed before the 1840's, so that throughout the eighteenth century no English author would have been able to protect himself against being translated or reprinted in Germany. When the treaty was negotiated in Hanover, it was pointed out that German reprints of English books were widely disseminated in Germany, whereas few Hanoverian, or even German, books were known in England.[111]

Some of the most interesting arguments were advanced by the Göttingen professor Johann Stephan Pütter in *Der Büchernachdruck nach ächten Grund-sätzen des Rechts geprüft*. Pütter rejected reprinting in general but would permit reprints in special circumstances. In foreign countries, he thought, reprinting should be allowed as long as the circulation of the reprint was confined to that country and the original publisher could not hope to sell his books on the foreign market. English books, for instance, should be allowed to be reprinted in Italy and Italian books in England; the less significant the book trade between two countries the more permissible the reprinting. By implication Pütter stated that no serious objections could be raised against reprints of English works in Germany.[112]

The strongest incentive to the reprinting of English books was an economic one. Books could be produced more cheaply in Germany than in England.[113] The quality of the print, the paper, and the binding was generally inferior to that of the books imported, but the lower price seems to have appealed so much to potential buyers that German editions could be made to sell.[114] Besides, these reprints appear to have been more easily available than imported books in places other than centers of book trade and learning.

A glimpse of some publishing strategies is afforded by advertisements in the *Göttingisches Magazin der Wissenschaften und Litteratur*.[115] This renowned journal was edited by Lichtenberg and Georg Forster. Its publisher, Johann Christian Dieterich, announced in 1783 that he planned to do a reprint of Johnson's *English Poets*, which was to be sold at half the price of the original edition.[116] In the subsequent number of the periodical he announced another plan. A huge collection of the classical poets and the best prose writers of England was to contain all of Johnson (including the *Lives*), though not in the same order as the original. The reprint was to be correctly edited and clearly printed on white de luxe writing paper. "Lovers and friends of English literature" were asked to avail themselves of this offer and to subscribe at their local booksellers. Whoever subscribed to ten copies would receive an eleventh gratis. Dieterich hoped that his proposal would be welcomed. Original editions, he pointed out, were difficult to supply and their prices were inevitably high.[117]

A two-volume edition of Milton (duly listed in Nicolai's *Handbibliothek* not under Milton but under *The Works of the English Poets*) was the first to come out.[118] The distinguished editor whom Dieterich had won for his plan, Georg Christoph Lichtenberg,[119] was complimented by an Irish friend on this "laudable and useful undertaking, and . . . excellent method of making the english language better known by rendering the acquisition of english books easier and cheaper." The letter added: "There are still many excellent ones which have not as yet reach'd the Continent, and which, I am persuaded, will when known there be well lik'd and well receiv'd."[120] The order of one copy for the son of the correspondent, which followed in the next letter,[121] could not be fully carried out: the plan was abandoned. Most probably Dieterich had overestimated the German market.

Dieterich's was not the only large project. Readers of the *British Mercury*, a German weekly, written in English, of miscellaneous information on England, were informed from Hamburg in May 1789 that

> Mr. *Gökingk* and Mr. *Bentzler,* two Gentlemen of great reputation in the literary World, propose to publish a new Edition of the best English periodical works in the original language. It will be a choice Collection of such pieces only as are calculated for posterity by their intrinsic worth and everlasting interest. They will begin with the *Tatler,* the *Spectator,* &c. and come down to the best modern works of this kind, the *Mirror,* the *Lounger,* and others. The first Volume of about 24 sheets neatly printed will be published in September 1789, and delivered to those Subscribers who till the end of June shall pay 16 Groschen, but the money must be sent free of postage to Wernigerode, where the Editors reside.[122]

Again, nothing seems to have come of this project.[123] Benzler had been successful as a translator of *The Spectator* and *The Adventurer,* but he obviously had no luck as an editor.[124]

The most ambitious and ultimately most successful project was launched by the Basel publisher and bookseller Johann Jacob Thurneysen when, in 1787, he began reprinting what had until then appeared of Gibbon's *Decline and Fall of the Roman Empire.*[125] Unlike other products that issued from the presses of reprinters, this was so careful a piece of work that the six volumes were not only applauded by the German reviewers but also graciously accepted by the author.[126] Obviously encouraged by the success of this edition, Thurneysen proceeded, until the end of the century, to reprint a collection of humanistic literature and belles-lettres which ultimately constituted a well-chosen library of British authors for the German, if not for the Continental, reader. Gibbon was followed by Bolingbroke's *Letters on the Study and Use of History,* Robertson's *History of the Reign of the Emperor Charles V,* Blair's *Lectures on Rhetoric and Belles Lettres,* Kippis' *Life of Captain James Cook*—all published in 1788. The reprinting of English belles-lettres began in 1796 with *Tristram Shandy* and ended, a fitting conclusion of the whole series, in 1803 with Warton's edition of Pope. In all, 187 volumes appeared.[127] The *Göttingische Gelehrte Anzeigen* was full of praise: "Eine jede Privatbibliothek, welche diese schöne Folge von Drucken . . . enthält, wird als ein Heiligthum des guten Geschmacks betrachtet werden können."[128] Thurneysen's reprints, though not inexpensive, apparently sold well. Of some works second and even third editions were called for. Regardless of whether Thurneysen made his own choice or received advice on the selection of titles, he must be regarded as an important literary intermediary between England and Germany. His reprints, well advertised and marketed from Basel and from Gotha,[129] found their way into a considerable number of private and institutional libraries.

Bookselling

I shall not here be concerned with translations from English. With certain
exceptions, they were published in Germany and can thus be regarded as German
books distributed through the normal channels of the German book trade, whatever these were at a given time during the period.[130] Reprints of English books
as produced in Germany fall much into the same category and can likewise be
omitted. Original English books, however, for which the demand grew as the
century progressed, need special attention. They had to be imported and posed
a number of problems to both bookseller and reader.

At the beginning of the eighteenth century the German trade in English
books appears to have been practically negligible.[31] Though there was an interest
in England and English literature, the catalogues of the Leipzig Book Fair
between 1705 and 1720 do not list a single English title among the "libri
peregrini idiomatis"—only a French translation of Locke and some language
instruction manuals written in German.[132] At least up to 1740 the German book
market seems to have been oriented toward the traditional scholarly reader. In
that year more than a quarter of all new publications were in Latin, then still
the vehicle of international communication for the scholarly reading public.[133]
A sidelight on the situation is Zacharias Conrad von Uffenbach's remark (about
1710) that since English books were not sent abroad he had to learn English
from the Bible, the only book in English he was able to obtain in Frankfurt.[134]

Complaints about the paucity or the inaccessibility of English books in
Germany were frequent throughout the century. The *Neue Zeitungen von
gelehrten Sachen,* published in Leipzig, repeatedly pointed out that English
books were for various reasons hardly obtainable in Germany. One reviewer
found them too expensive; another complained that owing to publication on
subscription they were so rare as if they had never been published.[135] Toward
the middle of the century Friedrich von Hagedorn suggested to Johann Arnold
Ebert that he should translate Steele's *Conscious Lovers.* But the translation did
not appear, probably because Ebert could not buy a copy of the play in Leipzig
and it took too long to order one from Holland.[136] Joh. Christ. Eschenbach had
to base his translation of Berkeley's *Dialogues between Hylas and Philonous* on
the French translation because he could not get hold of the English text.[137] At
the end of the century Johann Gottlob Immanuel Breitkopf's *Magazin des Buch-
und Kunst-Handels* was delayed because he had difficulties in obtaining the
material for his bibliography from England.[138] The first issue of *Annalen der
neuesten englischen und französischen Chirurgie und Geburtshülfe* contained
fewer English contributions than originally intended because the English journals
had not been sent for half a year.[139] In general, the shortage of English books
appears to have been most acutely felt inland. Hamburg or Bremen were better
provided for owing to their trade relations with England.[140]

These and similar complaints furnish at least a partial background for two important developments. One is the reprinting of English books in the later decades of the century. It would probably not have been done to the same extent if English books had been more readily accessible to the individual reader through an international book trade. Johann David Michaelis, for instance, undertook his reprint of Lowth's *De sacra poesi Hebraeorum* because of the scarcity of the work in Germany: "librum apud nos rarum, multo auctiorem et tamen multo minore pretio parabilem."[141]

The other is the wide currency in Germany of French translations of English books. Of course, the knowledge of French was far more widespread than that of English, but there can be little doubt that those who had a command of both would frequently have preferred to read the original if it had been as easily obtainable as the French translation or the Dutch reprint of it. Some Germans, among them Friedrich Heinrich Jacobi, philosopher and novelist, ordered them directly from Amsterdam—Thomson's *Seasons*, Brown's *Estimate*, Tillotson's *Sermons*—and sometimes he sent an impatient inquiry: "A-t-on déjà en françois une traduction d'un ouvrage anglois, *Voyage sentimenteux* de Yorick? J'en suis enthousiasmé."[142]

Some of the more uncommon, if not outstanding, collections of English books in private German possession were, at least partially, bought in England. Mostly they were acquired during a sojourn in London. The list of German visitors to eighteenth-century Britain is long and distinguished and includes a large number of scholars and men of letters.[143] Of the three I want to mention, the first is the great collector Uffenbach. On his famous tour (1709–1711), during which he added 4,000 volumes to his collection,[144] he first went to Amsterdam, where, to his disappointment, hardly any English books could be had: "In Amsterdam ist die einzige *Weduwe Swaart*, so mit Englischen Büchern gleich hinter der Börse handelt. Sie hat aber nichts als *Sermons* und dergleichen."[145] Therefore Uffenbach bought a large stock of English books in London, particularly historical works. He went to several auctions and acquired "etliche Englische Historicos und nur ein einziges lateinisches Werk, nemlich den Mabillon" from Christopher Bateman.[146] Latin books, Uffenbach found, could be better obtained in Holland.

The second is Albrecht von Haller, polymath and one-time editor of the *Göttingische Gelehrte Anzeigen*. Haller was not a bibliophile, though interested in books and printing. During his short stay in England he went to one of the eminent London booksellers from whom he bought a few books. As he noted in his diary, they were splendid but expensive, and better printed than any other contemporary books.[147] Finally, there is Johann Georg Hamann, one of the leading Storm-and-Stress *littérateurs*, who came to London on business and assembled there a small library of fascinating variety. Not only did Hamann read the Bible in English when he experienced his conversion; he bought everything from Addison's *Miscellaneous Works* (1736) to Wickham's *Utility and Advantages of Broad, High Wheel Carriages, Demonstrated Rationally and Mathematically* (1755), and from Browne's *Religio Medici* (ed. 1656) to Vernon's *Considerations upon the White Herring and Cod Fisheries* (1749). Even though we do not know where he bought these books, the fact remains that he brought together the most unusual English library in Königsberg, frequently made use of by Herder.[148]

One of the natural consequences of the visits of German scholars and men of letters to England was the gradual emergence of fairly close-knit circles of colleagues and friends who would assist each other in procuring the books they needed for their work. The frequent offers for help in their correspondences seem to imply that then (as now) the supply of books across the Channel in either direction was not without difficulties and that these could best be overcome by a personal call for help. Much of this story can be left to the biographers of Lichtenberg, Michaelis, and others,[149] but the role which government officials occasionally played should be mentioned here. When, for instance, a new Syriac lexicon came out in Germany, Robert Lowth, then bishop of Oxford, arranged for an Oxford bookseller to subscribe for twelve copies, and payment was made through Herr Best, Legationsrat in the Ministry for Hanover in London, who acted as the publisher Dieterich's agent.[150] Conversely, the impressive amount of information on England and English letters which Goethe had at his disposal in Weimar early in the nineteenth century would scarcely have been available without Johann Christian Hüttner, Herzog Karl August's representative in London, who supplied books and journals.[151]

The most significant institutional book buyer of the period, the library of the University of Göttingen, made use of much the same channels.[152] Founded in the 1730's, on a then revolutionary plan, as a large-scale research and reference library, it was intended to include comprehensive collections of foreign publications on a wide variety of subjects.[153] From the late 1740's onward English books were imported in increasing numbers. At first they were supplied by several Dutch booksellers.[154] Later it was thought more expedient to place orders directly with London booksellers. The library became one of the best customers of Thomas Osborne.[155] In transacting business, Freiherr von Münchhausen, curator of the university, relied on Hanover's diplomatic mission in London. There is evidence that after 1753 Legationsrat Best acted as the library's representative. The books came to Göttingen via Hamburg.

The scheme apparently worked so well that Christian Gottlob Heyne, when he became librarian in 1763, saw no reason for changing it. Lists of desiderata were regularly compiled in Göttingen, sometimes by Heyne himself, forwarded to Hanover and from there sent to Herr Best through the quarterly courier. In actually ordering the books (after Osborne's death in 1767 mostly from John Ridley in St. James's Street),[156] Best had the occasional assistance of Joseph Planta, a Göttingen student who became, in 1773, assistant librarian at the British Museum.[157] The lists are still extant, so that the formation of the greatest repository of English books in Germany can be followed almost step by step.[158]

There appears to have been a widespread awareness among booksellers and their customers that the German trade in foreign, especially English, books left much to be desired. The archives of the University of Göttingen contain a memorandum, to be dated about 1751, in which the situation is outlined:

Denen teutschen Buch-Laden fehlet es auswärts fast durchgehends an
Credit und an Correspondentz mit denen Französischen, Englischen,
Spanischen, Italienischen und Holländischen Buchhandlungen und
Gelehrten. Aus diesen Reichen kommt kein Buchhändler auf die Leipziger
Messe, und die Leipziger Messe ist das *non plus ultra* der meisten
teutschen Buch-Händler. Hieraus folget, daß wir die besten Werke der
auswärtigen nicht anders als mit großer Mühe und Kosten sehr langsam
erhalten, die Werke teutscher Gelehrter aber bleiben denen Ausländern
fast gäntzlich verborgen.[159]

One could not wish for a clearer diagnosis. The German book trade of the mid-
eighteenth century was provincial and without international business connections.
Its rallying point, the semiannual Leipzig Book Fair, apparently held little
attraction for the foreign publisher and bookseller. Some Dutch booksellers,
particularly the Amsterdam firm of Arkstée en Merkus, were active in the 1730's
and 1740's, but most of them stopped coming to Leipzig in the latter decades,
partly on account of the increasing number of German reprints.[160] The French
and the English booksellers stayed away, as for them Leipzig was apparently
not a big enough market. Twenty years after the Göttingen memorandum only
C. Heydinger, a dealer in French and German books, came from London to
Leipzig,[161] and he is said to have been unsuccessful in business.[162] A few years
later the Leipzig publisher Dyk recalled a single Englishman—"he came once,
and cheated"—and concluded: "Whoever does considerable business in Paris and
London certainly does not come to Leipzig."[163] In 1751 the solution appeared to
lie in the foundation of a big German international bookselling corporation, and
this is what the author of the memorandum suggested. But his plan, grandiose as
it must have appeared, failed to find support.

The actual demand for English books in mid-eighteenth-century Germany
is difficult to estimate, and it may prove impossible to unearth the kind of evidence
that could provide statistics. But there are indications that after 1750 the demand
increased and that, as a consequence, the trade in English books entered upon a
new phase. Language learning manuals and dictionaries make a more frequent
appearance in the book fair catalogues and testify, as do some anthologies, to a
broader interest in English as a second foreign language. Imports of French
translations of English authors—from Desaguliers's *Cours de Physique Experi-
mentale* to *Histoire de Tom Jones*, and from *Voyage d'un Chretien . . . par I.
Bunian* to *Lettres du Duc de Newcastle*[164] were soon followed by larger imports
of original English books. The firm of Johann Wendler in Leipzig appears to
have been among the first to offer a variety of English books in the original
language.[165] In the autumn catalogue of 1755 Wendler announced, in one large
entry, the availability of

D. Akenside the pleasures of imagination a Poem.8. Bangorian Contro-
versi, 7 Vol.8. Bolingbroke the philosophical Works, 5 Vol.8. The Centaur
not fabulous in five Lettres to a friend.8. Denis select fables.8. Gay fables,
2 Vol.8. Gray Poems.fol. Grandison the History, 6 Vol.8. The History of

Sir Harry Herald and Sir Edward Haunch.8. History of a Young Lady of
distinction.8. Iones, miscellanies in prose and verse.8. Milton's Paradise
Lost and Paradise regaind. 4 & 8. Alex. Pope the Works, 10 Vol.8. The
Rambler, 8 Vol.8. Roder.Rondom the aventures.8. The Spectator, 9 Vol.8.
Thomsons the Works, 4 Vol.8. Young's complaint, or night thoughts.8.
Youngs Love of fame.8. Monthly review, a periodical work by several
hands from May 1749 to 1755. Leipz. by Ioh. Wendler.

And he added: "Bey welchem auch ein Catalogus von Engl. Büchern gratis
ausgegeben wird."[166] This may well be the first catalogue of English books ever
prepared for the German reader by a German bookseller.

The attempt to introduce English books must have been successful, or at
least promising. In the following year Wendler published the first number of
Brittische Bibliothek, a review journal devoted exclusively to books published in
England.[167] In addition to the announcements, which Wendler continued to
insert in the book fair catalogues, several lists of books said to be for sale in
the publisher's bookshop appeared in this periodical.[168] They consist of as many
as thirty-two items, with a strong bias toward philosophy, history, medicine, and
natural philosophy. Of the seventeen items of the first list only three can be
classified as belles-lettres. In many ways the lists counteract the impression,
created by the first announcement, that the imports were predominantly, or even
exclusively, of literature in the narrow sense of the word. If they are in any way
representative, there must have been a fairly strong interest in nonliterary and
nonhumanistic books.

Toward the end of its existence (1767) the journal was taken over by
another publisher, who had already made a modest contribution to the publication of English humanistic literature in Germany. He appended to the last volume
a thirty-two-page "Catalogue of English Books Sold by Caspar Fritsch at
Leipzig,"[169] which brings together several hundred items from virtually all fields
of knowledge. It is difficult to believe that he had all these books in stock. But
even if he ordered them from England, his catalogue remains impressive for its
range and comprehensiveness. It contains seventeenth- and early eighteenth-
century books and cannot have been compiled only from the "Recent Books"
sections of those English periodicals Fritsch also offered for sale. It must be seen
as a genuine attempt to market English books in the center of the German book
trade.[170]

By the 1770's the market seems to have been large enough for English
books to be stocked and to be listed in catalogues as immediately available.
Fritsch's catalogue, published in 1767, was followed by a number of others. In
Berlin, Friedrich Nicolai issued his *Verzeichniß einer Handbibliothek.*[171] In
Vienna, Trattner brought out his *Catalogue des livres françois, anglois, italiens.*[172]
In Göttingen, Johann Christian Dieterich inserted a number of advertisements
in his *Göttingisches Magazin der Wissenschaften und Litteratur* to give notice
of a stock of English books from which the scholarly reader could make his
choice.[173] Dieterich's lists contain more titles from the belles-lettres category

than the earlier Leipzig ones, but still medicine and science are strongly represented. Dieterich's was an academic bookshop, and this may account for the specialized items he occasionally offered.[174]

For a full assessment of the imports of English books a large number of booksellers' catalogues will ultimately have to be searched. Even if other exclusively English catalogues should turn up, most of the titles will have to be extracted from the *Catalogi Universales* which the more important booksellers tended to bring out from time to time. Two questions are likely to emerge from the study of these catalogues. First, what precisely were the channels through which English books reached the individual bookseller? Did he, like the big Leipzig firms, order them directly from England? Did particular London booksellers specialize in exports? Did some German booksellers act as agents for others? Part of the answer will perhaps be found in the Leipzig Book Fair catalogues. And second, were there enough books offered for sale to satisfy the demands of the ordinary as well as of the fastidious customer? There may be no simple answer. At any rate, as a local bookseller in Göttingen, Dieterich could not meet the requirements of the University Library.[175] Occasionally private persons acted as agents. In 1773, Hofrat Ring in Karlsruhe collected individual subscriptions for the Baskerville edition of Ariosto, which he apparently sent to Birmingham.[176] (The current analysis of the eighteenth-century subscription lists[177] is likely to reveal the names of those who availed themselves of such opportunities.) As late as 1795, C. Timaeus, "Hofmeister und öffentlicher Lehrer an der Ritterakademie Lüneburg," publicly offered his services in procuring English books for German scholars who had reason to complain of the "difficulty of the literary traffic with England."[178]

Throughout the century the demand for French books in Germany no doubt exceeded that for English books, and the predominance of French culture for most of the period made it possible for several Frenchmen to do business as dealers in French books. In Berlin, for instance, the first purely French bookshop was opened shortly after the turn of the century, and by 1750 five out of thirteen bookshops were French.[179] The only attempt to open an English bookshop in Germany came late in the eighteenth century, in a place where the impact of England had always been strong, and at a time when the vogue of English culture had apparently reached a climactic point.

On 1 January 1788, *The British Mercury, or Annals of History, Politics, Manners, Literature, Arts, etc. of the British Empire* (published in Hamburg) carried the following announcement:

English Library, *established* at Hamburgh.
The Public are hereby acquainted, that a valuable Library of new, old, and many very scarce English Books, in all Arts and Sciences, is now opened by William Remnant, at his House in the Gaense-Markt, Hamburgh; where Gentlemen may be sure of being supplied with any Quantity, *for ready Money,* at a cheaper Rate than they can procure them themselves from England. Orders for any Quantity of English Books not in his

Catalogue, and also for Maps, Globes, mathematical, astronomical, chirur-
gical and other Instruments, Music, Copper-Plates &c. punctually and
expeditiously executed; and sent to any Distance, on previous Security
being given for the Payment on Delivery at the Post. Good Allowance to
Booksellers; and all Letters post-paid, duly answered.

  Catalogues, Price 6 Pence, may be had at the Place of Sale.[180]

Only three months later the same paper carried gratifying "News of the English
Library at Hamburgh":

It will be pleasing to the Lovers of English Literature to hear, that this
usefull Undertaking, the only one on the whole Continent, that is, or ever
was to be found, is prospering beyond all expectation. The Orders for
English Books pour on Mr. R. from all parts of Germany, and he is pro-
moting this zeal of the Public by making reasonable prizes. Considering
the difficulties by which new English Books were formerly procured, Mr.
R. deserves the highest encouragement.[181]

  The two announcements neatly summarize the situation in the second half
of the century. English books were difficult to obtain; they were expensive; and
ordering them from England, obviously a widespread practice, proved unsatis-
factory. Thus William Remnant[182] (who came to Hamburg as a language teacher)
appears to have provided a much-needed service for Hamburg (where only two
or three foreign bookshops seem to have existed)[183] and for Germany in general.
After some initial troubles caused by a severe winter and the envy of less enterprising German colleagues, the shop was well established by March 1789, when
Remnant publicly challenged others to supply English books faster than he
could. His trade expanded and he claimed to have customers also in Switzerland,
Denmark, Sweden, Poland, and Russia—areas traditionally served by the large
Leipzig firms. He repeatedly offered his assistance to German booksellers, and
his intention seems to have been to become a large-scale importing agent for
English books. He also claimed to export German books to England and to
Scotland: Latin, Greek, and other scholarly works.[184] Though there is as yet no
direct evidence, it seems possible that his ambitious plans were coordinated with
plans to improve the English trade in German books. At any rate, in 1800 a
James Remnant, calling himself a German bookseller, was doing business in London and promised that "every Article of Literature published in *Germany, Denmark, Switzerland,* and *Russia,* [could be] speedily procured to any amount for
prompt payment on delivery."[185] It would seem that this export-import business
was a cooperative effort of relatives.[186]

  At least for some time William Remnant issued catalogues fairly regularly.
They were "to be delivered *Gratis,* every Month" with *The British Mercury.*[187]
The first was a retrospective catalogue, the later ones were lists of current pub-
lications and divided into sections such as "Medicine, Arts, History, etc.,"
"Theology," "Politics and Miscellanies," "Poetry," "Plays," "Novels," and "Mag-
azines." The number of items varies but is generally less than one hundred. The

grouping may appear odd, but it should perhaps be taken as a businessman's synopsis of the late eighteenth-century German interest in English books. Catalogue IX, which is unusually comprehensive, contains 30 items of the first category, 22 theological, 25 political and miscellaneous, 26 poetical titles, 4 plays, 12 novels, and 6 magazines. The poetry ranges from Darwin's *Botanic Garden* to *Sick Laureate, or, Parnassus in Confusion,* and from Polwhele's *English Orator* to the Reverend J. Sterling's *Poems,* with Goldsmith's *Deserted Village* as the only standard title. The list of novels is hardly better and equally illustrative of the apparently indiscriminate reception in Germany of late-eighteenth-century English belles-lettres. By contrast, the medical books deal with fairly specialized topics and suggest that there was a continued demand for information in this field.

Remnant announced that he wanted to attend the Easter Book Fair in Leipzig in 1790 "with a considerable stock of the very best English, Hebrew, Greek, Latin, and other books printed in Great Britain."[188] Regardless of whether or not he revived the trade in English books in Leipzig, he supplied everything that issued from the press in England—the serious book, the fashionable engraving,[189] and such paraphernalia of the "English style" as "*Ladies* Pocket books . . . bound in red Morocco, with plates, a pencil and silver cap."[190] Besides, his shop, which moved several times,[191] was also a meetingplace for writers and readers. On 22 September 1798, Coleridge, just arrived in Hamburg on his German tour, found "delightful young men in it—fine heads of Jacobi, Wieland, Schiller, & Goethe."[192] William and Dorothy Wordsworth also called, and Dorothy "bought Percy's ancient poetry, 14 marks."[193] Thus Remnant served both the old era and the new, until his shop, continued after his death in 1810 by his widow, finally closed in 1812 or 1813. Though by that time other channels for English books had been opened up, his name will remain connected with one of the earliest and most energetic attempts to market them in Germany.

Reviewing

The beginnings of the reviewing of English literature in Germany can be traced back to the first learned journal, the *Acta Eruditorum,*[194] published from 1682 onward as one of the imitations of the *Journal des Sçavans.*[195] It was intended to document the most recent state of scholarship in all fields. Though it had a scientific bent, it offered, besides original articles, reviews of new publications in each of its six sections: "Theologica & ad Ecclesiasticam Historiam spectantia"; "Juridica"; "Medica & Physica"; "Mathematica"; "Historica & Geographica"; and "Philosophica & Philologica Miscellanea."

In preparing the journal, its founder, Otto Mencke, traveled abroad to establish connections with foreign scholars.[196] In London he met Isaac Vossius, Robert Boyle, and Thomas Gale (dean of York), in Oxford John Fell (bishop of Oxford), Edward Bernard (professor of astronomy), and John Wallis (mathematician and theologian). Such connections and good relations with booksellers made it possible for Mencke to establish the *Acta* as a leading European review organ.[197] He procured the *Philosophical Transactions* regularly, and important English books, such as Locke's *Essay,* Toland's edition of Milton, Dryden's *Fables,* or a Leipzig reprint of Bacon's *Works,* were speedily reviewed.[198] References to English scholars abound in the early volumes,[199] but Mencke had difficulties in getting English publications reviewed. Few German scholars, particularly in Leipzig, knew English, and those who did were often not experts in the field.

From the present point of view the importance of *Acta Eruditorum* must be seen in the fact that it continued the tradition of international scholarship, based on Latin as the medium of communication, into the early eighteenth century. Modern students tend to be unaware of this aspect, and as a result the often crude and primitive criticism of English authors in the vernacular receives closer attention than the more sophisticated criticism in Latin. Dryden, for instance, who is generally treated as one of the literary discoveries of the mid-eighteenth century, was ably reviewed in 1700, and Shakespeare was not only mentioned by Morhof in 1682[200] but also compared to Dryden a few years later in the *Acta.*[201]

Shortly after the *Acta* the first vernacular reviewing organ appeared: Christian Thomasius' *Monatsgespräche,*[202] which holds a unique place in the history of German journals and in the history of German reviewing.[203] Thomasius did not pay particular attention to English works, but they did not escape his notice. Milton, Dryden, Hobbes, Burnet, and Thomas Stanley are among the authors he mentions, quotes, or criticizes.[204] David Abercromby's *Fur Academicus* and Robert Knox's *Historical Relations of the Island of Ceylon* he reviewed at length,[205] so that these two books seem to be the first English works of which reviews written in German appeared in a journal.

A survey of the early reviews must include a third periodical: *Neue Zeitungen von Gelehrten Sachen.*[206] It was published in Leipzig from 1715 almost to the end of the century. Intended as a companion piece to *Acta Eruditorum,*[207] it initiated the reporting of scholarly news, an activity which had throughout the century a close affinity to reviewing. *Neue Zeitungen,* first published weekly, later at shorter intervals, reported from the centers of learning in Europe under the names of the respective towns and cities—a feature also to be found in many later publications of this type. In 1785, one thousand copies were printed,[208] an impressive number. For some time (1718–1723) a Latin edition was brought out twice a month for the benefit of those foreign scholars who could not read German.[209]

From the beginning, England was covered extensively. In the first year there were no less than thirty-four reports from London, four from Oxford, and one each from Cambridge and Aberdeen. Though English books were difficult to obtain and bibliographical sources rare, every effort was made not only to include British achievements in the general surveys of European scholarship that preceded each volume but also to draw attention to significant authors and important publications. At any rate, Pope—then about to translate Homer—was singled out as an author to be watched.[210]

While Thomasius was inimitable and made his impact only insofar as reviewing in the vernacular became the standard practice as the century progressed, the *Acta* and *Neue Zeitungen* set the pattern for subsequent developments. They lasted longer than most periodicals and thus could serve as a model for the many learned journals that sprang up in the first decades of the eighteenth century. By 1720 the number of scholarly periodicals had increased to fifty-four, which made up more than 22 percent of the total production of journals at the time.[211]

The reviewing activities of each journal cannot be analyzed here, but two general points should be made. First, the trend toward the journal written in German implied that reviewing meant reviewing for the German public and for the German market. The international tendency did not completely and immediately disappear. However, editors and reviewers seem to have become increasingly aware that the function of a journal was to collect information for the smaller circle of readers served by it. Though some journals had a national circulation, many regional reporting organs followed in the wake of *Neue. Zeitungen:* in Zurich, Hamburg, Frankfurt, and elsewhere.[212]

Second, the tendency toward regionalism and sometimes even toward parochialism was deliberately counteracted by a number of journals in that their editors drew attention to significant foreign publications. When, in the 1730's and 1740's, the era of international scholarship had in many ways come to a close, certain journals apparently took the lead in opening new perspectives on the intellectual life abroad. In that period the number of translations was still small, and original English books had not yet gained wide currency. But the works of British authors were in increasing numbers brought to the notice of the German reader. By treating them not in the older tradition as contributions to an international body of scholarly literature, but in a more modern fashion as the products of a foreign literature, some editors appear to have played a prominent part in preparing the ground for the large-scale reception of English literature in the later decades of the eighteenth century.

One example is furnished by *Zuverläßige Nachrichten von dem gegenwärtigen Zustande, Veränderung und Wachsthum der Wissenschaften* (1740–1757),[213] a journal of high standing and general circulation.[214] Like its predecessor, *Deutsche Acta Eruditorum, oder Geschichte der Gelehrten, welche den gegenwärtigen Zustand der Litteratur in Europa begreifen* (1712–1739),[215] it was edited by Christian Gottlieb Jöcher, author of the well-known *Gelehrten-Lexikon.*[216] While *Deutsche Acta,* as is apparent from the title, is still firmly rooted in the tradition of European scholarship, *Zuverläßige Nachrichten* belongs to a transitional period. Jöcher felt that new contexts had to be established. Accordingly, he stated that as part of his editorial policy rare and precious foreign books, especially from England, would be reviewed since these were least known and read by German scholars.[217]

Another example is *Neuer Büchersaal der schönen Wissenschaften und freyen Künste,* edited from 1745 to 1750 by Johann Christoph Gottsched.[218] It was an attempt to break away from the scholarly journal and to provide, both for the expert and for the emerging "general" reader, a survey of new publications in belles-lettres and fine arts. Like Jöcher, Gottsched felt that the journal should not be restricted to German publications: "Nicht nur deutsche, sondern auch englische, französische und italienische Sachen werden hier ihren Platz finden; wenn sie ihn durch ihre Wichtigkeit, oder andrer Umstände wegen, verdienen werden."[219] The reviews in the first volume of Young's *Love of Fame*, Ayre's *Memoirs of the Life and Writings of Alexander Pope* and Harris' *Three Treatises* set the pattern. Though some translations are noted and some excerpts and shorter pieces newly translated into German, the majority of the "English" contributions are reviews of original publications.

About the middle of the century the early scholarly journals lost much of their former importance.[220] Just as in England a new element entered the literary scene with the appearance of *The Monthly Review* and *The Critical Review*, so the German scene was changed with the emergence of the great reviewing organs that were to dominate the later decades of the eighteenth century and, in some cases, also the early decades of the nineteenth. During the sixties and seventies a marked tendency toward specialization resulted in a large number of professional journals, and the increased literary activity of the period accounts for the publication of the first truly critical journals, among them Lessing's famous *Briefe, die neueste Literatur betreffend*. Between 1760 and the end of the century about 240 new journals of a more general scholarly nature have been recorded. The number of literary and critical journals increased by nearly 200, and that of historical and geographical journals by more than 300.[221] Though many were short-lived, the major ones continued for decades and produced thousands of articles and reviews.[222]

Since the reviewing of translations and original English books presented different problems to the contemporary reviewer, the two activities, though frequently joined in the same journal, are best considered separately. Once more, translations were, for the intents and purposes of the editor and reviewer, German books. Through the book fair catalogues, particularly the sections on forthcoming books, they were subject to bibliographical control, and owing to their physical presence in Germany they were readily accessible—two qualities that became all-important when the haphazard reviewing in the early part of the century gave way to attempts at systematic reviewing in the last thirty or forty years.

The transition is marked by the first volume of the *Allgemeine deutsche Bibliothek*.[223] Founded in 1765 by Friedrich Nicolai, the Berlin bookseller, it was openly modeled on the leading English review organs.[224] Nicolai intended it to be a journal "like the *Monthly Review* . . . , in which all new German publications should be reviewed." This would include, as the statement of editorial policy announced, translations from foreign languages, though the rule was that they should be reviewed more briefly than original German books: "Schriften von minderer Wichtigkeit, und Uebersetzungen wird man nur kürzlich anzeigen, doch mit Beyfügung eines kurzen Urtheils, über den Werth derselben." Thus the *Allgemeine deutsche Bibliothek* would inform its readers four times a year what new translations had been undertaken. Given the circulation of 2,500 copies in the late seventies and early eighties—the peak period of translations from English—one can say that they were given excellent publicity. Of the 1,200 copies about which the printer reported in 1783, 184 went to Hamburg, 111 to Frankfurt, 40 to Zurich, 55 to Breslau, 23 to Vienna, 60 to Nuremberg. Even if this is a partial record, it shows the national distribution of the *Allgemeine deutsche Bibliothek*.

From the beginning the journal covered all branches of literature with uncommon thoroughness. Considering the amount of editorial work involved, the achievement is indeed impressive, even in the field of translations, which was not central to Nicolai's interest. There is no printed index, but my own preliminary index to the translations from English comprises more than a thousand items, most of them short notices of two or three pages. With the limited information that is at present available there is no saying what percentage of all translations was actually listed and reviewed in the *Allgemeine deutsche Bibliothek*. It was no doubt high, though the coverage cannot have been complete.

In the first year (1765) only about a dozen reviews appeared. The number was soon to rise, though not continuously, and reached between fifty and seventy in 1770 and 1775 as well as between 1787 and 1792. The range of subject matter is extremely wide; from theology to horticulture, from surgery to chronology, and from drama to world history; hardly any field was left out. Belles-lettres and humanistic literature did not by any means dominate. There were years, like 1790, when roughly one half of the translations reviewed were of medical and scientific books.

The success of the *Allgemeine deutsche Bibliothek* called forth competitors. As early as 1772 the *Auserlesene Bibliothek der neuesten deutschen Litteratur* was founded.[225] Though brought out by a respectable publisher, it lasted for only ten years and was discontinued when Nicolai's periodical was at its height. More serious and ultimately more successful a rival was the *Allgemeine Literaturzeitung*, which appeared in Jena from 1785 onward. It was likewise dedicated to the principle of comprehensiveness, and for the first few years an attempt was made to include all German publications listed in the book fair catalogues and many foreign publications.[226] When this proved impossible, a change of policy occurred in the 1790's. From 1796 onward the *Intelligenzblatt* of the *Allgemeine Literaturzeitung* included large-scale review articles of English publications intended to survey a variety of new books. These ranged widely through scholarly, belletristic, and technical literature. Soon these articles tended to specialize, and the readers were presented with concise accounts of recent work in such fields as theology, history, statistics, or natural history. These continued well into the nineteenth century.[227]

The reviewing of original English books, though attempted by a variety of German journals, could only in rare cases be done on a large scale over a longer period. Not that the public did not support such journals. Throughout the second half of the century the interest in English literature hardly ever abated, and the demand for information about England and its literary and political life appears to have continually increased. The problem was the supply of books from England. As I have indicated, it was limited and frequently so sporadic that it must have been difficult, if not impossible, for the individual editor to establish a long-term policy for reviewing English books.

One, perhaps the only, scholarly journal that succeeded in regularly reviewing new English publications on a high level of achievement without exhausting its resources was the *Göttingische Anzeigen von gelehrten Sachen* (1753–1801).[228] It had its modest beginnings in *Göttingische Zeitungen von gelehrten Sachen* (1739–1752),[229] founded in 1739 as one of the regional academic newsletters modeled upon the Leipzig *Neue Zeitungen.* Under the editorship of Albrecht von Haller (1747–1753), it soon became the leading scholarly review organ, respected both in Germany and abroad throughout the latter half of the century.[230]

The distinctive feature of the *Göttingische Anzeigen* was a universality which was hard to match. As its historian says: "Der Gedanke der wissenschaftlichen Weltlitteratur ist von den Göttinger gelehrten Anzeigen lebhafter und unbefangener erfasst worden, als in irgend einem andern gelehrten Blatte der Zeit, insbesondere auch des Auslands."[231] This bold approach to reviewing, which is revealed in almost every volume, was backed by the unique library which the Göttingen reviewers had at their disposal. In fact, one of the functions of the library was to assemble those books needed for review purposes. The curator of the university took a personal interest in the supply of books which could be of use for the journal, and lists of new accessions were compiled for Johann David Michaelis when he was editor, so that reviews could be written at the earliest possible date. The union between the library and the journal was perfect when, in 1770, the librarian himself (Christian Gottlob Heyne) became editor of the *Göttingische Anzeigen.*[232]

Of the numerous contributors to the *Göttingische Anzeigen* only Haller has so far been given attention as a reviewer.[233] His literary (as distinct from scientific) reviews between 1746 and 1778 have been identified, and though these are only a small portion of the about 9,000 reviews he is supposed to have written, Haller emerges as an interesting critic of English belles-lettres. He reviewed Young's *Night Thoughts* (*The Consolation*), Richardson's *Clarissa,* Gray's *Odes,* Johnson's *Rasselas,* Lyttelton's *Dialogues,* Gibbon's *Essai sur l'étude de la littérature,* Lord Kames' *Elements of Criticism,* and other works within one or two years of their first appearance. But noteworthy as these critiques are from the literary point of view, they were not quite in the mainstream of the reviews issuing from Göttingen.

The *Anzeigen* was first and foremost a scholarly journal, and though "scholarly" was liberally interpreted, it was mainly humanistic and scientific literature from England that concerned the Göttingen reviewers. In 1753, when the first volume appeared under the new title, some forty original English books were reviewed, and this number tended to become larger in the following years. There are, almost inevitably, some items of less than permanent interest, but the majority of the reviews are of contemporary standard works, and the concentration, in one volume, of books of unusual interest is indeed surprising: Orrery's *Remarks on Swift*, Hume's *Philosophical Essays* and *Political Discourses*, Fielding's *Examples of the Interposition of Providence*, Hill's *General Natural History*, Bolingbroke's *Letters on the Study and Use of History*, Kennicott's *State of the Printed Hebrew Text of the Old Testament*, and, finally, Lowth's *Praelectiones*, appraised by Johann David Michaelis.[234] Even if not every volume is of the same caliber, the one hundred-odd eighteenth-century volumes of the *Göttingische Anzeigen* are basic documents for the student of the reception of English writers in Germany. Until now they have largely been disregarded.[235]

Concurrently with the early volumes of the *Göttingische Anzeigen* the first specialized review journal appeared—*Brittische Bibliothek* (1756–1767).[236] Published by Johann Wendler in Leipzig, it was obviously intended for the general reader whom Wendler had begun to supply with imported English books.[237] Its editor, Karl Wilhelm Müller,[238] a minor local *littérateur*, aimed at combining "lengthy extracts and critiques" of books[239] with biographies of famous English men of letters[240] and with translations of smaller pieces. A characteristic feature of the transitional period during which the first volumes appeared was the inclusion of reviews of older works. Of those that were brought to notice in the first number—Hutcheson's *System*, Long's *Astronomy*, Mary Jones' *Miscellanies*, Jortin's *Ecclesiastical History*, and Cibber's *Lives*—the oldest had come out fourteen years earlier.

As the demand for current information grew, Müller announced in 1759 that in the future the *Brittische Bibliothek* would, in addition to reviews, carry briefer notices of new books, which had been extracted and translated from the English monthlies. Taken in conjunction with the initial promise that only those books would be reviewed which the contributors themselves had read, the announcement reveals a typical predicament of many German reviewers at the time. They were expected to be *au courant* but it was obviously impossible for them to get hold of the English books they wanted to review or to write their reviews in due time.[241] The way out of this difficulty was the transmission of information gained secondhand from English sources.

In general, the dependence on *The Monthly Review*, *The Critical Review*, and other magazines appears to be heavy. Though it is hardly possible to identify, except in rare cases, individual German subscribers, it must be assumed that these organs had a strong influence on the reviewing and the subsequent reception of English literature in Germany. Two examples are furnished by major periodicals. One is the *Bibliothek der schönen Wissenschaften und der freyen Künste*,[242] founded by Nicolai prior to the *Allgemeine deutsche Bibliothek* but soon edited, at his request, by Christian Felix Weiße.[243] The journal was divided into a section of longer reviews and a section called "Vermischte Nachrichten," which consisted of shorter notices of domestic and foreign books. The longer reviews were of major books, mostly in literature and aesthetics, and though their selection does not show a particular intention to document new trends in England and France, they were nevertheless valuable accounts for the contemporary reader of such works as Lord Kames's *Elements of Criticism* or Duff's *Essay on Original*

Genius. The other section, praised by Herder and recommended by the *Göttingische Anzeigen,* is in its English and French parts almost entirely taken from foreign magazines. Weiße, who wrote much of the journal himself, frequently worked under pressure and simply translated, sometimes in abridged form, from the *Critical Review* and *Monthly Review* whatever seemed of interest and would fill his pages. Thus of the more than 800 notices that appeared in the *Bibliothek* under Weiße some 740 can be traced back to either of these periodicals.[244] The borrowings, if they can be so called, remained undetected for a long time.[245]

The second instance is the *Frankfurter Gelehrte Anzeigen,* a sequel to the *Franckfurtische Gelehrte Zeitungen* (1736–1771).[246] The famous first volume of 1772[247] (to which Goethe and Herder contributed) made, among other things, a fresh start in the reviewing of English literature. The publisher's announcement read:

> In addition to all useful works on higher learning those on history, philosophy, belles lettres, and the arts will receive particular attention, and in all branches of learning a special effort will be made to ensure that nothing worth noting escapes the lover of English literature. Part of this effort will consist of short notices of bad or mediocre English books in order to put a curb on the rage for translating.[248]

In all, seventy-one reviews of original English books appeared (as against sixty-four of French books). Thus the program was carried out, though at the sacrifice of intellectual independence. Even the distinguished contributors to this volume obviously found it beyond their powers to write their own reviews of all new English books. A large number of reviews were simply translated, again from *The Monthly Review,* occasionally from *Gentleman's Magazine;* others were taken as guides by the German reviewers; and still others were used as sources for critical judgments, as in the case of *Humphry Clinker,* though the reviewer, Johann Heinrich Merck, knew the book. With rare exceptions, the reviews were not labeled as translations but presented as original contributions.[249]

The practice of translating reviews was fairly widespread. It had previously occurred in the *Franckfurtische Gelehrte Zeitungen,* and it is also to be found in the short-lived *Samlungen aus der neuesten britischen Literatur,* published in Bremen in 1771.[250] Here the authors openly confessed that most of the reviews came from *The Monthly Review* and *The Critical Review*—only to be attacked by Merck, who had pilfered these sources in much the same way.[251] A few years later the time came for a journal whose sole purpose was the speedy dissemination of the contents of the leading London reviews. In 1775 the Leipzig publisher Weygand brought out *Englische allgemeine Bibliothek, von mehrern Gelehrten in England ausgefertigt.*[252] Its first number was no more than a near complete translation of the January issue of *The Monthly Review,* rendered into German instantly, so that the translation could appear in the same month. Appended were lists of new or projected translations into German and (a possible indication that English at least for some readers had become a familiar foreign language) of translations from other languages into English. Conversely, the February issue was partly based on *The Critical Review*. And so on for twelve presumably not very successful numbers: the journal was discontinued at the end of the year.

A little later the same publisher made a second, and more successful, attempt to bring out a digest of English reviews in German translation: Johann Joachim Eschenburg's *Brittisches Museum für die Deutschen*.[253] In the six volumes which appeared between 1777 and 1780 Eschenburg improved on the pattern of the *Brittische Bibliothek*, combining selected translations and an anthology of new poems with extensive reviews and shorter classified notices. He began with Pearce's *Commentary on the Four Evangelists*, Chandler's *Paraphrase and Notes on the Epistles to the Galatians and Ephesians*, Beattie's *Essays*, Hume's *Life*, and Forster's *Voyage Round the World*—all publications of the same or the preceding year. The number of longer reviews increased in the subsequent issues, but Eschenburg always managed to present his readers with information on recent books. In this the *Brittisches Museum* is a typical product of a new era of greatly accelerated Anglo-German communication.

The shorter notices are variously grouped under at least six headings: theology, law, pharmacy, natural history and economics, history and politics, and belles-lettres.[254] While the translation section of the journal is confined to literature, criticism, and biography, the division of the reviewing part indicates once more the impressive breadth in the reception of English authors in Germany. Of course, Eschenburg relied on the London reviews, but he did not merely reproduce them under his name. In many cases he offered a synthetic account of a new book based on several original reviews plus his own reading. In addition, he often translated generous excerpts from the books themselves.[255]

In 1781, Eschenburg replaced the *Brittisches Museum* by a still more ambitious project: *Annalen der Brittischen Literatur, vom ganzen Jahre 1780*.[256] He dropped the translations and the anthology and concentrated on reviews in an effort to present his German readers with a year's work in English literature. In addition to forty full reviews (ranging from an edition of Beaumont and Fletcher to Ingenhousz's *Experiments upon Vegetables*, and from Sheridan's *Dictionary* to the *Account of Arnold's Pocket Chronometer*) there are one hundred brief mentions (with thirty-eight titles from belles-lettres and theatrical literature). There is also an annual list for 1780 of German translations from the English, citing fifty-six titles from all fields; it appears to be the only compilation of this kind attempted by a contemporary.[257]

No second volume was published, but the tendency toward systematic surveys did not disappear. In 1789, Johann Wilhelm von Archenholz brought out the first of twenty volumes of *Annalen der Brittischen Geschichte*.[258] Intended as a series of annual supplements to his previously published book on England,[259] the work was divided into such sections as Parliament, government, colonial affairs, and so forth. Two sections were reserved for literature and the arts. The first literary surveys were written by no less an expert on England than Georg Forster.[260] After Forster's death Archenholz invited Eschenburg to continue these accounts.[261] What was expected of Forster and Eschenburg was the presentation, in a suitable context, of a synopsis of a year's literary production in the

widest sense of the word.[262] This went beyond the large-scale reviewing which
Eschenburg had tried, but was the logical extension of it. As miniature literary
histories these accounts cannot properly be dealt with here. They should be
considered with the late eighteenth-century German attempts to write the literary
history of England.

It is tempting to set this concept of a regular survey of English letters
against the background of the statistical ideals of the period as expounded by
historians like Johann Christoph Gatterer[263] and of the ideals of general or even
universal bibliography as conceived and at least partly realized by Johann Samuel
Ersch.[264] Such a study is unfortunately impossible here, but even so it should not
be overlooked that, regardless of the contents and quality of these review essays,
the idea of an annual history of English literature marks a culminating point in
the reception of English authors in eighteenth-century Germany. Only a century
earlier the first rudimentary account of English literature had appeared in Daniel
Georg Morhof's *Unterricht von der teutschen Sprache und Poesie.*[265]

Collecting

In considering collections of books by British authors which were formed
in eighteenth-century Germany, I shall in the first place be concerned with
private libraries. For the greater part of the century the private library was
dominant and many of the important private libraries were superior to such
public institutions as were then in existence. Besides, the relation between the
private library and the reader is, as a rule, close and immediate. Even if it cannot serve as an infallible guide to what was actually read, it can at least be taken
as evidence of what, in the individual case, seemed worth acquiring from the
literature of a foreign nation.

As a whole, the private libraries of the period were a most heterogeneous
group of collections. They include small sets of books which may contain a single
English title as well as great and famous collections built up by distinguished
bibliophiles. General statements can hardly be made, at least at the present
moment, but it is possible to indicate the range of material that awaits the
historian who wants to analyze in detail the dissemination of English books in
eighteenth-century Germany. The number of remarkable private libraries has
been estimated as well over two hundred—most of them being known to have
contained up to 10,000 volumes, many over 20,000, and some over 30,000.[266]

On the lowest level, primitive lists of books can be found in the inventories preserved in town archives of middle-class or lower middle-class households.
As is to be expected, these lists are of small collections only and it cannot in each
case be assumed that the owner of the books assembled them as a personal
library. At any rate, the inventories constitute a class of source material which
can be searched systematically for information about the distribution of English
writers in the lower strata of eighteenth-century German society. Below this

level, the student has to rely on sources that turn up only occasionally and often in unexpected places.

Of the relatively few inventories that have so far been investigated, those extant in Tübingen[267] do not contain a single English book in the original language for the period between 1750 and 1760, and only two between 1800 and 1810. An occasional translation of Bunyan or William Penn is perhaps better classed with devotional literature than with English literature, and a German Ferguson owned by a merchant in 1806 or a *Robinson Crusoe* in the hands of a baker in 1808 are not particularly noteworthy. But an interesting collection is that of the mayor. In 1756 he possessed, among 146 books, five on English history, two in German, three in French, as well as *Le Spectateur* and *Il Negoziante di Venezia*, an unspecified title which one would like to take as a translation of the *Merchant of Venice*. A reader, in other words, with a strong interest in English history, but one who read about England in German and French.

Frankfurt inventories, which have been searched with the intention of documenting the relationship between vocation and the possession of books,[268] show traces of English books as early as the 1750's. Thus in 1755 a bell-founder owned not only *Robinson Crusoe* but also *Pamela* in four parts (presumably the Leipzig translation of 1743), two works in German on English history, and the translation of James Anderson's book on the Freemasons. *Robinson Crusoe* was no uncommon possession, but otherwise the bell-founder had an exceptional library since it was customary in his circles to have both smaller and more restricted collections. About the same time the sizable nonhumanistic library of a merchant was apparently not better stocked with English authors; it contained Locke, *Le Christianisme raisonable*, *Pamela*, and "l'Antipamela." Original English books, which are absent from the mid-century inventories, turn up in later lists, though not in large numbers. An apparently unusual library of a merchant in 1801 contained *Tom Jones*, Goldsmith's *Roman History*, a selection from Pope, the *Persian Tales*, and *The Sentimental Journey*, some in London editions, some in the Altenburg reprints of Richter. Though the general picture is not a clear one,[269] English authors do not appear to be strongly represented in these inventories; German and French translations dominate. Original English books appear late, and more frequently in libraries of merchants than in those of civil servants.

The next level is represented by medium-sized collections which constitute genuine private libraries in the sense that they reflect the tastes and interests of an educated general reader, often of higher or high social status. Some of these libraries still exist, mostly in country mansions, where they are not generally accessible.[270] Many others have been destroyed or dispersed or incorporated in large institutional libraries and cannot now be identified.[271] Attempts have recently been made to reconstruct a few of them and to catalogue them retrospectively.[272]

An example of this type of noteworthy, though not exceptional, library is that of the Herzogin Caroline von Pfalz-Zweibrücken-Birkenfeld, who resided in the southern part of the Palatinate and had, both personally and geographically, close contacts with French culture.[273] She died in 1774, so that her library (sold after her death) can be said to have been formed in the transitional middle decades of the century. It consisted of more than 1,500 titles. The English section accounts for nearly 120 titles and is remarkable for consisting of predominantly French translations. The ratio of French to German translations is about two to one, and there is not in the whole collection a single title in English.

The library has a strong bias toward religious and devotional literature. English authors in this section (Bunyan, Baxter, Doddridge, Watts, and others) are mostly in German translation. In all other sections, of which history, literature, and travel books contain a fair number of English authors, French translations prevail. The philosophers are represented by Locke and Shaftesbury, the historians mainly by Burnet, Hume, Bolingbroke, and Robertson. English literature (only twenty-four titles as against more than 200 from French literature) seems to be restricted to a fashionable collection of standard authors: Addison, Chesterfield, Fielding, Lady Mary Montagu, Pope, Richardson, Swift, and Young, with Coventry, Glover, and Anthony Hamilton as additional embellishments.

The fact that French translations figure so prominently is of great significance. It shows in impressive detail the role which French played as a vehicle in the reception of English literature in eighteenth-century Germany. At least in the early part when the knowledge of English was not widespread, French translations (which frequently preceded those into German) appear to have contributed to a wider and earlier dissemination of English authors than would otherwise have been the case. On a certain level the knowledge of French was ubiquitous, and the fact that the presumably large number of Germans who read French translations of English books included not only a duchess but also a small-town mayor and Frederick the Great (whose small collection of English literature was nearly all in French translation)[274] would seem to justify a special study of this phenomenon.

Another example is furnished by the library of Freiherr Ludwig Carl von Weitolshausen, genannt Schrautenbach.[275] It is smaller than the Birkenfeld library (832 titles) and different in character. Schrautenbach died in 1783, a highly educated man, a diplomat, and a member of the Herrnhuter circle. He had been in London, and he read English, though perhaps not too well.[276] His English and Scottish philosophers (Bacon, Cudworth, Ferguson, Gerard, Hartley, Hume, Lord Kames, Newton, Shaftesbury) are, except Shaftesbury, all in translation—Latin, French, and primarily German. The theological works are also in several languages; those in English include Tillotson's *Sermons* in an Amsterdam reprint and Sterne's *Sermons* in a German reprint. Among Schrautenbach's ancient authors is a Foulis edition of Sallust, and in ancient history five of the thirteen titles are translations from Laurence Echard, Gibbon, Goldsmith, and William Robertson's *History of Ancient Greece,* itself a translation of a French work by P. A. Alletz. The section on English history is not large but another example of the importance of French translations. As for belles-lettres, Schrautenbach owned more English titles than French, and these were for the most part in the original language. Except for Thomas Amory, John Barclay, and Richard Tickell there are no deviations from what appears to have been the German standard catalogue of eighteenth-century authors. From the bookselling point of view it is interesting that of 17 titles 8 are London editions, 5 Scottish editions, and 4 German reprints.

With the new interest being taken in the history of private and institutional libraries in Germany it is to be expected that in due course more information will become available.[277] It should enable us to say with more precision than is at present possible which English authors were actually selected, read, and appreciated. Tantalizing questions, however, are likely to remain. Of many libraries we shall probably not be able to learn more than what summary accounts provide. In his all-too-brief contemporary report on private libraries between 1750 and 1760 Johann Georg Meusel refers to the "pretty library" of Pastor Mylius in Hamburg, which contained sixty volumes of seventeenth- and eighteenth-century English sermons and other English books, and to the "nice library" of Subrektor Overbek in Lübeck, which comprised "everything that the wit of modern German and foreign authors had produced."[278] To select Königsberg libraries as further examples, that of Professor Quandt (in all, 8,000 volumes) is said to have included 400 English and 300 Dutch works; that of Professor Waga, a teacher of law, complete sets of the English, French, and Dutch editions of the ancient classics; that of Professor Walther, a theologian, a rare collection of English and other bibles;[279] that of Herr Dunker, "ehemaliger Inspector des Stipendienhauses," many precious English books; that of Herr Meyer Friedländer, a merchant, a collection of English engravings and a large number of books in English and Hebrew; and that of Herr Wulf Friedländer, also a merchant, even more travel books and other books in English than the preceding collection.[280] Finally, the library of Lessing's father in Kamenz in Saxony appears to have contained the collected works of leading English theological writers.[281] The number of such libraries is difficult to estimate, but it seems to have been considerable.

On the third level those collections are to be considered for which—for reasons of size or importance or association—full-scale contemporary catalogues or extensive sales-catalogues were compiled. There is as yet no master list of these catalogues.[282] Future students of the reception of English authors in eighteenth-century Germany will have to proceed step by step in establishing the significance of these collections in the context of Anglo-German literary relations. Since the usual criteria for assessing the status of a large collection do not here apply, some changes in the accepted pattern are likely to occur. Some collections generally regarded as great may be given a lower status in this particular hierarchy because their holdings of English books are small or undistinguished. Others that are usually accorded a lesser stature may considerably rise in importance.

A few examples will have to suffice. One of the outstanding collections of the early eighteenth century was that of Zacharias Conrad von Uffenbach (approximately 12,000 volumes).[283] Uffenbach, it will be remembered, was one of the presumably few German customers of London booksellers in the Queen Anne era.[284] He was an ardent bibliophile, but his library was not, in the prevalent fashion of the day, a mere accumulation of showpieces but a working library whose usefulness and bibliographical accessibility he constantly tried to improve. British authors as such were not one of Uffenbach's primary interests, so that as a respository of original English books his library is perhaps not quite as great as it is in other respects.

Nevertheless, the *Catalogus Librorum*[285] contains (II, 444–70) a twenty-five-page section of "Anglicæ historiæ scriptores," in all more than 150 volumes. Most of the works are in English, but Uffenbach occasionally bought the Latin, French, and German translations in addition to the English original, as in the case of Burnet's *History of the Reformation* (II, 448, 464–65). As a whole, this section is impressively far ranging. Chronologically it extends from Polydore Vergil's *Anglicæ historia* (Basel, 1555) to John Asgill's *The Succession of the House of Hannover Vindicated* (1714), with a few later additions of translations, like *Hertzogs von Marlbouroughs Leben und Helden-Thaten* (1723). Most of the books are of seventeenth-century origin. There are standard authors such as Camden, Stow, Hooker, Burnet, Stillingfleet, and Clarendon and a host of minor writers on special topics. There are collections of sources as well as memoirs, and there is even an occasional lapse such as Mrs. Manley's *Memoirs of Europe.* Other sections of Uffenbach's catalogue contain some English titles as well, for example, "Atheistica, profana ac relligionem evertentia" (I, 761–71) or "Libri critici et grammatici" (I, 577–606; apparently Uffenbach did not collect poets). One section, "Quackerorum, Anabaptistarum &c. scripta" (I, 833–87), is replete with English titles; and another, though short, lists some English titles—"Machiavellistica, Hobbesiana et similia scripta" (I, 966–67). Thus historical and theological works dominate—in keeping with the general character of Uffenbach's collection.

A second library, that of Graf Heinrich von Bünau,[286] has been justly famous since the eighteenth century for its comprehensiveness (40,000 volumes) and for its great catalogue, compiled by Johann Michael Francke.[287] Graf Bünau, himself a historian, conceived of his collection primarily as a scholar's library. Its classification,[288] an outstanding achievement at the time, was devised with the scholar's needs in mind.[289] Bünau began collecting on a large scale in the 1720's and thus could bring together what is probably the most inclusive early eighteenth-century private collection of English books in Germany. Published between 1750 and 1756, the *Catalogus Bibliothecae Bunavianae* appeared at a time when other great collections, not excepting that of the University of Göttingen, were still in the early stages of their formation.

Unlike Uffenbach's, Graf Bünau's library was strong in literature and literary history (in the contemporary sense of the term). The pertinent general sections of the catalogue are well interspersed with English authors. The section on the ancients and moderns controversy includes Temple, Wotton, Blackwall, and Addison (I, 453 f.); the "Ivdicia critica de avctoribvs et libris" duly list Blount's *Censura* (I, 481), and the only treatise on pastoral poetry is Pope's, in French translation (I, 694). All important reference books on the history of literature and learning in England were assembled: Leland, Bale, Fuller, Winstanley, Langbaine, Mackenzie's *Writers of the Scots Nation,* and others (I,

595ff.). In a similar manner the catalogues of the libraries of London, Oxford, and Cambridge (I, 854 f.), as well as the major works on the universities, were brought together, with Anthony à Wood in two editions (I, 971–73).

Among the "Scriptores vitarvm Ervditorvm particvlares" there is biographical literature not only on Bacon, Boyle, Halley, and Newton, on Hobbes, Locke, Shaftesbury and others, but also on Donne ("Theolog. Anglicanus"), Milton, Pope, and Shakespeare, though not on Dryden (I, 1054 ff.). The "Poetae Anglici" (I, 2091–94) are represented collectively by such anthologies as *Poems on Affairs of State* or the *Miscellanies* of Swift, Arbuthnot, Pope, and Gay, and individually by no less than twenty-five authors, beginning with Addison and ending with Ned Ward. A few are of the sixteenth and early seventeenth centuries, but the majority are Restoration and early eighteenth-century writers, such as Butler, Blackmore, Prior, Steele, and Glover. The longest entry is for Pope, followed by those for Milton and Dryden. The literary and scholarly review organs of the period—from *Weekly Memorials for the Ingenious* to *The History of the Works of the Learned*—are put together in a separate section (I, 492–93), and works such as *Gulliver's Travels* (in English and French) are found among the "Descriptiones regionvm fictarvm et itinera ficta" (I, 2110).

The elaborate and sometimes labyrinthine system of Graf Bünau's collection does not permit comment on all sections. The few that have been selected do not fully represent the holdings. Other fields were equally well provided for. To pass over history, the "Ephemerides literariae, ad physicam et medicinam spectantes," for instance, include not only a complete run of the *Philosophical Transactions of the Royal Society* but also selected volumes of their French translation and their seventeenth-century Latin translation, published in Leipzig (I, 762 f.).

Three other libraries to which I shall draw attention were built up in the second half of the century. They belonged to *littérateurs* or professional scholars who in some way or another acted as intermediaries in the process of the dissemination of English literature in Germany. Hence they reflect a pronounced interest in English books. The first is that of Johann Georg Schlosser, Goethe's brother-in-law. Schlosser is a figure of some consequence in the reception of English literature, if only as a translator of Pope and Shaftesbury.[290] Of Schlosser's library no catalogue survives, but his own books and those of his brother Hieronymus Peter[291] appear to form the eighteenth-century nucleus of a great nineteenth-century German library, that of Friedrich Johann Heinrich Schlosser, Johann Georg's nephew.[292] Its manuscript catalogue is a model of its kind and from it can be extracted a wider and more inclusive collection than is found in comparable libraries.[293] To indicate its scope briefly, titles range from Tickell's edition of Addison to Wood's essay on Homer, from Bacon's works to Steele's *Christian Hero* (in German translation), from Blair's *Sermons* to Shaftesbury's *Characteristics*, from Smollett's *History of England* to Stanley's *History of Philosophy* (in Latin), from Isaac Hawkins Browne's *De animi immortalitate* to Hogarth's *Analysis of Beauty* (in German), from Bolingbroke's *Study and Use of History* to Jones' *Life of Nader Shah*, from Lowth's *Carmina Latina*, to Lyttelton's *History of Henry II*. In all, several hundred titles, which include even such authors as John Pordage, Isaac Barrow, John Berington, and Thomas Pope Blount. All four languages in which eighteenth-century Germans read English authors are represented. And not a few original-language editions in this library were Basel reprints produced by Thurneysen.[294]

Another remarkable library belonged to Johann Georg Hamann, the well-known "Magus des Nordens," who is one of the key figures of that significant phase in the impact of English literature, the *Genieperiode*. Hamann, as I have pointed out, brought books back from his visit to England,[295] but the publication dates suggest that many of the English works in his library were assembled after his return. In 1776, when he was close to being forced to sell his collection, he printed, as *Biga Bibliothecarum*, a catalogue that comprised his own library and that of his friend Lindner.[296] From this catalogue and additional documents his collection has been reconstructed and brought into that orderly system which it appears to have badly wanted when it was in actual use.[297]

The collection comprised approximately 2,000 titles. Most of the six categories into which it has been divided are strong in English books. An enumeration of even a fraction of them would be bewildering, but some features should be noted. Though theology, in keeping with Hamann's interests, is a fairly extensive section, there are fewer English titles here than among the philosophical works, which include unusual items like Collins' *Discourse on Freethinking* or Herbert of Cherbury's *De veritate* (marked "Lib. rar."). English literature is a full section (fuller than the French), with poetry dominating. Hamann possessed many eighteenth-century poets both major and minor (down to the infamous *Essay on Woman*), and a surprising number of Restoration poets. Except for Sterne and Goldsmith, there are no major novelists, but the collection includes satirists such as Swift and the less common Mandeville. Criticism and literary history comprise, quite naturally, authors of interest to the student of Homer, Ossian, and related subjects, but also such unexpected items as Rymer's *Tragedies of the Last Age*.

As in almost all libraries of this type, the historical and geographical sections are interspersed with English books, but not excessively so, whereas the politics and economics sections abound with them, mostly in original-language editions published in England. Regardless of what Hamann acquired in England, his collection is of exceptional range, and it might prove difficult to find another German library of similar size which surpasses it in the area of English poetry. The final section, natural history and mathematics, contains disappointingly few English titles, as does Hamann's collection of journals, which is devoid of any of the monthlies that one would like to find as evidence of an interest in current literary events.

The third library is the large collection of Johann Joachim Eschenburg.[298] Since Eschenburg, as the eleventh *Britannica* has it, "is best known by his efforts to familiarize his countrymen with English literature," there is no need to explain why his library should hold a place of distinction among eighteenth-century German collections of English authors. Eschenburg compiled his own manuscript catalogue. It still survives[299] and differs in some respects from the printed sales catalogue issued in 1822.[300] In the sales catalogue two sections are devoted entirely to English literature: "Englische Dichter" and "Schriften von und über Shakespeare."[301] The first, which lists 240 volumes of almost exclusively original-language editions, is a mixed assortment of poetry, drama, prose, and criticism, mainly of the seventeenth and eighteenth centuries, though Eschenburg also owned the works of Chaucer, Lydgate, Drayton, and Spenser. It was in the first place a working collection, consisting of many complete editions of the poets from Suckling to Jerningham, and of the dramatists from Vanbrugh to Lillo. In addition, there are collections and anthologies, which Eschenburg apparently made use of for the minor authors in his *Beispielsammlung zur Theorie und Literatur der Schönen Wissenschaften*. Prose writers are scantily represented; the collection includes a Dublin edition of Swift, but the absence of Addison and other essayists is surprising.

Eschenburg's Shakespeare collection is headed by a Third or Fourth Folio (it lacked the title page) and consists, as one would expect from a translator of Shakespeare, of editions and such critical studies as can be of help in translating. The number of editions, however, is small and all date from after the appearance of Eschenburg's own translation. The critical works (mostly in English, some in German translation) include nearly all of the important late-eighteenth-century contributions to Shakespearian studies: Richardson, Malone, Douce, and so on. Earlier critical essays, except Rymer's *Short View of Tragedy*, are curiously absent. A good deal of the collection is filled by the German translations of Eschenburg and his fellow translators. Other sections of the catalogue— "Aesthetik und Wissenschaftskunde," "Künste," "Romane, Satyren und scherz-hafte Schriften in verschiedenen Sprachen"—are likewise of interest.

Libraries of this type, if not exactly numerous, were by no means rare in eighteenth-century Germany. They range from those of well-known men of letters with strong ties to England and English literature, such as Wieland,[302] to those of little-known local celebrities, such as the Hamburg professor Michael Richey, who taught Greek but owned a sizable collection of English books.[303] As a whole, the catalogues or sales catalogues of these libraries form a body of source material of paramount importance in any attempt to determine the extent to which British authors permeated the intellectual life of the country.

In addition to private libraries, at least two other kinds of collections must be mentioned briefly. One comprises the various accumulations of printed material assembled by reading societies.[304] These societies sprang up in many places throughout the country (both in larger and smaller communities) in the latter part of the century. More than four hundred can be traced before 1800, and of about one tenth of them full records are preserved. The first foundations date back to the 1730's, and one of the earliest societies indicates their significance in the present context. It was established in Stralsund in Pomerania in 1750 and called "Privatverein zum Studium der englischen Sprache und Literatur."[305]

The aims—literary, social, political—of the reading societies were variously defined by their contemporaries, but their chief historical interest lies in the fact that they contributed substantially to the dissemination of books and to establishing the habit of reading in what is vaguely called the middle classes of society. Their members represented the bourgeoisie and were composed of civil servants, physicians, merchants, officers, professors, clergymen and also tended to include, from the lower strata of this group, teachers, clerks, and artisans. Many joined because they could not afford to buy books privately, others only because they wanted to keep up with new publications, modern ideas, and recent information. Frequently one of the leading motives was the "enlightenment" of themselves and others, so that the reading societies were also an important factor in the political and social changes of the period.[306]

The simplest form of organization was the reading circle, in which members associated for the sole purpose of sharing subscriptions to periodicals or acquiring, as common property, expensive works. Thus in the early 1750's some Bremen clergymen jointly subscribed to English moral weeklies—"aus besonderem Triebe zur Verbesserung ihrer Gelehrsamkeit."[307] The leading members of this circle were Johann Henrich Tiling and Johann Philipp Cassel. Putting the subscriptions to good use, Cassel soon became a prolific translator,[308] and together the circle brought out the *Bremisches Magazin zur Ausbreitung der Wissenschaften, Künste und Tugend . . . mehrentheils aus den englischen Monatsschriften gesammelt und herausgegeben* (1756–1765).[309] In a similar manner other Bremen readers combined in 1774 in order to buy J. F. Schiller's translation of John Hawkesworth's *Account of the Voyages Undertaken . . . for Making Discoveries in the Southern Hemisphere,* published in Berlin in 1774 (3 vols.).[310]

Sometimes the reading circles developed into more closely organized societies with special meeting places, which also housed their common possessions. In other cases, reading societies were from the beginning established as a club, frequently called *Lesekabinette,* with rooms or even a house used by members for reading, discussion, and social gatherings. They had their rules of admission and proceeding, and in many cases the libraries supported by these societies were formed, not by suggestions for acquisitions that came from the intellectual elite among its membership, but by democratic voting.

A few of the library lists of the reading societies have been published, others are still in manuscript. Though English authors were, as a rule, not numerous, a fair selection of them was available to the members. In Wunstorf, near Hanover, for instance, then a small town of 1,600 inhabitants, two reading societies existed.[311] One had, among 133 titles, about ten that were translations of English novels, travel books, and historical works or, as in the case of *Annalen der Brittischen Geschichte,* sources of current information. The other, which owned twenty journals and thirteen books, counted Schubart's *Englische Blätter* as well as translations of Burke's *Reflections* and Moore's *Journal during a Residence in France* among its holdings. The reading society in Trier (seventy-seven members) was better supplied with English books.[312] Though there were no English magazines, Archenholz's work on England and his *Annalen der Brittischen Geschichte* had been acquired in addition to translations of Cook's *Travels,*

Hume's *History,* Milton's *Paradise Lost* and *Paradise Regained, Ossian,* Pococke's *Description of the East,* Pope's and Shakespeare's *Works,* Fielding's *Tom Jones,* Sterne's *Sentimental Journey,* and Young's *Works.* Interestingly, all of the classical English authors are represented in the Mannheim editions of Anton von Klein.[313]

While some of these collections appear modest, there were also more opulent institutions for communal reading. These were founded by booksellers as large-scale *Lesekabinette,* and some even went by the name of *Museum.*[314] One of the first was founded by the Vienna publisher and reprinter Thomas Edler von Trattner as early as 1777 and was conceived of, like its German counterparts, as a commercial enterprise with no strict rules of membership.[315] Its catalogue of 1780[316] comprises more than 1,600 items, among them many English books. In Frankfurt the bookseller Wilhelm Fleischer opened, in 1795, a "Lese-Institut in- und ausländischer Werke" and promised the prospective reader to make available twice a year all new publications offered at the Leipzig book fairs.[317] In Dresden (famous for its many libraries) the firm of Arnold and Pinther announced, in the following year, the opening of their *Musuem,* which was to consist of a music cabinet, a discussion room, a gallery of paintings and engravings, and finally a library of more than eight thousand volumes, containing "the most recent and most interesting works of German as well as of French, English, and Italian literature."[318] Twelve English and French journals were regularly available to patrons. The Leipzig Museum, founded by the bookseller Beygang, was the largest. It offered a choice from 167 periodicals, and the library is said to have consisted of no less than seventy thousand volumes.[319] All these institutions, which were combinations of reading societies and lending libraries, catered to the "general" reader who would consume what was new and interesting.

Hamburg, which boasted the first English bookshop on the Continent, was apparently also the first city with a purely English reading society or reading institute. In July 1802 the *Privilegierte wöchentliche gemeinnützige Nachrichten von und für Hamburg* carried the following advertisement:

New British circulating library, no. 16 Neuenburg.

The undersigned has the honor of obediently informing the lovers of English literature that the above institution will be opened on the 25th of this month. The annual subscription is only 16 marks, for which the owner may select two books, which he can exchange twice a week. The British lending library comprises a selection of the most famous works of older and recent literature, in particular the most famous accounts of travels and voyages, the British Theater, the most popular poets, the most excellent works in history and biography, and also a collection of acclaimed novels and periodicals. The catalogue is now in press and will upon completion be sent gratis to every subscriber. 19 July [*sic*] 1802. Thomas Hartbridge.[320]

Only a few months later William Remnant made a countermove in the same paper:

At the repeated Request of many Friends to English Literature, on the 2d
of January next will be opened, a very valuable and extensive English
Circulating Library, which shall vie with the best similar Institution in
London; including all the interesting newest English Books, Pamphlets,
Journals &c, as soon as they can be procured. Plans and Catalogues may
be had Gratis of the Proprietor William Remnant, English Bookseller,
No. 52, next Door to the golden A.B.C., near the Exchange, Hamburgh.[321]

Thus the reading of English authors, once the concern of the few and the
cognoscenti, had reached the level of the circulating library.

I must pass over general public libraries, most regrettably that of Wolfenbüttel[322] with its great seventeenth- and early eighteenth-century collection, but
I should like to comment briefly on another type, the institutional library. I take
this as a collective term for libraries connected with institutions of higher education. Their range extends from the small Gymnasium library to the full-scale
university library. The number of these libraries is large, and their variety
considerable. They deserve attention for their contributions, on all levels of
advanced education, to the reception of English literature in Germany.

There are manuscript catalogues of many Gymnasium libraries. An
example is that of the Gymnasium Paulinum in Münster, compiled in the early
or middle nineteenth century.[323] Considering the fact that this was an old
grammar school with special emphasis on the teaching of Latin, it contains a
surprising number of English books: medical and scientific works in original editions and translations, many travel accounts and historical and geographical
works as well as English editions of the classics. The eighteenth-century standard
authors were generously selected, predominantly in German translations: Addison,
Burke, Defoe, Dryden, Goldsmith, Hume, Locke, Pope, Richardson, Sterne,
Swift, Thomson, and Young. The absence of Fielding and Smollett seems to
suggest that the emphasis was on the moral and instructional value of the library.

Other libraries of this type have a special interest from their association
with translators and literary mediators. One such library is that of the Collegium
Carolinum in Braunschweig,[324] an academic institution between the Gymnasium
and the university, at which Friedrich Wilhelm Zachariä, the translator of
Milton, Johann Arnold Ebert, the translator of Young, and Johann Joachim
Eschenburg, the translator of Shakespeare, taught at various times.[325] The
Collegium was founded by Abt Johann Friedrich Wilhelm Jerusalem, who wanted
it to have "a choice library of the most useful, newest, and best books in each
branch of learning."[326] The collection, begun in 1748, did not grow rapidly, but
its nearly four thousand volumes were apparently well selected and its English
contents should be representative of what knowledgeable and enlightened
teachers in the second half of the century considered as worth acquiring for an
institution which placed special emphasis on the teaching of English. Two
catalogues of the library are preserved and remain to be studied.

Among the university libraries priority must in every respect be given to
that of the University of Göttingen, which was the greatest repository of English

books in eighteenth-century Germany.[327] Like other university libraries it was part of the intellectual environment of a more general educated reading public. At the same time it was a research center that surpassed all others during the last decades of the century. From Göttingen issued one of the most incisive accounts of literature and learning in England that were written in eighteenth-century Germany, Johann Gottfried Eichhorn's *Litterärgeschichte* (1799).[328] From Göttingen also came the first full bibliography of eighteenth-century English authors, Jeremias David Reuss's *Alphabetical Register of all the Authors Actually Living in Great-Britain, Ireland, and in the United Provinces of North-America, with a Catalogue of their Publications* (1791).[329] Reuss was under-librarian in Göttingen and wrote about his work with a curious mixture of pride and modesty:

> The project appears to be a bold one for a foreigner to do; but if he is in the possession of most of the literary resources upon which an English author could draw and if he uses these with industry and care, it may perhaps not be too daring if he attempts to supply a work which the English have not yet produced.[330]

In other words, toward the end of the century the library of the University of Göttingen was fully equipped even for the most detailed work on contemporary English literature in the widest sense of the word. Only the unusual dearth of work in the history of scholarship and scholarly institutions can account for the fact that not only the circumstances of the origin of Reuss's bibliography but the very fact of its existence is unknown even to specialists in eighteenth-century studies.

Reading

Who read English authors in eighteenth-century Germany is a question for which there seems to be no simple and satisfactory answer. A variety of factors has to be taken into account, and none of them can be assumed to have been stable in this period of rapid change. To establish a straightforward relationship between a clearly defined literature and a clearly definable reading public proves impossible. More likely, a series of answers will have to be given, each referring to a different group of readers or to a different group of books.

So far only one small group of readers has been given attention: some leading men of letters.[331] Their reactions to individual works have been recorded, and their appreciations of these works have been analyzed. But since they were studied primarily as key figures in a process of literary interaction they have been considered as critics rather than as readers. Thus in spite of all we know about their familiarity with English letters in the context of literary history, there is relatively little information about such aspects as the scope of their reading and the resources that were in each case at their disposal.[332]

Practically nothing is known about the reception of English writers by the

German reading public at large. The topic is particularly difficult to investigate, no doubt, since some of the classic sources in the documentation of reading habits and reading vogues are here not, or not readily, available. Contemporary observers ranked Germany (or at least Prussia) high on the scale of literacy in Western Europe,[333] but the number of readers was, of course, still limited.[334] According to modern estimates, no more than about 10 percent of the population over the age of six could read in the earlier and middle part of the century, at best 15 about 1770, and 25 around 1800.[335] Since the ability to read does not automatically make a person a reader, the number of actual readers was apparently much smaller. For the small town of Wunstorf it has been established that the potential membership of the two reading societies can hardly have exceeded sixty (i.e., less than 4 percent of the total population).[336] Membership lists of other reading societies likewise suggest that only a small fraction of the population can be considered readers in the sense that they habitually read.[337] About the turn of the century it was judged that the German reading public— certainly taken in a narrow sense—consisted of about 300,000 persons.[338] Even if this is a conservative estimate, the number is large enough to pose numerous problems to the student in search of the readers of English authors.

I should like to consider three aspects only.[339] One is the kind of information that can be obtained from subscription lists. Another is the relation of English literature to the "general" reader of the period. The third is the emergence of a reading public that actually read English.

Subscription lists, always a welcome complement to library inventories,[340] are unfortunately not plentiful. Most of the translations do not appear to have been published by subscription. If they were, the lists were not included in the books. The books in the potentially most interesting category—the reprint of an original-language edition—per se tended to appear without the names of subscribers or *Pränumeranten*.

Among the few subscription lists one of exceptional interest is found in Johann Joachim Bode's translation of *Tristram Shandy*. The novel had first been unsuccessfully translated by Johann Friedrich Zückert,[341] so that Bode's translation, which followed his German version of the *Sentimental Journey*, was apparently expected to be a literary event. It was brought out in Hamburg by Bode's own publishing house in 1774.[342] The subscription list comprises more than 650 names of individuals, booksellers, and libraries.[343] It is led by "Ihro Kayserlichen Hoheiten, der Großfürst und die Großfürstinn von Rußland" (six copies) and includes a galaxy of famous names: Goethe, Hamann, Herder, Klopstock, and Wieland, surrounded by Boie, Jacobi, Matthias Claudius, Bertuch, and Carl Philipp Emanuel Bach. The chief interest of the list, however, does not derive from the great names but from the ordinary subscribers who supplied, with their names, their occupations and places of residence.

As might be expected, most of the subscribers, about a quarter, are from Hamburg and the adjoining Altona. Schleswig-Holstein is also represented, but not strongly with, for instance, 9 subscribers from Schleswig or 11 from the small Itzehoe. The second largest number of subscribers (35) lived in Mitau, a minor but apparently very active cultural center in Courland, with a predominantly German population.[344] Another 29 subscriptions were received from Petersburg and 16 from Königsberg, as against 24 from Göttingen, 15 from Weimar, and 2 from Zurich. Only 4 subscribers can be located in Vienna, 3 in Stuttgart, 5 in Frankfurt. Merely 6 were in Berlin, but a Berlin bookseller subscribed for 30 copies, the largest number on the list. Thus by far the majority of the subscribers lived in northern Germany and the Baltic region.

Social and professional groups are easily identifiable. Less than 11 percent appear to belong to the nobility or the equivalent of the landed gentry.[345] About one-fifth, the largest single group, are higher civil servants (sometimes titled), government officials, or administrators (including, for instance, a "Hof- und Kammerrath in Weymar," a "herzogl. würtemb. Hofgerichts-Assessor und Renten-kammerexpeditions-Rath" or a "kön. Großbrit. Hof und kanzeley Rath, zu Hannover"). The second largest group, about 90, are merchants, mostly from Hamburg. Roughly 10 percent belong to the legal profession, somewhat more than 3 percent to the medical profession. About 5 percent are military men, and about 7 clergymen. There are also artists, musicians, professors and teachers as well as students.[346] Sixteen of the subscribers would seem to belong to the lower administrative personnel (clerks, etc.). No less than 43 are women, provided "Mad. A*** geb. O**" or "Mad. v. B. geb. v. B.—" are not Shandyan entries like "N.N.—".

The group from Mitau[347] should not be passed over, regardless of whether or not it was a community of Sternean enthusiasts. It represents, in microcosmic form, certain tendencies that seem to be of larger significance. The appearance in the subscription list of twelve women from the nobility and bourgeoisie demonstrates the strong presence, if not predominance, of the feminine element in the reading public that took an interest in English belles-lettres. The prevalence of members of the civil service and legal profession, though natural in an administrative center, suggests a notable social and professional compactness in the reading public of the period, especially in smaller communities. The additional presence of a major, two captains, the local bookseller, a pastor, and a professor suggests its range. At the same time, there is an indication, also observable elsewhere, that such a homogeneous group of educated readers set a pattern which was followed by socially inferior groups. This at least appears to be the explanation for the (more unexpected) appearance on the list of a "Kammermusikus," a "Concertmeister," and a "Commißion Sekret." Communal reading of *Tristram Shandy* was made possible by a subscription from the library of the Freemasons in Mitau.

Though general conclusions can hardly be drawn from a single list, the subscribers to Bode's translation do not seem to have been untypical readers. A second subscription list, to which I want to draw attention, reveals a comparable group. It is prefixed to Archenholz's *Annalen der Brittischen Geschichte*,[348] and though it does not identify the readers of a particular author, it defines a reading public with pronounced English interests. Besides the general note that 370 copies were ordered by booksellers, it contains more than 180 names, many again with occupations and nearly all with places of residence. Summarily, Archenholz's subscribers are composed of members of the nobility (thirteen) and such representatives of the bourgeoisie as are also prominent in Bode's list. Merchants and civil servants are numerous. Among the relatively few uncommon subscribers a "Herzogl. Curländischer Hofsänger und Schauspieler in Mietau," a "Caffee-Gastwirth in Danzig," and an "Ober-Salz-Inspector beim Salzwesen der Königl. Preußl. Seehandlungs-Societät in Neu-Fahrwasser" are perhaps noteworthy. The geographical distribution of the *Annalen* was wide; many copies seem to have gone to private libraries in smaller places all over the country. Vienna (28 subscriptions), Danzig (26), and Hamburg (19) stand out among the large towns and cities.

Such lists, then, provide one detailed answer to the question of who read English authors in Germany. Yet from the type of book with which they are associated they cannot be expected to give an exhaustive answer. The educated reading public that emerges from them was apparently only a section of the entire reading public. At any rate, Jean Paul suggested, in a footnote to his *Konjektural-Biographie* of 1799, a tripartite division among those that could then be considered as habitual readers:

> In Germany there are three publics or *publica:* (1) the general, almost uneducated and unlearned, of the lending libraries; (2) the learned, consisting of professors, candidates, students, and reviewers, and (3) the educated, which is composed of men of the world and educated women, of artists, and the higher classes educated at least through social intercourse and travel. (There are certainly frequent interrelations between these three publics).[349]

This survey is certainly not complete, and by modern standards it may be found lacking in precision. But it offers a broad and authentic view of the contemporary reading scene.

According to this pattern, Bode's and Archenholz's subscribers must be taken to come from the two categories of the learned readers and the educated readers (*Weltleute* being a convenient term for merchants, civil servants, and the professional classes). They may even be seen as a homogeneous group of readers when opposed to the first category of the uneducated and unlettered reader associated with the then already numerous circulating libraries.[350] Though there is little specific information, this clientele of the circulating libraries must be supposed to have been large. Possibly some of Bode's subscribers that appear to belong to a lower social class represent, both intellectually and educationally, the top stratum of Jean Paul's first category.

In any event, it must be assumed that the "large, almost uneducated and unlearned public of the circulating libraries" also came into contact with British authors. In the absence of a full-scale survey of the contents of such libraries, it is pointless to speculate on their range of English works. However, many of the second-, third-, and fourth-rate novels that were then translated must have been among them. *Geschichte der Miss Charlotte Jarvis in Briefen* or *Geschichte eines englischen Jubeliers und Mahlers, von ihm selbst aufgesetzt* or *Miss Whiting oder Das kurzweilige Mädchen, eine Frühlingsbegebenheit* are examples of the kind of fiction that appeared at the same time as Bode's *Tristram Shandy*.[351] It is difficult to believe that such works were aimed exclusively at the educated reader and found their place in his collections only.

The problem that here confronts the student of the reception of English literature is perhaps best illustrated from an anecdote. Visitors to the Dresden Gallery always found the soldier posted at the court gate inattentive to his duties as a guard. His rifle was comfortably rested against the wall, and he himself was reading a novel from a circulating library[352]—a perfect image of the late-eighteenth-century rage for reading in the middle and lower strata of German society. Can we be sure he was *not* reading a novel translated from English? In other words: If there was an English contribution to the reading matter intended for mass consumption, how large was it? And was it felt, by readers or critics or both, to be a distinctly English contribution? There is no satisfactory answer yet.

My comments on the second aspect—the relation of English literature to the so-called "general reader" of the period—are only intended to outline a field that needs further investigation. The figure of the general reader, often invoked, has seldom been defined. It must be seen in connection with one of the great changes in the history of reading: the transition from what has been called the period of intensive reading to that of extensive reading.[353] Up to the middle of the century the general pattern of reading outside the courts, the patrician houses, and the circle of scholars was characterized by the fact that few books were available and that these books were read time and again. The normal middle class or upper middle class household provided its members at best with a small collection of books (often of a predominantly devotional nature) which was neither continually added to nor likely to be exchanged against other collections. It remained a fixed stock of reading matter, so that the prevalent mode of reading was inevitably that of intensified repetitive reading.

In the second half of the century this pattern disappeared. Though the older attitudes toward reading were partly retained or, at a later date, consciously revived, a new pattern emerged. It was characterized by noniterative reading. As a rule, books were read once and once only. The most decisive single factor in bringing about this change appears to have been the proliferation of newspapers and other periodical publications. By appearing at fixed intervals they fostered the habit of recurrent reading; and by providing new reading matter they created a craving for novelty at the same time that they satisfied it.[354] Reading became extensive in the sense that the reader, instead of concentrating on a small collection of books, continually reached out for more material in search of new information and novel entertainment.

The habit appears to have originated with the scholarly reader and to have spread with the expansion of the reading public in the second half of the century. It produced a division of readers that cuts across the stratification observed by Jean Paul. If the increase in literacy led to a public of uneducated readers in addition to the traditional public of scholarly readers and the more recent public of educated readers, the chief result of the adoption of the habit of extensive reading appears to have been the emergence of a wide spectrum of readers that qualified as "general" in the sense that their reading was unspecific from a social and educational point of view.

This process, simple in principle, was highly complex in actual fact. Among the several factors that entered into it, the conspicuous presence, within the larger corpus of English literature, of certain kinds of works which were eminently susceptible to a "general" reception appears to have been one of great importance. As the immediate success of these genres suggests, there seems to have been a latent demand for them, a demand, however, that could neither be stimulated nor satisfied by original German publications. Identical or equivalent genres did not exist and came into being, if at all, only after foreign prototypes had established themselves with the German reading public. In some cases, a great many imitations followed, in others the models proved inimitable for various reasons. The grounds on which these types of literature achieved prominence and significance were not, or not in the first place, literary. What gave them their "general" interest was their immediate human appeal, the fact that they embodied or mirrored human experience either actual or fictional.

Three genres appear to have been principally concerned. Chronologically the first is the periodical essay or, in the terminology preferred in Germany, the moral weekly. A selection from *The Tatler* and *The Spectator* was translated under the title of *Der Vernünfftler* by Johann Mattheson as early as 1713.[355] In the imitations that followed[356] the first attempts can be traced to envisage a reading public beyond the categories of the learned and even the educated reader. The new reading public was to be educationally and, by implication, socially indifferent. Thus the Hamburg *Patriot,* one of the earliest German followers of Addison and Steele, proclaimed: "Weil sie aber insgemein und überhaupt entweder Gelehrte sind, oder Ungelehrte; so will ich allezeit jedweden Auffsatz dahin einrichten, daß er weder für die Gelehrten zu schlecht und zu niedrig, noch für die Ungelehrten zu hoch und unbegreifflich, sondern vielmehr jedermann verständlich sey, und bloß den ordentlichen Gebrauch Menschlicher Vernunfft erfordere."[357] This public, the *Patriot* felt, could and should include even artisans and farmers. The fact that instead of four hundred, six thousand copies of this work had ultimately to be printed clearly indicates the power of the genre to generate a "general" public of extensive readers.[358]

The second genre is the novel, whose influence on German literature and the German reading public can hardly be overestimated. The concept of the novel as it developed in Germany in the later decades was to a large extent derived from the English novel. In his *Versuch über den Roman* (1774) Friedrich von Blanckenburg, perhaps the most representative theoretician, proceeded on the proposition, adapted from Fielding, that man and human nature, irrespective of rank and position, should be the theme of the novel.[359] The popularity of the genre seems to have been even greater than in England. Whether of English origin or in the English manner, the novel had the widest appeal during the second half of the century. Up to the 1750's and 1760's novels of various types have so far been traced only in the libraries of educated readers, but whatever sources are available for the latter and last decades indicate the seminal role of the novel in extending the reading public and establishing the habit of extensive reading.[360]

The beginning and the end of this process can conveniently be viewed from Göttingen. When, in 1748, Johann David Michaelis, an Orientalist, translated *Clarissa* he assured his readers that the book was so inoffensive that it was suitable for everybody.[361] When, in 1800, Jeremias David Reuss (in his capacity as censor for the government in Hanover) described the reading scene in Göttingen he pointed out: "Drey Leihbibliotheken . . . von *Romanen und Schauspielen* scheinen für Göttingen zu viel, und doch sieht man den Büchern, die nur eine Messe überlebt haben, es an, wie fleißig sie gelesen worden sind. Es ließt aber auch hier fast alles, bis auf Krämerjungen und Mägde herab. Dieses übermäßige Lesen ist erst seit etwa 10 Jahren eingerissen."[362] By then the novel was universally accepted, and the reading of novels had become so absorbing that it found its place in Immanuel Kant's philosophical anthropology among habits that produced "Gemüthsschwächen im Erkenntnißvermögen."[363]

Finally, there is the travel book (as distinct from the geographical treatise). It appears to have been one of the most distinctive English contributions to eighteenth-century German reading. Apart from the continued success of the early stories of actual or fictitious adventure, the numerous accounts of voyages, above all the reports of Cook's discoveries,[364] enjoyed an ever-widening public. Of the reading societies that have so far been investigated hardly any was without the classic works of the genre, and some had considerable collections.[365] Many attempts were made to imitate the genre, but most of them inevitably failed.[366] The eighteenth-century German traveler could not and did not venture to proceed beyond the neighboring countries, and none of the great explorations was achieved by Germans. They had to be read about in English books. It has been suggested, and the suggestion has much to commend it, that despite great changes in Germany the traditional patterns of European life were transformed in France (by the French Revolution) and in England (by the expansion of trade and industry and the exploration of unknown or little known parts of the world). Germany participated in the revolutionary changes from afar, and lived through them vicariously by reading about them.[367] The experience came secondhand, but its reception through the printed page caused what might be called a general reading revolution.[368]

The third aspect—the emergence of an English-reading public—is in many ways the most intriguing. Though there were, of course, German readers of English books in the early eighteenth century (predominantly scholarly readers), the formation of a homogeneous group which can be said to constitute a public in the sense that it provided a market for original-language books is definitely a phenomenon of the last few decades. In 1762, Friedrich Nicolai complained: "Das deutsche Publikum begünstigt meinen Anschlag auf die Engländische Schriftsteller bisher eben nicht sehr."[369] This seems to imply that there was as yet hardly any awareness of English letters as a distinct corpus of foreign literature.

As I have indicated, the first attempts to import English books for the Leipzig book fairs date from the 1750's. Though the availability of these books no doubt contributed toward the formation of a special group of readers, it is the beginning of the reprinting of English books that most clearly indicates the existence of a reading public. In 1775 the *Frankfurter Gelehrte Anzeigen* advertised Johann Heinrich Merck's edition of *Ossian*. The note recalls the time when a proposal by the Leipzig publisher Dyk of an English-language edition of Shakespeare drew three subscribers from all over Germany. Meanwhile a drastic change had occurred: "Jetzt liefert die Richterische Buchhandlung zu Altenburg (zierliche aber fehlerhafte) Abdrücke Engl. Schriften in Menge."[370] Thus it would seem that in the mid-1770's this public had come into being.

The process was a gradual one, and it must be seen as a breaking away from the established rule of French literature and French culture in Germany, which still held its sway in the 1760's.[371] In retrospect Johann Wilhelm von Archenholz gave what appears to be the best concise description of the change that occurred in the late 1760's and 1770's:

> We Germans have known the British for not more than thirty years. We had seen their troops in our country; . . . we admired their industrial products. But still, we did not know more of the British than if their island had belonged to another part of the world. We knew neither their constitution nor their laws, neither their customs nor their literature. No lesser men than Wieland and Lessing were required to acquaint the Germans with this extraordinary people, whose character, moral history, and culture are so very individual. The admiration for Corneille and Voltaire, which Gottsched had implanted in the Germans, diminished considerably when Shakespeare and Milton became known, who through their powerful genius as it were monopolized literary fame. The desire to read the works of these and other great British writers in the original language initiated the study of the English language, which has since made continuous progress in Germany. It was found that in respect of their mentality and civil virtues as well as in view of their literary and philosophical works, the Germans had more in common with the English nation than with any other. Since this discovery our respect for everything English has increased. . . . The character of the English accounts for the fact that no other literature combines pleasure and instruction to the same degree.[372]

In other words, England ceased to be a *terra incognita,* and as the passage suggests, the German discovery of England was by no means confined to her literature, though some of the strongest impulses came from the German men of letters.

The point that is of special interest in the present context is the spread of the knowledge of the English language in Germany and the interdependence of language learning and reading. As a rule, it can be supposed that, unlike the knowledge of French, the knowledge of English was restricted to the scholarly and the educated reader. There were in all probability very few readers of English below the level of the upper middle class. It is rare that one finds a technician and inventor like Johann Conrad Fischer from Schaffhausen, who is certainly not typical enough of his social group to pass for an artisan, with a good command of English.[373]

Two categories of readers should perhaps be distinguished: those that had received some formal training in English, and those that were self-taught. Members of the first group belong, by and large, to a younger generation which had profited from the attempts made in eighteenth-century Germany to establish English as an academic subject.[374] Occasional courses were taught early, but it was not before the 1750's or 1760's that more systematic procedures appear to have been introduced.[375] Detailed information about the teachers and their courses is, with exceptions, hardly available before 1780. By that time, however, the encouraging results of language teaching must have been visible, at least in Göttingen (where John Thompson had taught successfully since 1735 and been made full professor in 1762).[376] Christian Gottlob Heyne, the famous librarian, wrote in 1781: "Enfin nous commençons à pouvoir nous passer de traductions, depuis que le françois & l'anglois ont pour ainsi dire obtenu chés nous le droit de bourgeoisie & que l'on conduit notre jeunèsse à la connoissance des originaux mêmes."[377] In other words, a fairly large public of potential readers of English must have existed when in the later eighties Thurneysen began his series of reprints.

The other group is more diversified and represents a wide spectrum of readers. Though there are exceptions, it comprises mainly those that had already received their formal education at the time when it became either desirable or fashionable to acquire English as a new foreign language. (Most of the members of this group can be supposed to have been readers if not speakers of French.) I can only try to indicate the range and variety of the group by selecting a few examples. Apart from men such as Georg Forster, who received part of his education in England and whose mastery of English was supreme, it includes Johann Wilhelm von Archenholz, who spent six years in England and was subsequently able, as an early journalistic writer, to write and edit an English journal for Germans, *The British Mercury*. It also includes Johann Georg Hamann, both as a *littérateur* and as a representative of that presumably large number of traders and merchants who either went to England or came into contact with Englishmen in Hamburg, Bremen, Königsberg (which had a small English colony), and elsewhere. It further includes Johann Heinrich Merck, who not only translated the English reviews but also taught English to Princess Louise, later the wife of Duke Carl August of Weimar. It includes Klopstock, who learned English from *Night Thoughts*, Goethe, who used both tutors and Dodd's *Beauties of Shakespeare* and made "english verses, that a stone would weep," as well as Frau von Stein, who in 1776 relied on Goldsmith and Shakespeare as her manuals of instruction. And it includes, lastly but not finally, that nameless old gentleman whom Voltaire encountered in Colmar (then French but German-speaking): he began learning English at the age of seventy and had made sufficient progress to read the best English authors.[378]

Though, in 1772, Johann Christoph Gatterer affirmed that there had never been on earth another nation that was so keen on learning foreign languages as the Germans at that particular moment,[379] it must not be supposed that every reader of English was highly proficient. Many of those who taught themselves seem to have had an imperfect command of the language, and not a few may have had difficulties in reading and understanding the books they praised so highly. Some of the deficiencies, especially in pronunciation, found their way into print and may serve as indications of the limitations which should be taken into account. If Goethe gave his well-known oration the title "Zum Schäkespears Tag," this may have been an attempt at *Eindeutschung*. But if Johann Jakob Bodmer, who translated Milton, wrote "Sasper" instead of "Shakespeare," this must be taken as an unsuccessful effort to spell phonetically.[380] What could occasionally be observed in the fringe zones of this reading public William Mason reported from Hamburg to Thomas Gray, quoting a woman admirer who compared *Night Thoughts* to Gray's *Elegy:* "Je lu, & elle est bien Jolie & Melan-cholique mais elle ne touche point La Cœur comme mes tres cheres Nitt toats."[381]

As a whole, this reading public was small enough to remain a kind of elite. Shortly after 1800 a list of reviewers for the *Allgemeine Literatur-Zeitung* includes 516 names with notes on subjects and language qualifications. While somewhat more than half of the reviewers expressed an interest in foreign books, only 139 stated that they would review English publications.[382] Though no general conclusions can be drawn from this list, the knowledge of English does not appear to have been very widespread, even in the later decades. This is confirmed by the hierarchy of translators, which Friedrich Nicolai sketched in *Das Leben und die Meinungen des Herrn Magister Sebaldus Nothanker* in 1776: "Ein Uebersetzer aus dem Engländischen ist vornehmer, als ein Uebersetzer aus dem Französischen, weil er seltener ist. Ein Uebersetzer aus dem Italiänischen läßt sich schon bitten. . . . Einen Uebersetzer aus dem Spanischen aber findet man fast gar nicht."[383] Again a rough indication which needs support from other sources.

One point can, however, be made. If English as a new foreign language in Germany required a collective effort on the part of those that learned it both as readers and as translators, this effort left permanent traces. To quote once more Heyne: "Comme la langue angloise était moins généralement connue, ce ne furent que des gens d'un gout plus cultivé qui se mêlerent de traduire de l'anglois, & voilà d'où vient les traductions d'ouvrages anglois que notre Professeur *Ebert* a faites sont devenues elles mêmes des modèles accomplis de style dans notre langue."[384] This is certainly not true of all translations,[385] but it has been established in a general way that the reading of English in Germany and the attempts at translating carefully from English into German made a significant contribution to the emergence of German as a literary language.[386]

In sum, then, the reception of English authors in eighteenth-century Germany must be seen as an intricate process. In the assimilation through translation and republicàtion of a whole literature, which took place, not in a period of stability, but in one of rapid intellectual development and cultural change, more factors can be seen at work than the historian is usually able to find. He can follow the interplay of various cultural traditions and trace the transmission, through a complicated system of distribution, of texts in several languages. Above all, he can watch the formation, within a fairly short period, of a public that acquired, through the printed page, an impressive familiarity with a foreign literature and can be said to have become, if I may use the expression, literate in a foreign culture.

NOTES

1. The standard accounts are Lawrence Marsden Price, *English Literature in Germany,* California Publications in Modern Philology, 37 (Berkeley and Los Angeles, 1953), and Horst Oppel, *Englisch-deutsche Literaturbeziehungen,* Grundlagen der Anglistik und Amerikanistik, 1 and 2 (Berlin, 1971), 2 vols. Neither is concerned exclusively with the eighteenth century. In the German translation of Price's book the important bibliography of secondary sources is brought up to 1960: *Die Aufnahme englischer Literatur in Deutschland, 1500–1960* (Bern and Munich, 1961).

2. Various aspects of French *anglophilie* have been explored. The history of German *Anglophilie* and *Anglomanie* remains to be written. Travel literature is especially pertinent here. For specific studies see notes 125 and 143.

3. The earliest survey is Max Koch, *Über die Beziehungen der englischen Literatur zur deutschen im achtzehnten Jahrhundert* (Leipzig, 1883).

4. See page x. The second list also contains additions and corrects certain entries in the first. Vicesimus Knox, for instance, though a writer of literary essays, appears in the second volume.

5. Approximate figures deduced from the Price checklists.

6. *Literature,* p. 20.

7. *Allgemeines Bücher-Lexikon* . . . (Leipzig, 1812–1894).

8. *Vollständiges Bücher-Lexikon* . . . (Leipzig, 1834–1836), 6 vols.

9. Hans-Joachim Koppitz, "Zur Bibliographie der deutschen Buchproduktion des 18. Jahrhunderts," *Zeitschrift für Bibliothekswesen und Bibliographie,* 9 (1962), 18–30. See also Koppitz, "Bibliographien als geistes- und kulturgeschichtliche Quellen im deutschen Sprachgebiet," *Börsenblatt für den deutschen Buchhandel,* Frankfurter Ausgabe, 19 (1963), 818–28, and the remarks in Robert F. Arnold, *Allgemeine Bücherkunde zur neueren deutschen Literaturgeschichte,* 4th ed. (Berlin, 1966), p. 214. For an earlier period see M. Spirgatis, *Die litterarische Produktion Deutschlands im 17. Jahrhundert und die Leipziger Messkataloge* (Leipzig, 1901) [rpt. from *Sammlung bibliothekswissenschaftlicher Arbeiten,* Heft 14].

10. The best recent introduction is Rudolf Blum, *Vor- und Frühgeschichte der nationalen Allgemeinbibliographie* (Frankfurt, 1959); rpt. from *Archiv für Geschichte des Buchwesens,* 2 (1959).

11. For the use of the book fair catalogues in an earlier period see Irene Wiem, *Das englische Schrifttum in Deutschland von 1518–1600,* Palaestra 219 (Leipzig, 1940).

12. Reinhard Wittmann, "Die frühen Buchhändlerzeitschriften als Spiegel des literarischen Lebens," *Archiv für Geschichte des Buchwesens,* 13 (1973), 613–931, draws attention to the fact that certain book-trade journals, particularly the *Magazin des Buch- und Kunst-Handels* (1780–1783), contain important supplementary lists of publications that appeared between the book fairs.

13. So far the only extensive study of some eighteenth-century fair catalogues is Rudolf Jentzsch. *Der deutsch-lateinische Büchermarkt nach den Leipziger Ostermeß-Katalogen von 1740, 1770 und 1800 in seiner Gliederung und Wandlung,* Beiträge zur Kultur- und Universalgeschichte, 22 (Leipzig, 1912).

14. From the point of view of Franco-German literary relations Martin Fontius has drawn attention to the fair catalogues: "Zur literarhistorischen Bedeutung der Messekataloge im 18. Jahrhundert," *Weimarer Beiträge,* 7 (1961), 607–16.

15. Dresden: Georg Conrad Walther, 1745.

16. Braunschweig: bei sel. Ludolph Schröders Erben, 1760. See Harold Forster, "Edward Young in Translation I," *Book Collector,* 19 (1970), 495, no. 1760a. The edition was completed in 1769.

17. *Verzeichniß einer Handbibliothek der nützlichsten deutschen Schriften zum Vergnügen und Unterricht* . . . ([Berlin], 1787).

18. See *Allgemeines Verzeichniß* . . . (Leipzig, 1800), pp. 228–50. Most of these items were Basel editions published by Decker. None of them is listed in Price, *Humaniora.*

19. A notable exception is J. E. Norton, *A Bibliography of the Works of Edward Gibbon* (Oxford, 1940, rpt. 1970).

20. English books were imported by German booksellers as early as the middle of the sixteenth century and some of the problems that confront the bibliographer in the eighteenth century exist for earlier periods as well. The only study so far is Max Spirgatis, "Englische Litteratur auf der Frankfurter Messe von 1561–1620," in *Beiträge zur Kenntnis des Schrift-, Buch- und Bibliothekswesens,* 7 (= *Sammlung bibliothekswissenschaftlicher Arbeiten,* 25) (Leipzig, 1902), 37–89.

21. I hesitate to go beyond this question, but there are certain indications that special editions were in existence.

22. See Nora Imendörffer, *Johann Georg Hamann und seine Bücherei,* Schriften der Albertus-Universität, 20 (Königsberg and Berlin, 1938), p. 137.

23. Some aspects have been investigated by Marce Blassneck, *Frankreich als Vermittler englisch > deutscher Einflüsse im 17. und 18. Jahrhundert,* Kölner anglistische Arbeiten, 20 (Leipzig, 1934).

24. See E. Audra, *Les Traductions françaises de Pope (1717–1825): Etude de bibliographie* (Paris, 1931), p. 38, no. 54; p. 47, no. 69; p. 49, no. 73; p. 58, no. 86; p. 66, no. 100; and p. 72, no. 112.

25. Audra, p. 62 f., no. 93.

26. Altona: Iversen, 1758–1764, 5 vols. Price, *Literature,* p. 177.

27. *Works Complete* (Berlin: Nicolai), 10 vols. Price, *Literature,* p. 177.

28. See Charles Alfred Rochedieu, *Bibliography of French Translations of English Works 1700–1800* (Chicago, 1948), p. 30.

29. See *Catalogus Universalis* (Leipzig), Easter Fair 1750, sig. G_{2v}: "Edinb. in Commißion in der Weidmannischen Handlung." This appears to be identical with the edition "Édimbourg: Aux dépens de la Compagnie" (Rochedieu, ibid.). See also Giles Barber, "Some Uncollected Authors XLI: Henry Saint John, Viscount Bolingbroke, 1678–1751," *Book Collector,* 14 (1965), 535 (no. 18).

30. *Briefe vom Geiste des Patriotismus* (Jena, 1764). See Price, *Humaniora,* p. 156.

31. Price, *Humaniora,* p. 156; Rochedieu, *Bibliography,* p. 30, lists an edition *s.l.,* 1752. See also Barber, p. 536, no. 20.

32. Leipzig: Eurich, 1758. See Price, *Humaniora,* and Barber (note 29), who supplements Price.

33. *Allgemeines Verzeichnis* (Leipzig) (autumn 1777), p. 366.

34. Leipzig: Weidmann, 1777–1801, 3 vols. Price, *Humaniora,* p. 151.

35. *La Dunciade, poeme en dix chants* (1771), 2 vols. No publisher is given, and

it does not appear in Audra and Rochedieu. Heinsius, I, col. 715, lists "Lond. (Varrentrapp, Francof.)" See also Price, *Literature*, p. 178.

36. See Wiem (note 11) and Gilbert Waterhouse, *The Literary Relations of England and Germany in the Seventeenth Century* (Cambridge, 1914; rpt. New York, 1966).

37. *De praestantia classicorum auctorum commentatio: Latine vertit atque animadversionibus instruxit G. H. Ayrer.* It does not appear in Price, *Humaniora*.

38. *Expositio Philosophiæ Newtonianæ* (Viennae: Typis Joannis Thomæ Trattner, 1761).

39. Some titles are recorded in Gottfried Erich Rosenthal, *Litteratur der Technologie* (Berlin and Stettin, 1795; rpt. Hildesheim, 1972). Of the later bibliographical sources Wilhelm Engelmann's *Bibliotheca historico-naturalis* (Leipzig, 1846), *Bibliotheca mechanico-technologica* (Leipzig, 1834), and *Bibliotheca medico-chirurgica* (Leipzig, 1848) are the most important.

40. See Joachim Kirchner, *Bibliographie der Zeitschriften des deutschen Sprachgebiets bis 1900*, I (Stuttgart, 1969), nos. 3531, 3538, 3541, 3549, 3616, 3648, 3677, 3721, 3740.

41. See Hans Hecht, *T. Percy, R. Wood and J. D. Michaelis: Ein Beitrag zur Literaturgeschichte der Genieperiode*, Göttinger Forschungen, 3. Heft (Stuttgart, 1933), pp. 19–31. Two of apparently six copies (see p. 25) are preserved in the British Museum (C.116.h.8) and in the Library of the University of Göttingen (4⁰ Auct. gr. II, 2168).

42. Stettin: I. S. Leich, 1797. *A Supplement to the View* . . . appeared in 1801. Rpt. New York: Burt Franklin, n.d.

43. The first edition to contain Michaelis' additions was published in Göttingen by Johann Christian Dieterich, 1758–1761, 2 vols. Under the title of *Roberti Lowth Praelectiones de Sacra Poesi Hebraeorum Notae et Epimetra* all of Michaelis' additions were, obviously at Lowth's request, reprinted by the Clarendon Press in 1763.

44. In addition to J. G. Buhle, ed., *Literarischer Briefwechsel von Johann David Michaelis*, 3 parts (Leipzig, 1794–1796) Hecht has printed a number of letters in *T. Percy, R. Wood and J. D. Michaelis*. A fairly large number are still in manuscript.

45. No attempt has yet been made to list translations published in periodicals. Some material is to be found in the two contemporary indexes to eighteenth-century German periodicals: Johann Samuel Ersch, *Repertorium über die allgemeinen deutschen Journale und andere periodische Sammlungen für Erdbeschreibung, Geschichte und die damit verwandten Wissenschaften* (Lemgo, 1790–1792), 3 vols., and [Johann Heinrich Christian Beutler and Johann Christian Friedrich Gutsmuth], *Allgemeines Sachregister über die wichtigsten deutschen Zeit- und Wochenschriften* . . . (Leipzig, 1790).

46. See Hermann Bräuning-Oktavio, "Johann Heinrich Merck als Drucker, Verleger, Kupferstecher und Mäzen," *Philobiblon: Eine Vierteljahrsschrift für Buch- und Graphiksammler*, 13 (1969), 99–122, 165–208, and "Goethe und Johann Heinrich Merck: Die Geschichte einer Freundschaft," *Goethe: Neue Folge des Jahrbuchs der Goethe-Gesellschaft*, 12 (1950), 190.

47. Göttingen, 1782. Emmert also compiled *The Theatre: or, a Selection of Easy Plays* (Göttingen, 1789), and *The Novelist: or, a Choice Selection of the Best Novels* (Göttingen, 1792–1793), 2 vols.

48. From vol. 1 (1777) onward.

49. I leave aside plays based on English novels, listed by Price.

50. See Konstantin Muskalla, *Die Romane von Johann Timotheus Hermes: Ein Beitrag zur Kultur- und Literaturgeschichte des achtzehnten Jahrhunderts*, Breslauer Beiträge zur Literaturgeschichte, 25 (Breslau, 1912), and Johannes Buchholz, *Johann Timotheus Hermes' Beziehungen zur englischen Literatur* (diss. Marburg, 1911; Göttingen, 1911).

51. See Wilhelm Engelmann, *Bibliothek der neueren Sprachen* . . . (Leipzig, 1842).

52. Graph 1 shows the gradual increase of translations in humanistic literature, Graph 2 that in belles-lettres. Both are based on the Price checklists. Only first translations have been counted. I am grateful to Ursula Alsleben for preparing these and the two other graphs.

53. On the reception of *Robinson Crusoe* see Hermann Ullrich, *Robinson und Robinsonaden: Bibliographie, Geschichte, Kritik* . . . , Litterarhistorische Forschungen, 7 (Weimar, 1898), and Otto Deneke, *Robinson Crusoe in Deutschland: Die Frühdrucke 1720–1780*, Göttingische Nebenstunden, 11 (Göttingen, 1934); on the reception of *Gulliver's Travels* see Matti M. Rossi, "Notes on the Eighteenth-Century German Translations of Swift's *Gulliver's Travels*," *Library Chronicle of the Friends of the University of Pennsylvania Library*, 25 (1959), 84–88.

54. "Allgemeine Uebersicht der ganzen teutschen Litteratur in den letzten 3 Jahren: zu mehrerer Erläuterung der am Ende beygefügten 12 Tafeln," *Historisches Journal*, 1 (1772), 266–301.

55. Owing to a slight inconsistency in "9. Schöne Litteratur" (p. 279) the actual number is 707 (including six "Miscellanschriften").

56. Jentzsch, *Büchermarkt* (note 13), p. 337.

57. Ibid. In 1770 only 35 percent of the total number of translations were from English, in 1800 44 percent.

58. Ibid.

59. Graph 3 shows the relative importance of the various places of publication. It is again based on Price, *Humaniora*. Graph 4 attempts the same for belles-lettres on the basis of Price, *Literature*. If a book was simultaneously published in two towns (e.g., Frankfurt and Leipzig) both have been counted as places of publication. Sometimes "Frankfurt und Leipzig" served to conceal the real place of publication.

60. Christlob Mylius' translation of Hogarth's *Analysis of Beauty* under the title of *Zergliederung der Schönheit* appeared in 1754 with the imprint "London. Bey Andreas Linde, I. K. H. der verwittweten Prinzessin von Wallis, Buchhändler, und in Hannover bey J. W. Schmidt." Price, *Humaniora*, has for Matthew Henry's *Anweisung zum Gebete durch Schriftstellen* "London, Heidinger, 1769" and for John Almon's *Staatsverwaltung des Herrn W. Pitt* "London and Berlin, 1764."

61. See Felix Reichmann, *Christopher Sower Sr., 1694–1758, Printer in Germantown: An Annotated Bibliography*, Bibliographies on German American History, 2 (Philadelphia, 1943).

62. *Die medicinischen Versuche und Bemerkungen, welche von einer Gesellschaft in Edinburgh durchgesehen und herausgegeben werden*, 1749–1752, 5 vols., with *Zusätze* . . . , 1755 ff., and *Neue Versuche und Bemerkungen*, 1756 ff. This was followed by *Medicinische Bemerkungen und Untersuchungen*, 1759 ff.

63. A preliminary list of these has been compiled by Giles Barber, "J. J. Tourneisen of Basel and the Publication of English Books on the Continent c. 1800," *Library*, 5th ser., 15 (1960), 194, from a catalogue in *Sermons of Mr. Yorick*. Several of these titles appear to have been imports, not reprints. Thus the 1776 edition of *Paradise Lost* is listed in the autumn fair catalogue of that year (p. 175) as "printed for Johnson and sold by Richter," whereas the imprint for *Letters of the Late Rev. Mr. L. Sterne to his most intimate Friends* is given as "Altenbourgh, printed and sold by Richter" (ibid., p. 173).

64. See Ernst Weißbrodt, *Die Meyersche Buchhandlung in Lemgo und Detmold und ihre Vorläufer: Festschrift zum 250 jährigen Bestehen der Firma* (Detmold, 1914). This includes a list of publications.

65. Figures derived from Price, *Humaniora*.

66. On Weidmann see Ernst Vollert, *Die Weidmannsche Buchhandlung in Berlin, 1680–1930* (Berlin, 1930). On Weygand see Herbert Koch, "Johann Friedrich Wey-

gand, Buchhändler in Leipzig," *Archiv für Geschichte des Buchwesens,* 9 (1969), 433–48, and Reinhard Wittmann, "Der Verleger Johann Friedrich Weygand in Briefen des Göttinger Hains," ibid., 10 (1970), 319–44. On Gleditsch and Dyk see Rudolf Schmidt, *Deutsche Buchhändler, deutsche Buchdrucker: Beiträge zu einer Firmengeschichte des deutschen Buchgewerbes* (Berlin, 1902–1903), pp. 322–24 and 195.

67. On Nicolai see Ernst Friedel, *Zur Geschichte der Nicolaischen Buchhandlung und des Hauses Brüderstr. 13 in Berlin* (Berlin, 1891), and Karl Löffler and Joachim Kirchner, *Lexikon des gesamten Buchwesens* (Leipzig, 1936), II, 532–33; on the Vossische Buchhandlung, ibid., III, 540.

68. On Bohn see Löffler-Kirchner, *Lexikon,* I, 236. On Hoffmann (later Hoffmann & Campe) see Schmidt, *Deutsche Buchhändler,* pp. 129 ff., and Löffler-Kirchner, II, 106. Two important general surveys are Hermann Colshorn, "Hamburgs Buchhandel im 18. Jahrhundert," *Börsenblatt für den deutschen Buchhandel,* Frankfurter Ausgabe, 27 (1971), A 185–91, A 354–64, and Werner Kayser, *Hamburger Bücher, 1491–1850 . . . ,* Mitteilungen aus der Staats- und Universitätsbibliothek Hamburg, 7 (Hamburg, 1973).

69. On Vandenhoeck (later Vandenhoeck & Ruprecht) see Wilhelm Ruprecht, *Väter und Söhne: Zwei Jahrhunderte Buchhändler in einer deutschen Universitätsstadt* (Göttingen, 1935), and Erich Carlsohn, "Vandenhoeck & Ruprecht, 1735–1960," *Börsenblatt für den deutschen Buchhandel,* Frankfurter Ausgabe, 16 (1960), 157–61. On Orell see Martin Bircher, "Shakespeare im Zürich des 18. Jahrhunderts," in *Geist und Schönheit im Zürich des 18. Jahrhunderts* (Zurich, 1968), pp. 59–65, and Theodor Vetter, *Zürich als Vermittlerin englischer Literatur im achtzehnten Jahrhundert* (Zurich, 1891), pp. 25 f.

70. "J. Dodsley und Compagnie" became a cause célèbre when Lessing discontinued his *Hamburgische Dramaturgie* because of a reprint published by "Dodsley." See Gustav Wustmann, "Dodsley und Compagnie," in *Aus Leipzigs Vergangenheit: Gesammelte Aufsätze* (Leipzig, 1885), pp. 236–49. There were also translations with this imprint, e.g., of William Gilpin's *Essay upon Prints: Abhandlung von Kupferstichen . . .* ("Frankfurt und Leipzig: bey J. Dodsley und Compagnie, 1768").

71. Two of the exceptions are the translations of *Clarissa,* published by Vandenhoeck, and of *Sir Charles Grandison,* published by Weidmann.

72. See Karl Baerent, "Kataloge der Weidmannschen Buchhandlung aus der ersten Hälfte des XVIII. Jahrhunderts," *Zeitschrift für Bücherfreunde,* N. S. 5 (1914), 236–41.

73. *Verlags-Verzeichniß von Johann Friedrich Gleditsch, Buchhändler in Leipzig . . . Bis Michaelis-Messe 1815.* The copy which I have used is preserved in the Deutsche Bücherei, Leipzig.

74. Price, *Humaniora,* lists twenty-two items as published by Gleditsch. As the *Verzeichniß,* according to a note on the title page, also includes some items formerly published by Junius and other publishers, the discrepancy is probably not so large as it first appears.

75. According to the titles listed in Price, *Humaniora,* Weidmann published seven titles in 1776 and 1777, Weygand six in 1779. On further aspects of the translations business, which I cannot here deal with in detail, see Helmut Knufmann, "Das deutsche Übersetzungswesen des 18. Jahrhunderts im Spiegel von Übersetzer- und Herausgebervorreden," *Archiv für Geschichte des Buchwesens,* 9 (1969), 491–572; Walter Fränzel, *Geschichte des Übersetzens im 18. Jahrhundert,* Beiträge zur Kultur- und Universalgeschichte, 25 (Leipzig, 1913); and Edna Purdie, "Some Problems of Translation in the 18th Century in Germany," *English Studies,* 30 (1949), 191–205.

76. This and the following paragraph is based on Karl Buchner, *Aus dem Verkehr einer Deutschen Buchhandlung mit den Geschäftsgenossen.* 2nd ed. Beiträge zur Geschichte des Deutschen Buchhandels, 2 (Gießen, 1874), pp. 117 f.

77. That other publishers also had their agents in London appears, for instance,

from a note by Johann Gottlob Immanuel Breitkopf in *Magazin des Buch- und Kunst-Handels*, 3 (1782), sig. A$_{1r}$.

78. *Dictionary of National Biography*.

79. A fuller list of his translations than in Price, *Humaniora*, p. 213, can be found in Johann Jacob Gradmann, *Das gelehrte Schwaben: oder Lexicon der jetzt lebenden schwäbischen Schriftsteller* ([Ravensburg], 1802), pp. 564 f.

80. In addition to Gradmann see Balthasar Haug, *Das gelehrte Wirtemberg* (Stuttgart, 1790), pp. 162 and 238.

81. See *Dictionary of National Biography;* Rudolf Hallo, *Rudolf Erich Raspe: Ein Wegbereiter von deutscher Art und Kunst,* Göttinger Forschungen, 5 (Stuttgart-Berlin, 1934); and John Carswell, *The Prospector: Being the Life and Times of Rudolf Erich Raspe (1737–1794)* (London, 1950).

82. Raspe called Reich the "Grandison unter den Buchhändlern." See Karl Julius Hartmann and Hans Füchsel, eds., *Geschichte der Göttinger Universitäts bibliothek* (Göttingen, 1937), p. 67.

83. The date is given by Buchner as 1770, but this is obviously a mistake.

84. Raspe gives the title as *History of Modern or English Gardening.* This and the remark that he would send "auch die Bogen von Smeathman [*Some Account of the Termites,* 1781?], wie sie herauskommen," seem to imply that the decision to translate a book was at least in some cases made before it had been published. Whether or not textual or bibliographical problems arise from the fact that advance sheets or advance copies were used for translations remains to be seen.

85. An example is John Hawkesworth's *Account of the Voyages Undertaken by . . . Captain Cook* (1773). Translations were planned by Weidmann in Leipzig and Spener in Berlin (where it appeared in 1774, translated by Johann Friedrich Schiller). A lengthy account is found in Karl Buchner, *Aus dem Verkehr einer deutschen Buchhandlung mit ihren Schriftstellern,* Aus den Papieren der Weidmannschen Buchhandlung (Berlin, 1873), pp. 15 f.

86. See Buchner, *Geschäftsgenossen* (note 76), pp. 30–34, also Vollert, *Die Weidmannsche Buchhandlung* (note 66), pp. 39–40.

87. See Buchner, *Geschäftsgenossen,* pp. 118 f.

88. Weidmann, for instance, inserted an announcement in the Book Fair Catalogue (autumn 1797, p. 429).

89. Thus, to give but one example, "Nachricht und Proben von einer neuen Uebersetzung des verlornen Paradieses" appeared in *Freymüthige Briefe über die neuesten Werke aus den Wissenschaften in und außer Deutschland,* 1 (1759), 42–47. Sometimes translations began to appear in periodicals and were discontinued when a translation in book form was announced; e.g., Hume's "Geschichte Königs Jakobs des Ersten" in *Carlsruher Beyträge zu den schönen Wissenschaften* (see 2, 1761, 570).

90. Examples will be found in *Göttingisches Magazin der Wissenschaften und Litteratur,* in *Brittisches Museum für die Deutschen,* and elsewhere.

91. On the history of this feature see Werner Kienitz, *Formen literarischer Ankündigung im 15. und 16. Jahrhundert* (diss. Cologne, 1930; Köslin, 1930). The French entries in this section have been found to provide interesting information on publishing trends and literary relations. See Fontius (note 14).

92. See *Neues Archiv für Gelehrte, Buchhändler und Antiquare,* eds. Heinrich Bensen and Johann Jacob Palm, 1 (1795), 46–47.

93. See the note concerning "Planta's History of the Helvetic Confederacy," inserted by Weidmann in the Book Fair Catalogue (autumn 1800), pp. 451–52.

94. *Leben und Thaten der Admirale und anderer berühmter Britannischer Seeleute. . . .* Part I has the imprint "Göttingen, in Elias Luzac des jüngern Verlage, 1755", part II "Leipzig in der Weidmannschen und zu Göttingen in Elias Luzac Handlung. 1755." The entry in Price, *Humaniora*, p. 42, is misleading.

95. See note 60.

96. Compare, for instance, items 1760a, 1765a, and 1767a in Forster, "Edward Young in Translation I" (note 16).

97. See Horst Kunze, "Buchkunde und Literaturgeschichte," *Buch und Schrift*, N.S. 1 (1938–1939), 113. More explicit on this point is the revised version of this study, published as introduction to *Lieblings-Bücher von dazumal . . .* (Munich, 1938); second edition as *Gelesen und Geliebt . . .* (Berlin, 1963).

98. *Des Herrn Admirals Lord Ansons Reise um die Welt . . .* , first published 1749, revised edition 1763; see Ruprecht, *Väter und Söhne* (note 69), p. 81, quoting from the unfinished fragment of Hollmann's history of the University of Göttingen. *Sittenlehre für die Jugend in den auserlesensten aesopischen Fabeln,* first published 1757, further editions 1761, 1773, 1783; see Buchner, *Schriftsteller* (note 85), p. xiv, and *Geschäftsgenossen* (note 76), p. 83. *Grandison,* first published 1754–1755, further editions 1759, 1764, 1770; see Buchner, *Geschäftsgenossen,* p. 84. *Allgemeine Weltgeschichte von der Schöpfung an bis auf die gegenwärtige Zeit,* 1765–1808; see Buchner, *Schriftsteller,* p. 5, and *Geschäftsgenossen,* pp. 104 f. *Reisen in Kleinasien,* 1776; see Buchner, *Schriftsteller,* p. 22.

99. No. 36, 7 September 1724, p. [2]. See also Joachim Kirchner, "Der Hamburger Patriot: Eine Untersuchung zur Frühgeschichte der Zeitschrift," in *Ausgewählte Aufsätze . . .* (Stuttgart, 1970), pp. 179 f.

100. Henry Pettit, ed., *The Correspondence of Edward Young, 1683–1765* (Oxford, 1971), p. 534.

101. See Forster, "Edward Young in Translation I," nos. 1751a, 1752a, 1753a, 1754a, 1756a, 1760a. The last two volumes of the revised edition of 1760 (no. 1763a) had not yet appeared.

102. It is impossible to discuss the problem of eighteenth-century German reprinting in any detail. See Kapp-Goldfriedrich, *Geschichte des deutschen Buchhandels,* III (Leipzig, 1909, rpt. 1970), and Hellmut Rosenfeld, "Zur Geschichte von Nachdruck und Plagiat: Mit einer chronologischen Bibliographie zum Nachdruck von 1733–1824," *Börsenblatt für den deutschen Buchhandel,* Frankfurter Ausgabe, 25 (1969), 3211–28.

103. Quoted from Eduard Berend, "War Jean Paul der meistgelesene Schriftsteller seiner Zeit?" *Hesperus,* 22 (1965), 11.

104. See Bernd Breitenbruch, "Der Karlsruher Buchhändler Christian Gottlieb Schmieder und der Nachdruck in Südwestdeutschland im letzten Viertel des 18. Jahrhunderts," *Archiv für Geschichte des Buchwesens,* 9 (1969), 643–732.

105. See Hermine Cloeter, *Johann Thomas Trattner: Ein Großunternehmer im Theresianischen Wien* (Graz-Cologne, 1952). The various reprints are listed in the bibliography appended to Ursula Giese, "Johann Thomas Edler von Trattner: Seine Bedeutung als Buchdrucker, Buchhändler und Herausgeber," *Archiv für Geschichte des Buchwesens,* 3 (1960), 1013–1454.

106. This information comes from the only detailed but in many respects inadequate study of Karl Krükl, *Leben und Werke des elsässischen Schriftstellers Anton von Klein: Ein Beitrag zur Geschichte der Aufklärung in der Pfalz* (Strasbourg, 1901). See pp. 43 ff., 111 ff. See also Wilhelm Bergdolt, "Mannheimer Verleger," *Badische Heimat,* 14 (1927), 176–77.

107. See below, pp. 165–75.

108. *Allgemeine deutsche Bibliothek,* 26, i (1775), 283.

109. Translated from Buchner, *Geschäftsgenossen,* p. 38.

110. See Julius Jolly, *Die Lehre vom Nachdruck* (Heidelberg, 1852), pp. 46–59.

111. Georg Sommer, *Die Zensurgeschichte des Königreichs Hannover* (diss. Münster, 1928; Quakenbrück, 1929), pp. 68–73.

112. Göttingen, 1774, p. 84. See also p. 100.

113. So far as these titles can be found in the bibliographies of Kayser and Heinsius prices are usually added. A comparison of English and German book prices

does not seem to have been made. Some information will be found in Walter Krieg, *Materialien zu einer Entwicklungsgeschichte der Bücher-Preise und des Autoren-Honorars vom 15. bis zum 20. Jahrhundert* (Vienna, 1953).

114. This is borne out by a note in *Der Teutsche Merkur* concerning the reprints published by Richter: "Der jüngere Hr. Richter in Altenburg macht sich ein wahres Verdienst um unser Publikum, dadurch, daß er uns Nachdrucke von den besten neuen Engl. Werken, die an Schönheit des Papiers, Eleganz und Correcktion des Drucks den Originalen theils im mindsten nicht weichen, theils auch sie noch übertreffen, und in Ansehung der Preiße um ein Beträchtliches wohlfeiler sind, als die Originale; wenigstens in Teutschland" (5, 1774, 368–69).

115. My information comes from the original wrappers preserved in the copy of the municipal library of Trier.

116. Vol. 3, no. 3, carried the following note: "Von den *Works of the english poets by Johnson 68 Vol. 12.* werde ich nach und nach einen saubern und correcten Abdruck besorgen, der um die Hälfte wohlfeiler als das Original seyn wird.—Mit *Miltons Works* ist bereits der Anfang gemacht. Man kann in allen Buchhandlungen darauf unterzeichnen." The format "12." appears to be an error. Dieterich's reprint was also an octavo edition.

117. The advertisement appeared in vol. 3, no. 4.

118. See *Verzeichniß* (note 17), p. 271.

119. For Lichtenberg's part see also Friedrich Lauchert, *G. Chr. Lichtenberg's schriftstellerische Thätigkeit in chronologischer Uebersicht dargestellt* (Göttingen, 1893), pp. 84 f.

120. Hans Hecht, ed., *Briefe aus G. Chr. Lichtenbergs englischem Freundeskreis . . .* , Vorarbeiten zur Geschichte der Göttinger Universität und Bibliothek, 2 (Göttingen, 1925), 39 f. The correspondent was Ed. Baron de Harold, who was "in the Service of H.M.S.H. The Elector Palatin, in Garrison at Dusseldorf" and wrote on 6 June 1783.

121. Ibid., p. 41; 7 July 1783.

122. Vol. 9, no. 18 (2 May 1789), p. 160.

123. It is not listed among Göckingk's literary plans in Goedeke's *Grundriß zur Geschichte der deutschen Dichtung* (Dresden, 1896), IV, 1, p. 971.

124. See the entries in Price, *Literature*, p. 270.

125. See Martin Germann, *Johann Jakob Thurneysen der Jüngere, 1754–1803: Verleger, Buchdrucker und Buchhändler in Basel . . .* , Basler Beiträge zur Geschichtswissenschaft, 128 (Basel, 1973). Germann was apparently unaware of Giles Barber's article on Thurneysen (note 63).

126. See Germann, pp. 114 ff.

127. For lists of Thurneysen's reprints see Barber and Germann. Their possible relation to others that were about the same time published by Decker in Basel remains to be established. In certain projects the two firms collaborated. There are also reprints with the imprint "Basil: Printed by J. J. Tourneisen. Paris: Sold by Pissot, Bookseller, Quai des Augustins," which have not been listed by Germann (e.g., that of Blair's *Lectures*, 1788).

128. 1793, II (26 August), p. 1368.

129. His business associate in Gotha was the bookseller Ettinger.

130. On the German book trade of the eighteenth century and the changes that occurred see a series of articles by F. Hermann Meyer in *Archiv für Geschichte des Deutschen Buchhandels:* "Die genossenschaftlichen und Gelehrten-Buchhandlungen des achtzehnten Jahrhunderts" (2, 1879, 68–124); "Die geschäftlichen Verhältnisse des deutschen Buchhandels im achtzehnten Jahrhundert" (5, 1880, 175–255); "Der deutsche Buchhandel gegen Ende des 18. und zu Anfang des 19. Jahrhunderts" (7, 1882, 199–249); and "Reformbestrebungen im achtzehnten Jahrhundert" (12, 1889, 201–300, and 13, 1890, 213–44).

131. British book exports to the Continent are listed in Giles Barber, "Books from

the Old World and for the New: The British International Trade in Books in the Eighteenth Century," *Studies on Voltaire and the Eighteenth Century,* 155 (1976), 185–224.

132. *Catalogus Universalis* . . . , autumn 1714, sig. G_{3v}. The earliest entry for a manual is in the autumn catalogue of 1710, sig. F_{1v}.

133. Jentzsch, *Büchermarkt* (note 13), p. 318 and tables.

134. *Merkwürdige Reisen durch Niedersachsen Holland und Engelland* (Frankfort and Leipzig, 1753), II, 443. The part of the work in which it is contained was translated as *London in 1710: From the Travels of Z. C. von Uffenbach,* tr. and ed. W. H. Quarrell and Margaret Mare (London, 1934).

135. *Neue Zeitungen von gelehrten Sachen,* 9 December 1737, p. 893, and 28 August 1715, p. 273. See also January 1717, p. 60, and June 1735, p. 408.

136. Friedrich von Hagedorn, *Poetische Werke,* ed. Johann Joachim Eschenburg. Part Five: *Briefwechsel* (Hamburg, 1825), pp. 133–35.

137. *Samlung der vornehmsten Schriftsteller die die Würklichkeit ihres eignen Körpers und der ganzen Körperwelt läugnen* . . . (Rostock, 1756), sig. $)($$_{2v}$. See also Blassneck, *Frankreich als Vermittler* (note 23), p. 41.

138. Vol. 3 (1782), sig. A_{1r}.

139. Vol. 1 (1799), p. 8.

140. See *Bremisches Magazin zur Ausbreitung der Wissenschaften, Künste und Tugend* . . . , 1 (1757), 3 ff.

141. *De sacra poesi Hebraeorum,* ed. E. F. C. Rosenmüller (Oxford, 1821), p. 389.

142. See J. Th. de Booy and Roland Mortier, "Les Années de formation de F. H. Jacobi, d'après ses lettres inédites à M.M. Rey (1763–1771) avec Le Noble, de Madame de Charrière," *Studies on Voltaire and the Eighteenth Century,* 45 (1966), 5–204. Quotation p. 147.

143. See W. D. Robson-Scott, *German Travellers in England, 1400–1800,* Modern Language Studies (Oxford, 1953), and Rosamond Bayne-Powell, *Travellers in Eighteenth-Century England* (London, 1951).

144. See Carl Graf v. Klinckowstroem, "Zacharias Konrad von Uffenbachs Erfahrungen mit Buchhändlern," *Börsenblatt für den deutschen Buchhandel,* Frankfurter Ausgabe, 14 (1958), 1109–11.

145. *Merkwürdige Reisen* (note 134), p. 443.

146. Ibid., p. 442.

147. Erich Hintzsche, ed., *Albrecht Hallers Tagebücher seiner Reisen nach Deutschland, Holland und England, 1723–1727,* Berner Beiträge zur Geschichte der Medizin und der Naturwissenschaften, N.S. 4 (Bern, 1971), p. 93. The bookseller "Jung," whom Haller visited, was probably John Young.

148. See Imendörffer, *Hamann* (note 22), pp. 49–51, 126, 163.

149. See Hecht, *Briefe* (note 120), pp. 36, 38, 55, 65–67.

150. Lowth's letters to Michaelis of 28 May 1770 and 29 August 1770 are printed in Hans Hecht, *T. Percy,* pp. 84–86. It also appears from one of the letters that Mr. Velthusen, German chaplain to the king, occasionally acted as intermediary.

151. See Walter Wadepuhl, "Hüttner, a New Source for Anglo-German Relations," *Germanic Review,* 14 (1939), 23–27.

152. This and the following paragraph is mainly based on Hartmann and Füchsel, eds., *Geschichte der Göttinger Universitäts-Bibliothek* (note 82), pp. 31 f., 69, 71, 77.

153. See Johann Stephan Pütter, *Versuch einer academischen Gelehrten-Geschichte von der Georg-Augustus-Universität zu Göttingen* (Göttingen, 1765), I, 213.

154. Hartmann and Füchsel, *Geschichte,* p. 31. The reference to *Bijdragen tot de Geschiedenis van den Nederlandschen Boekhandel,* VI, 538, does not lead to further information.

155. On Osborne see H. R. Plomer, *A Dictionary of the Printers and Booksellers* . . . *from 1726 to 1775* (Oxford, 1932), 185 f. As early as 1744, Göttingen secured certain items from the sale of the Harley Library, which Osborne bought in 1742.

156. On Ridley see Plomer, *Dictionary*, p. 213. The orders placed by the library with Ridley can well support Plomer's supposition that "his shop must have been well known, and he probably did a high-class business."

157. See *Dictionary of National Biography.*

158. From 1763 onward the lists comprise more than 500 pages and are preserved in the Universitätsarchiv (A 8 d1 and A 9a and 9b). An early list like that of 7 June 1763 (A 9a, fol. 1r and v) comprises about forty items. The bibliographical sources for these lists remain to be established.

159. Quoted from Wilhelm Ruprecht, "Göttinger Gelehrtenbuchhandlungen: Pläne aus der Frühzeit der Georg August-Universität," *Archiv für Geschichte des Deutschen Buchhandels*, 21 (1930), 212–13.

160. See Albrecht Kirchhoff, "Der ausländische Buchhandel in Leipzig im 18. Jahrhundert," *Archiv für Geschichte des Deutschen Buchhandels*, 14 (1891), 155–82, and Kirchhoff, "Der Zeitpunkt des Wegbleibens der Holländer von der Leipziger Messe," ibid., 17 (1894), 363–65. The first article contains a survey of the Leipzig operations of Arkstée en Merkus, but does not give specific information about English books.

161. Pütter, *Nachdruck* (note 112), p. 141.

162. C. H. Timperley, *Dictionary of Printers and Printing* (London, 1839), p. 744.

163. *Archiv*, 17 (1894), 365.

164. See *Catalogus Universalis*, Easter Fair 1752, p. 269; Autumn Fair 1750, p. 104; Easter Fair 1752, p. 274; and Easter Fair 1753, p. 389.

165. Wendler appears to have been in business from 1744 to 1766, and was at first director of the Weidmann'sche Buchhandlung. See Albrecht Kirchoff, "Lesefrüchte aus den Acten des städtischen Archivs zu Leipzig: VI. Miscellen zum Buchhandels-Recht und -Brauch," *Archiv für Geschichte des Deutschen Buchhandels*, 15 (1892), 234 ff.

166. *Catalogus Universalis*, Autumn Fair 1755, p. 639.

167. See below, p. 151.

168. See 2 (1757), 436, 547–48, 655–56. There are no advertisements in vol. 3. Vols. 4, 5 and 6 contain sections headed "Neue Bücher."

169. Caspar Fritsch bought the firm of Wendler in 1766. See the notice in the Catalogue of the Easter Fair of 1766, p. 734.

170. Besides Fritsch, Gleditsch, Weidmann, and to a lesser extent Martini seem to have transacted foreign business on a larger scale. See Kirchhoff, "Der ausländische Buchhandel," p. 157.

171. See note 17.

172. *Catalogue des livres françois, anglois, italiens qui se trouvent en vente, à un prix raisonable, chez Jean-Thom. Nob. de Trattnern* . . . (Vienna, 1787). The English section, though small, comprises pp. 271–99. Supplements appeared in 1787 and 1791.

173. See vol. 1 (1780) nos. 2, 3, 4, and 5, and vol. 3 (1782–1783), nos. 2 and 3.

174. Mostly medical books. A number of titles have an Edinburgh imprint (e.g., a Hawkesworth edition of Swift). That there are also Foulis editions seems to suggest that good printing was appreciated.

175. For some time, apparently in the late 1760's and early 1770's, Dieterich tried to import English, French, and Italian books for the university library. After a short interval the library again ordered books directly from London. See Hartmann-Füchsel, *Geschichte* (note 82), p. 71.

176. Note in *Frankfurter Gelehrte Anzeigen*, no. 94 (1773), 779 f. Among the subscribers were some members of the German nobility; see *Orlando Furioso* (Birmingham, 1773), IV, sig. 2*v–2**r.

177. The "Book Subscription Lists Project" is carried out at the University of Newcastle by P. J. Wallis.

178. *Intelligenzblatt der Allgemeinen Literatur-Zeitung,* no. 110 (30 September 1795), 884-85.

179. Arthur Georgi, *Die Entwicklung des Berliner Buchhandels bis zur Gründung des Börsenvereins der deutschen Buchhändler 1825* (Berlin, 1926), pp. 76–79. See also Ernst Kundt, *Lessing und der Buchhandel* (Heidelberg, 1907), p. 22.

180. 4 (1788), 31.

181. Ibid., 17 March 1788, 383.

182. The only reference to Remnant as a bookseller is in Hermann Colshorn, "Hamburgs Buchhandel im 18. Jahrhundert," *Börsenblatt für den deutschen Buchhandel,* Frankfurter Ausgabe, 30 (1974), A 82. In "Vom Kunsthandel in Hamburg," ibid., 24 (1968), 3198–99, Colshorn drew attention to Remnant as an occasional publisher.

183. See J. M. Lappenberg, *Zur Geschichte der Buchdruckerkunst in Hamburg am 24. Juni 1840* (Hamburg, 1840), p. lv; Christi. Ludew. v. Griesheim, *Anmerk. u. Zugaben über den Tractat: die Stadt Hamburg . . .* (Hamburg, 1759), p. 308; and Griesheim, *Verbesserte und vermehrte Auflage des Tractats: die Stadt Hamburg . . .* (Hamburg, 1760), p. 263.

184. One of Remnant's catalogues (no. 9, pp. 43 f.) contains a lengthy note to the public, in which Remnant gives an account of his business activities.

185. See *A Catalogue of Foreign Books, Ancient and Modern, Containing Many scarce and valuable Articles* (London, 1800), p. [3].

186. William Remnant acted as agent for James Remnant when James published his *Universal European Dictionary of Merchandise;* see *Intelligenzblatt der Allgemeinen Literatur-Zeitung,* no. 90 (13 July 1796), 757–58.

187. *A monthly Catalogue of all the new Books, new Editions, Translations and Maps, published in the English Dominions . . . : To be had at the Prices affixed, of the Publisher, William Remnant, English Library, Hamburgh.* The first was published for July 1788, and announced in *The British Mercury,* on 21 July 1788 (p. 127). Thereupon the editor discontinued his own lists of new books. The catalogues appear to be preserved only in a few copies of the periodical. I have seen nos. i, iii, iv, and ix (March 1789) to xxiv (November and December 1790). The journal was discontinued in July 1791.

188. See Catalogues XIV and XVIII. In the latter Remnant announced a special catalogue of these books. Catalogue XVI contains classical authors in stock. Among these were "many of Baskerville's and Foulis's *Classics,* in 8.vo and 12.mo. mostly in new and very elegant bindings, at various prices."

189. These were very popular at the time. In *Magazin des Buch-und Kunst-Handels,* 1 (1780), insert, there is a fairly long "Verzeichnis von engländischen Kupferstichen, welche in der Bremerschen Kunsthandlung zu Braunschweig zu haben sind."

190. Catalogue XVI, item 42.

191. See Colshorn (note 182).

192. *Notebooks,* ed. Kathleen Coburn (London, 1957), I, entry 340. See also his *Collected Letters,* ed. Earl Leslie Griggs (Oxford, 1956), I, 417, 432, 446. There is an interesting remark in the first letter: "Johnson, the Bookseller, without any poems sold to him; but purely out of affection conceived for me, & as part of any thing I *might* do for him, gave me an order on Remnant at Hamburgh for 30 pound."

193. *Journals of Dorothy Wordsworth,* ed. E. de Selincourt (London, 1952), I, 31. See also *The Letters of William and Dorothy Wordsworth,* ed. Ernest de Selincourt and Chester L. Shaver (Oxford, 1967), I, 246, 248.

194. See Kirchner, *Bibliographie der Zeitschriften des deutschen Sprachgebietes* (note 40), p. 1, no. 1. Published in Leipzig from 1682 to 1731 and continued as *Nova Acta Eruditorum* from 1732 to 1782.

195. The standard history of the German journals is Joachim Kirchner, *Das*

deutsche Zeitschriftenwesen: Seine Geschichte und seine Probleme: Teil I: Von den Anfängen bis zum Zeitalter der Romantik, 2nd ed. (Wiesbaden, 1958).

196. Joachim Kirchner, "Zur Entstehungs- und Redaktionsgeschichte der *Acta Eruditorum,*" in *Ausgewählte Aufsätze* (note 99), pp. 153–72.

197. Fifty copies were sent to London. See Kirchner, p. 159.

198. Locke: 1691, 501–5; Bacon: 1694, 400; Toland: 1700, 371–79; Dryden: 1700, 321–25.

199. Up to 1700 the references are listed in Waterhouse, *Literary Relations* (note 36), pp. 125–27.

200. See *Unterricht von der teutschen Sprache und Poesie, deren Ursprung, Fortgang und Lehrsätzen* (Lübeck, 1700), p. 229.

201. With reference to Dryden the reviewer writes: "Certe inter Anglos hactenus præcipue eminuit, seu cetera spectes poëmatum genera, seu, quod difficillimum est, Tragœdiam, in qua neque Gallorum Cornelio cessit, neque Anglorum Shakespario, atque hoc tanto præstantior fuit, quanto magis litteras calluit" (1700, p. 322). Attention to this passage was first drawn by Waterhouse (p. 127).

202. See Kirchner, *Bibliographie* (note 194), p. 1, no. 4. The full title of volume I is: *Freymüthige Lustige und Ernsthaffte jedoch Vernunfft- und Gesetz-Mässige Gedancken oder Monats-Gespräche, über allerhand, fürnehmlich aber Neue Bücher.*

203. The history of German book reviewing is covered by Anni Carlsson, *Die deutsche Buchkritik von der Reformation bis zur Gegenwart* (Bern and Munich, 1969). See also Thomas Woitkewitsch, "Thomasius' 'Monatsgespräche': Eine Charakteristik," *Archiv für Geschichte des Buchwesens,* 10 (1970), 655–78.

204. See the various references in the indexes to vols. 1 and 2. In the series "Athenäum Reprints" a facsimile was published in 1972.

205. Abercromby: July 1689, pp. 523–80; Knox: July 1689, 580–98. Thomasius reviewed of Abercromby the Amsterdam edition of 1689 (not in Wing) and of Knox a German translation of 1689 (unrecorded in Waterhouse, *Literary Relations*).

206. See Kirchner, *Bibliographie,* p. 3, no. 41. Under this title the journal appeared until 1784. In 1785 the title was changed.

207. The editor, Johann Gottlieb Krause, made extensive use of the correspondence of Otto Mencke, the editor of *Acta Eruditorum.*

208. See Joachim Kirchner, *Das deutsche Zeitschriftenwesen,* p. 29.

209. *Nova litteraria . . . in supplementum actorum eruditorum divulgata.* Reference: Kirchner, *Bibliographie der Zeitschriften,* p. 4, no. 53.

210. See 1715, pp. ix and 430.

211. Kirchner, *Das deutsche Zeitschriftenwesen,* p. 22.

212. *Neue Zeitungen aus der gelehrten Welt* (Zurich, 1725; Kirchner, *Bibliographie,* p. 5, no. 74); *Niedersächsische neue Zeitungen von gelehrten Sachen* (Hamburg, 1729–1730; Kirchner, p. 6, no. 85); *Franckfurtische gelehrte Zeitungen* (Frankfurt, 1736–1771; Kirchner, p. 7, no. 109).

213. See Kirchner, *Bibliographie,* p. 8, no. 125.

214. See Kirchner, *Das deutsche Zeitschriftenwesen,* pp. 40, 63.

215. See Kirchner, *Bibliographie,* pp. 2–3, no. 27. For Jöcher's editorship of both journals, not noted by Kirchner, see Johann Christoph Adelung, *Fortsetzung und Ergänzungen zu Christian Gottlieb Jöchers allgemeinem Gelehrten-Lexicon* (Leipzig, 1787), II, 2292–93.

216. Leipzig, 1750–1751.

217. *Zuverläßige Nachrichten,* 1 (1740), sig. A₄ᵥ.

218. See Kirchner, *Bibliographie,* p. 246, no. 4395.

219. Vol. 1 (1745), 8.

220. Reviews tended to become longer, and fewer and fewer books were reviewed. Also, the reviews were delayed.

221. See Kirchner, *Bibliographie.*

222. An equivalent of the Morgan-Hohlfeld checklist of *German Literature in*

British Magazines, 1750–1860 (Madison, 1949) is one of the foremost bibliographical desiderata in the field.

223. Berlin und Stettin, 1765–1796 (Kiel, 1770 ff.). Continued as *Neue allgemeine deutsche Bibliothek,* 1793–1806. See Kirchner, *Bibliographie der Zeitschriften,* p. 16, no. 248, and p. 27, no. 444.

224. This paragraph is largely based on Günther Ost, *Friedrich Nicolais Allgemeine Deutsche Bibliothek,* Germanische Studien, 63 (Berlin, 1928; rpt. Nendeln, Liechtenstein, 1967). For details see pp. 9, 6, 24, 25. Second quotation from "Vorbericht," 1 (1765), i.

225. See Kirchner, *Bibliographie,* p. 18, no. 291.

226. Kirchner, *Bibliographie,* p. 24, no. 388, and *Allgemeine Literatur-Zeitung,* 3 January 1785, pp. 2 ff.

227. The series began in *Intelligenzblatt,* no. 40 (30 March 1796), 321.

228. See Kirchner, *Bibliographie,* p. 12, no. 187, and p. 29, no. 471.

229. See ibid., p. 8, no. 122. In 1802 the title was changed to its present form, *Göttingische Gelehrte Anzeigen.*

230. For the early history of the journal see Gustav Roethe, "Göttingische Zeitungen von gelehrten Sachen," in *Festschrift zur Feier des hundertfünfzigjährigen Bestehens der Königlichen Gesellschaft der Wissenschaften zu Göttingen: Beiträge zur Gelehrtengeschichte Göttingens* (Berlin, 1901), pp. 567–688.

231. Roethe, p. 582.

232. See Friedrich Leo, "Heyne," in *Festschrift,* pp. 153 ff., and Hartmann-Füchsel, *Geschichte* (note 82), p. 88. Much of the manuscript material connected with the editing of the *Anzeigen* is still extant. See *Verzeichniss der Handschriften im Preussischen Staate: I. Hannover: Die Handschriften in Göttingen,* III (Berlin, 1894), pp. 512–13.

233. See Karl S. Guthke, *Haller und die Literatur,* Arbeiten aus der Niedersächsischen Staats- und Universitätsbibliothek Göttingen, 4 (Göttingen, 1962). The following details come from this book.

234. See 1753, i, pp. 294–96; 540–44 and ii, 906–12; 687–88; ii, 860–2; ii, 1082–90; ii, 1147–52; ii, 947–50.

235. Price, *Humaniora,* lists selected reviews with individual titles. A copy with the names of the reviewers is preserved in the library of the University of Göttingen. For the period from 1783 to 1822 a general index is available: *Allgemeines Register . . . : Verfertigt von Johann Melchoir Hartmann . . . und beendigt von Johann David Ludwig Hess* (Göttingen, 1829), 8 vols. There is only one survey, and that insufficient, of the reviewing activities and the contents of the reviews: Heinrich Albert Oppermann, *Die Göttinger gelehrten Anzeigen während einer hundertjährigen Wirksamkeit für Philosophie, schöne Literatur, Politik und Geschichte* (Hanover, 1844).

236. See Kirchner, *Bibliographie,* p. 13, no. 208. Of vol. 7 only part I was published.

237. See above, pp. 141–42.

238. See *Leipziger Gelehrten- und Künstleralmanach auf das Jahr 1786* (Leipzig, n.d.), p. 35.

239. Sometimes the reviews include extensive translations. Thus the review of Johnson's *Dictionary* (vol. 3, part ii) is little more than a translation (hitherto unrecorded) of Johnson's preface.

240. Those which appeared were of Restoration and early eighteenth-century authors.

241. See 4 (1759), 219.

242. Leipzig, 1757–1767. Continued as *Neue Bibliothek der schönen Wissenschaften und der freyen Künste* (Leipzig, 1765–1806). See Kirchner, *Bibliographie,* pp. 247–48, no. 4430 and p. 248, no. 4446.

243. For Weiße's editorship see Richard Francis Wilkie, Jr., "Christian Felix Weiße

and His Relation to French and English Literature" (diss. University of California, 1953), pp. 479–565.

244. In Appendix II Wilkie has given "The Sources for the Reviews of English Books in the *Bibliothek der schönen Wissenschaften und der freyen Künste* and the *Neue Bibliothek* . . . , under Weiße's Editorship (1759–84)."

245. They were first pointed out by Charles Paul Giessing, "The Plagiarized Book Reviews of C. F. Weisse in the *Bibliothek der Schönen Wissenschaften*," *Modern Philology*, 16 (1918–1919), 21–32. See also Richard F. Wilkie, "Weisse's Borrowings for the *Bibliothek der schönen Wissenschaften*," *Modern Philology*, 53 (1955–1956), 1–7.

246. See Kirchner, *Bibliographie*, p. 7, no. 109, and p. 18, no. 288.

247. Rpt. in *Deutsche Litteraturdenkmale des 18. Jahrhunderts*, 7 (Heilbronn, 1882, rpt. Nendeln/Liechtenstein, 1968).

248. Quoted from: "Briefe von Boie, Herder, Höpfner, Glein, J. G. Jacobi und Anderen aus den Jahren 1769–1775," *Weimarisches Jahrbuch für deutsche Sprache, Litteratur und Kunst*, 6 (1857), 79 (translation).

249. The first study of the reviews was Otto P. Trieloff, *Die Entstehung der Rezensionen in den Frankfurter Gelehrten-Anzeigen vom Jahre 1772*, Münstersche Beiträge zur neueren Literaturgeschichte, 7 (Münster, 1908). His conclusions were somewhat modified by Hermann Bräuning, *Studien zu den Frankfurter Gelehrten Anzeigen vom Jahre 1772* (Darmstadt, 1911). Both have been superseded by the meticulous work of Hermann Bräuning-Oktavio, *Herausgeber und Mitarbeiter der Frankfurter Gelehrten Anzeigen 1772*, Freies Deutsches Hochstift: Reihe der Schriften, 20 (Tübingen, 1966). I have not seen William F. Roertgen, "The 'Frankfurter Gelehrte Anzeigen' in Relation to the Literature of the Time (1772–1790)" (diss. University of California, 1947).

250. See Kirchner, *Bibliographie*, p. 249, no. 4463.

251. *Allgemeine deutsche Bibliothek*, 22 (1774), 614. See also v.D., "Ueber die Diebstähle der Gelehrten," *Neues Hannöverisches Magazin*, no. 14 (1800), 205–20.

252. See Kirchner, *Bibliographie*, p. 19, no. 310.

253. See ibid., p. 252, no. 4504. On Eschenburg see Fritz Meyen, *Johann Joachim Eschenburg, 1743–1820, Professor am Collegium Carolinum zu Braunschweig: Kurzer Abriß seines Lebens und Schaffens nebst Bibliographie*, Braunschweiger Werkstücke: Veröffentlichungen aus Archiv, Bibliothek und Museum der Stadt, 20 (Braunschweig, 1957).

254. This is the division of no. 1. There are slight variations in later issues.

255. See *Annalen der Brittischen Literatur*, 1781, sig. 3_{r-v}.

256. See Kirchner, *Bibliographie*, p. 252, no. 4515.

257. Eschenburg began listing new translations in the *Brittisches Museum*, 3 (1778).

258. Not in Kirchner. 1789–1800, 20 vols., vol. 1 appeared in a "new edition" in 1790.

259. *England und Italien* (Leipzig, 1785), 2 vols. in 3 parts. The work was very popular; translations into several languages appeared.

260. Forster's contributions appeared in vol. 1 (new ed., 1790), 274–325, in vol. 3 (1790), 41–95, in vol. 5 (1791), 184–314, in vol. 7 (1793), 65–147; part II of this last contribution was only begun by Forster in vol. 9 (1794), 208–396. See also Horst Fiedler, *Georg-Forster-Bibliographie, 1767 bis 1970* (Berlin, 1971), p. 43, no. 141; p. 48, no. 180; p. 57, no. 212; p. 70, no. 265; p. 73, no. 284.

261. Apart from completing Forster's last contribution Eschenburg contributed surveys to vol. 11 (1795), 171–304; vol. 13 (1796), 272–354; vol. 16 (1798), 1–106; and vol. 19 (1799), 19–134. See Fritz Meyen, *Johann Joachim Eschenburg, 1743–1820*, p. 93, no. 227; p. 94, no. 240; p. 96, nos. 252 and 260; p. 98, no. 270.

262. Before Archenholz supplied the German reader with panoramic annual

surveys, he had provided brief weekly announcements of new books in the *British Mercury, or Annals of History, Politics, Manners, Literature, Arts, etc. of the British Empire.*

263. *Ideal einer allgemeinen Weltstatistik* (Göttingen, 1773).

264. See, among other works, *Allgemeines Repertorium der Literatur für die Jahre 1785 (bis 1800)* (Jena, 1785–1800), 8 vols.

265. Lübeck and Frankfurt, 1700, pp. 206–31.

266. These figures are given by Georg Leyh in his extensive survey of libraries in Milkau's *Handbuch der Bibliothekswissenschaft,* 2d ed., ed. Georg Leyh (Wiesbaden, 1957), III, part ii, pp. 15 f. A shorter survey is found in Richard Mummendey, *Von Büchern und Bibliotheken,* Belehrende Schriftenreihe der Buchgemeinde Bonn, 23 (Bonn, 1950), chap. 2.

267. This paragraph is based on Hildegard Neumann, "Der Bücherbesitz der Tübinger Bürger von 1750–1850: Ein Beitrag zur Bildungsgeschichte des Kleinbürgertums . . . (diss. Tübingen, 1955). Details on pp. 39, 53, 60, 67 ff., 92.

268. This paragraph is based on Walter Wittmann, *Beruf und Buch im 18. Jahrhundert: Ein Beitrag zur Erfassung und Gliederung der Leserlschaft im 18. Jahrhundert, insbesondere unter Berücksichtigung des Einflusses auf die Buchproduktion, unter Zugrundelegung der Nachlaßinventare des Frankfurter Stadtarchivs für die Jahre 1695–1705, 1746–1755 und 1795–1805* (diss. Frankfurt, 1934; Bochum-Langendreer, 1934). Details on pp. 53–56, 79–81, 91–93.

269. Wittmann gives only excerpts from the inventories and since he is not primarily concerned with foreign books, some information may have been omitted.

270. Some of these have been searched for novels by Marianne Spiegel, *Der Roman und sein Publikum im früheren 18. Jahrhundert, 1700–1767,* Abhandlungen zur Kunst-, Musik- und Literaturwissenschaft, 41 (Bonn, 1967).

271. Two examples are the Bibliothek Fürstenberg now incorporated in the library of the University of Münster and the library of the Markgräfin Friederike Sophie Wilhelmina von Bayreuth now incorporated in the library of the University of Erlangen.

272. See Hermann Bräuning-Oktavio, "Die Bibliothek der Großen Landgräfin Caroline von Hessen," *Archiv für Geschichte des Buchwesens,* 6 (1966), 681–876; "Zwei Privatbibliotheken des 18. Jahrhunderts: 1. Die Bibliothek der Herzogin Caroline von Pfalz-Zweibrücken-Birkenfeld, Mutter der 'Großen Landgräfin,' (gestorben 1774), 2. Die Bibliothek des Freiherrn Louis von Schrautenbach (gestorben 1783)," ibid., 10 (1970), 685–836; and "Der Katalog der Bibliothek des Landgrafen Ludwig IX. von Hessen-Darmstadt (1790)," ibid., 11 (1971), 1673–1728.

273. This and the next paragraph are based on Bräuning-Oktavio, "Zwei Privatbibliotheken," cols. 685–776.

274. See Bogdan Krieger, *Friedrich der Große und seine Bücher* (Berlin-Leipzig, 1914), p. 170. The main authors are Addison and Steele (*The Guardian*), Mandeville, Milton, Pope, Shaftesbury, Shakespeare, and Swift. There are other English authors in such sections as "Philosophie," "Memoiren, Biographien, Briefe," and "Länder- und Völkerkunde."

275. This paragraph is based on Bräuning-Oktavio, "Zwei Privatbibliotheken," cols. 777–836.

276. Schrautenbach owned Johnson's *Dictionary* (ed. 1778) and Bullokar's *English Expositor* (ed. 1707).

277. See, for instance, Karl-Heinz Haar, "Die Bibliothek des Heidelberger Historikers Friedrich Christoph Schlosser (1776–1861): Entstehung, Inhalt und Geschichte einer Gelehrtenbibliothek," *Bibliothek und Wissenschaft,* 8 (1972), 1–92. This library should be of special interest to eighteenth-century scholars, for Schlosser is the author of *Geschichte des achtzehnten Jahrhunderts in gedrängter Übersicht, mit steter*

Beziehung auf die völlige Veränderung der Denk- und Regierungsweise am Ende desselben (Heidelberg, 1823). An English translation, based on the later extension of the work, appeared in 1843–1852.

278. "Ueber Privatbibliotheken und ihre Besitzer, zwischen den Jahren 1750 und 1760," *Historisch-litterarisch-bibliographisches Magazin*, 1 (1788), 6–27; 2 (1790), 1–22; 4 (1791), 18–61. Mylius: 1, p. 24; Overbek: 2, pp. 13 f.

279. G. C. Pisanski, *Entwurf einer preußischen Literärgeschichte* (Königsberg, 1886), pp. 512, 515.

280. Ludwig von Baczko, *Versuch einer Geschichte und Beschreibung Königsbergs*, 2d ed. (Königsberg, 1804), pp. 352–54.

281. Lawrence Marsden Price, "English Theological Works in Pastor Lessing's Library," *Journal of English and Germanic Philology*, 53 (1954), 76–80.

282. Gustav Klemm, *Zur Geschichte der Sammlungen für Wissenschaft und Kunst in Deutschland* (Zerbst, 1837) has (pp. 131–35) a "Verzeichniß einiger der vorzüglichsten Privatbibliotheken seit 1700 . . . , sofern die Cataloge derselben gedruckt worden, oder sofern sie in andern Werken beschrieben werden." Lists can also be found in *Katalog der Bibliothek des Börsenvereins der Deutschen Buchhändler* (Leipzig, 1885–1902), I, 639 f. and II, 1249 ff. The important contemporary accounts of eighteenth-century libraries are Friedrich Karl Gottlob Hirsching, *Versuch einer Beschreibung sehenswürdiger Bibliotheken Teutschlands, nach alphabetischer Ordnung der Städte* (Erlangen, 1786–1791; rpt. Hildesheim, 1971), 4 vols., and Johann Georg Meusel, *Teutsches Künstlerlexikon oder Verzeichniss der jetztlebenden Teutschen Künstler: Nebst einem Verzeichniss sehenswürdiger Bibliotheken, Kunst- Münz- und Naturalienkabinete in Teutschland und in der Schweitz*, 2d ed. (Lemgo, 1808–1814), 3 vols. See also Robert Teichl, "Ein europäischer Bibliothekenführer um das Jahr 1780: Die Handschrift des Pfarrverwalters von Maria-Taferl, Adalbert Blumenschein," in *Festschrift Georg Leyh . . .* (Leipzig, 1937), pp. 172–79. For individual libraries the extensive notes in G. A. E. Bogeng, *Die großen Bibliophilen: Geschichte der Büchersammler und ihrer Sammlungen* (Leipzig, 1922), III, 121, are helpful.

283. On Uffenbach see Josef Becker, "Die Bibliothek des Zacharias Konrad von Uffenbach," *Festschrift Georg Leyh*, pp. 129–48; a shorter account is found in Bogeng, *Die großen Bibliophilen*, I, 256–58; see also Bogeng, "Über Zacharias Conrad von Uffenbachs Erfahrungen und Erlebnisse bei der Benutzung deutscher, englischer, holländischer öffentlicher Bibliotheken," in *Beiträge zum Bibliotheks- und Buchwesen: Paul Schwenke zum 20. März 1913 gewidmet* (Berlin, 1913), pp. 30–46.

284. See above, p. 139.

285. *Bibliotheca Uffenbachiana Universalis sive Catalogus librorum tam typis quam manu exaratorum, quos summo studio hactenus collegit Zach. Conradus ab Uffenbach, nunc vero ob rationes in proloquio deductas, venales prostant* (Frankfurt, 1729–1731), 4 vols. Title pages vary. Bogeng (III, 122) lists an addition to this catalogue: *Designation derjenigen Bücher . . .* (Frankfurt, c. 1735).

286. On Graf Bünau and his library see Heydenreich, "Die Bibliothek des Grafen von Bünau in Nöthnitz," *Neuer Anzeiger für Bibliographie und Bibliothekswissenschaft* (1877), 90–96, 124–30, and Werner Schultze, *Heinrich von Bünau: Ein kursächsischer Staatsmann, Gelehrter und Mäcen* (diss. Leipzig, 1933; Leipzig, 1933), particularly chap. 3.

287. *Catalogvs Bibliothecae Bvnavianae* (Leipzig, 1750–1756), 7 vols. Vols. I and III are in three parts each. The catalogue was not completed.

288. The interesting "Conspectvs Tomi I" is found in vol. I, part i, sig. $1C_{1r}$–$1G_{3v}$.

289. See the comments by Friedrich Adolf Ebert, *Geschichte und Beschreibung der Königlichen öffentlichen Bibliothek zu Dresden* (Leipzig, 1822), pp. 76 f. (Graf Bünau's library was later acquired by the Königliche Bibliothek.)

290. Alfred Nicolovius, *Johann Georg Schlosser's Leben und literarisches Wirken* (Bonn, 1844), contains a "Verzeichniß von J. G. Schlosser's schriftstellerischen

Arbeiten" (pp. 278–83). See also Hermann Bräuning-Oktavio, "Neues zur Biographie Johann Georg Schlossers," *Jahrbuch des Freien Deutschen Hochstifts,* (1963), 19–99; I have not been able to see Ingegrete Kreienbrink, "Johann Georg Schlosser und die geistigen Strömungen des 18. Jahrhunderts" (diss. Greifswald, 1948).

291. See *Allgemeine deutsche Biographie,* XXXI, 543 f.

292. See ibid., 541 f.

293. Preserved in the library of the Bischöfliches Priesterseminar, Mainz. The original catalogue is contained in seventy-seven boxes; from it the "Catalogus Bibliothecae Schlosserianae" (no shelfmark) was copied in the 1860's (2 vols. A-Iz in 167 fols. and J-Z in 195 fols.). Of the more than 20,000 titles some are preserved in the library, and a number of eighteenth-century books have the bookplate of Hieronymus Peter Schlosser. I am grateful to the Bischöfliches Priesterseminar for allowing me to use the catalogues.

294. Interestingly, many early nineteenth-century English authors were represented in this library in Paris reprints, mostly of collected works.

295. See above, pp. 139–40.

296. *Biga Bibliothecarum: Altera, Viri, Dum Viveret, Summe reverendi, Doctissimi, Excellentissimi Johann. Gotthelf. Lindneri, S. S. Theol. Doct. et Poeseos . . . Altera Amici Superstitis Qui Se Etiam Sine Illis Bene Victurum Sperat Praeconi Subiicienda Die Sept. MDCCLXXVI: In Aedibus Defuncti* (Regiomonti, Typis Driestianis). Quoted from Imendörffer (note 22), p. 62.

297. Imendörffer, *Johann Georg Hamann und seine Bücherei* (note 22).

298. On Eschenburg see note 253.

299. Niedersächsisches Staats-Archiv, Wolfenbüttel, shelfmark VI, 16, 61: "Verzeichniß der Büchersammlung des Professors J. J. Eschenburg in Braunschweig, von der Hand des Besitzers, abweichend von dem für die Auktion vom 7. Oktober ff. 1822. gedruckten Verzeichnisse."

300. *Verzeichniß derjenigen Bücher aus dem Nachlasse weil. Herrn Geheime-Justizraths und Professors Dr. Joh. Joachim Eschenburg, welche . . . auktionsmäßig verkauft werden sollen* (Braunschweig, 1822).

301. *Verzeichniß,* pp. 79–90 and 90–95.

302. *Verzeichniß der Bibliothek des verewigten Herrn Hofraths Wieland . . .* (Weimar, 1814). See also Werner Deetjen, "Wielands Bibliothek," in *Funde und Forschungen: Eine Festgabe für Julius Wahle zum 15. Februar 1921* (Leipzig, 1921), pp. 1–10.

303. *Catalogvs Librorvm et Collectionvm cvivslibet facvltatis ac scientiae qvas svo stvdio distincte ac systematice digestas ac compositas in bibliotheca sva habvit beatvs Michael Richey Prof. pvbl. Hamb.* (Hamburg, 1762), 4 vols. Title pages vary. On Richey see Hans Schröder und C. R. W. Klose, *Lexikon der hamburgischen Schriftsteller bis zur Gegenwart* (Hamburg, 1873), VI, 262–73.

304. This aspect of reading in eighteenth-century Germany has only more recently been investigated. A short general account is Herbert G. Göpfert, "Lesegesellschaften im 18. Jahrhundret," in *Dichtung, Sprache, Gesellschaft: Akten des IV. Internationalen Germanisten-Kongresses 1970 in Princeton,* ed. Victor Lange and Hans-Gert Roloff (Frankfurt, 1971), pp. 323–30. The most extensive general survey is by Marlies Prüsener, "Lesegesellschaften im 18. Jahrhundert: Ein Beitrag zur Lesergeschichte," *Archiv für Geschichte des Buchwesens,* 13 (1972), 370–594. Membership lists and holdings of selected reading societies have been studied by Barney M. Milstein, *Eight Eighteenth Century Reading Societies: A Sociological Contribution to the History of German Literature,* German Studies in America, 11 (Bern and Frankfurt, 1972). See also Irene Jentsch, *Zur Geschichte des Zeitungslesens in Deutschland am Ende des 18. Jahrhunderts* (diss. Leipzig; Leipzig, 1937). My general remarks on the reading societies in the following paragraphs are mainly based on Göpfert and Prüsener.

305. See Prüsener, col. 384. It existed until 1782.

306. See Klaus Gerteis, "Bildung und Revolution: Die deutschen Lesegesellschaften am Ende des 18. Jahrhunderts," *Archiv für Kulturgeschichte*, 53 (1971), 127–39.

307. See Rolf Engelsing, "Der Bürger als Leser: Die Bildung der protestantischen Bevölkerung Deutschlands im 17. und 18. Jahrhundert am Beispiel Bremens," *Archiv für Geschichte des Buchwesens*, 3 (1961), cols. 265 f.

308. See Johann Georg Meusel, *Lexikon der vom Jahr 1750 bis 1800 verstorbenen teutschen Schriftsteller* (Leipzig, 1803; rpt. Hildesheim, 1967), II, 59–66.

309. See Kirchner, *Bibliographie* (note 194), p. 290, no. 5253.

310. See Prüsener, "Lesegesellschaften," col. 390.

311. See Carl Haase, "Der Bildungshorizont der norddeutschen Kleinstadt am Ende des 18. Jahrhunderts: Zwei Bücherverzeichnisse der Lesegesellschaften in Wunstorf aus dem Jahre 1794," in *Festschrift Hermann Aubin zum 80. Geburtstag* (Wiesbaden, 1965), II, 511–25.

312. See Milstein, *Reading Societies*, pp. 51–73, 174–91. Among the members was Johann Peter Hermes, who later donated 22,000 volumes to the municipal library of Trier. This is one of the examples of members of reading societies who seem to have joined out of social and civil responsibility. Hermes' is an interesting eighteenth-century library with many items of English interest. See also Guido Gross, *Trierer Geistesleben unter dem Einfluß von Aufklärung und Romantik (1750–1850)*, Veröffentlichungen der Gesellschaft für nützliche Forschungen zu Trier (Trier, 1956).

313. They have not been identified as such by Milstein.

314. This paragraph is largely based on Prüsener, "Lesegesellschaften," cols. 517–19.

315. See Alois Jesinger, *Wiener Lekturkabinette* (Wien, 1928), pp. 67 ff.

316. Preface printed by Jesinger, pp. 119 ff.

317. See *Journal des Luxus und der Moden* (September, 1795), 425–34.

318. See *Einrichtung des Museums von Arnold und Pinther . . . auf das Jahr 1799;* preserved in Sächsische Landesbibliothek, Dresden (Hist. Saxon. G. 315,90). An account of the *Museum* was given by E. Bernard, "Ueber das Museum in Dresden," *Berlinisches Archiv der Zeit und ihres Geschmacks* (1799), ii, 445–51.

319. See F. G. Leonhardi, *Geschichte und Beschreibung der Kreis- und Handelsstadt Leipzig nebst der umliegenden Gegend* (Leipzig, 1799), pp. 613–14.

320. No. 49, 19 June 1802, p. 678 (translation).

321. No. 98, 8 December 1802, p. 1571.

322. There is no study as yet of the English holdings of this famous library. General studies include O. v. Heinemann, *Die herzogliche Bibliothek zu Wolfenbüttel: Ein Beitrag zur Geschichte deutscher Büchersammlungen*, 2d ed. (Wolfenbüttel, 1894), and Paul Raabe, "Das achte Weltwunder: Über den Ruhm der Herzog August Bibliothek," *Wolfenbütteler Beiträge: Aus den Schätzen der Herzog August Bibliothek*, 1 (1972), 3–25, and *id., Die Herzog August Bibliothek Wolfenbüttel: Bestände—Kataloge-Erschließung* (Wolfenbüttel, 1971), pp. 69–70.

323. Preserved in the archives of the library of the University of Münster (no shelfmark). I am grateful to Ursula Alsleben for excerpting this catalogue.

324. On its history see Johann Joachim Eschenburg, *Entwurf einer Geschichte des Collegii Carolini in Braunschweig* (Berlin and Stettin, 1812).

325. See Fritz Meyen, *Bremer Beiträger am Collegium Carolinum in Braunschweig: K. Chr. Gärtner, J. A. Ebert, F. W. Zachariä, K. A. Schmid*, Braunschweiger Werkstücke: Veröffentlichungen aus Archiv, Bibliothek und Museum der Stadt, 26 (Braunschweig, 1962).

326. Fritz Meyen, "Abt Jerusalem und die Gründung der Bibliothek des Collegium Carolinum zu Braunschweig," *Bibliothek und Wissenschaft: Ein Jahrbuch Heidelberger Bibliothekare*, 5 (1968), 158–73. Quotation, p. 164.

327. Apart from the general history of the university library there is no study of

the English collection. A few interesting points are made by J. Periam Danton, *Book Selection and Collections: A Comparison of German and American University Libraries* (New York and London, 1966). See also Bernhard Fabian, "Göttingen als Forschungs-bibliothek im achtzehnten Jahrhundert: Plädoyer für eine neue Bibliotheksgeschichte" (forthcoming in *Wolfenbütteler Forschungen*). Göttingen, though of paramount importance, is, of course, not the only university library that deserves attention; see Hugo Kunoff, "The Enlightenment and German University Libraries: Leipzig, Jena, Halle, and Göttingen between 1750 and 1813" (diss. Indiana University, 1972).

328. This is a general history of literature. A new edition appeared in Göttingen in 1812. The third volume has a special title page: *Litterärgeschichte der drey letzten Jahrhunderte*.

329. The work has an English and a German title page. The German version (*Das Gelehrte England oder Lexikon der jetztlebenden Schriftsteller*) indicates that it was conceived as a counterpiece to Hamberger-Meusel, *Das gelehrte Teutschland.* Johann Samuel Ersch in turn took Reuss as his model for *La France littéraire* or *Das gelehrte Frankreich.* Reuss also relied on his own great library. Its manuscript catalogue is preserved in the library of the University of Tübingen (MS. Mh 437). Since it is mainly a bibliographer's library I have not commented on it, despite its English interest.

330. Vol. I, sig.° 4ᵣ (translation).

331. Many studies that are here appropriate will be found in the bibliography appended to Price, *Die Aufnahme* (note 1).

332. Even more recent work is not quite satisfactory in this respect. An example is Shubael Treadwell Beasley, Jr., "Christian Friedrich von Blankenburg's (1744–1796) Relation to the English Language and Literature: A Contribution to the Reception of English Literature in Germany in the 18th Century" (diss. Cornell University, 1948).

333. See the chart in J. L. Ewald, *Über Volksaufklärung: Ihre Gränzen und Vortheile* (Berlin, 1790), p. 99. Prussia ranks third after England and France.

334. For brief surveys of the development of literacy see Carlo M. Cipolla, *Literacy and Development in the West* (Harmondsworth, 1969); *Lesen—Ein Handbuch: Lesestoff, Leser und Leseverhalten, Lesewirkungen, Leseerziehung, Lesekultur*, ed. Alfred Clemens Baumgärtner (Hamburg, 1973), chap. 2; and Rolf Engelsing, *Analphabetentum und Lektüre: Zur Sozialgeschichte des Lesens in Deutschland zwischen feudaler und industrieller Gesellschaft* (Stuttgart, 1973), a well-documented study.

335. See Rudolf Schenda, *Volk ohne Buch: Studien zur Sozialgeschichte der populären Lesestoffe, 1770–1910*, Studien zur Philosophie und Literatur des neunzehnten Jahrhunderts, 5 (Frankfurt, 1970), pp. 443–44. See also Rolf Engelsing, "Die Perioden der Lesergeschichte in der Neuzeit," in *Zur Sozialgeschichte deutscher Mittel- und Unterschichten*, Kritische Studien zur Geschichtswissenschaft, 4 (Göttingen, 1973), p. 141.

336. See Carl Haase, "Der Bildungshorizont" (note 311), p. 518.

337. See Engelsing, *Analphabetentum*, p. 63.

338. *Wahrheit aus Jean Paul's Leben*, Fünftes Heftlein (Breslau, 1830), p. 345.

339. For various reasons I disregard certain categories of readers. One of them is constituted by the readers of the translations of technical and scientific books.

340. Practically no work has yet been done on the subscription lists in German books. A modest beginning is Claude Miquet, "Les Lecteurs en Allemagne dans le dernier tiers du XVIIIᵉ siècle," *Dix-huitième siècle*, 1 (1969), 311–16.

341. Berlin, 1763–1767.

342. *Tristram Schandis Leben und Meynungen* (Hamburg: Bey Bode, 1774), 9 parts. Not listed in Price, *Literature*, and the *New Cambridge Bibliography of English Literature*, II, 951.

343. See I, sig. a$_{1r}$-b$_{8v}$.

344. For a short account see C. Mettig, *Baltische Städte: Skizzen aus der Geschichte Liv-, Est- und Kurlands*, 2nd ed. (Riga, 1905), pp. 311–24.

345. This is an approximate number. I have included those that from their places of residence appear to have belonged to the landed gentry. I have also counted "Kammerherren," if the title did not appear to be an honorary one.

346. Most of the subscriptions from Göttingen and Leipzig apparently came from students. The majority of the Leipzig students were Livonians.

347. Apart from these subscribers there is also a number from small places and country seats in Courland.

348. Vol. I, new ed. (Hamburg, 1790), ix–xviii. See also above, p. 153.

349. *Selberlebensbeschreibung, Konjektural-Biographie* (ed. Stuttgart, 1971), p. 129 (translation).

350. For accounts of the history of circulating libraries see Matthias Wellnhofer, *Die Anfänge der Leihbibliotheken und Lesegesellschaften in Bayern* [Traunstein, 1949]; Richard Schmidt, *Theorie der Leihbücherei: Ihr Wesen, ihre Geschichte, ihre Gestalt: Vorträge und Aufsätze*, ed. Wilhelm Vosskamp (Dortmund, 1954); and Bernd von Arnim and Friedrich Knilli, *Gewerbliche Leihbüchereien* (Gütersloh, 1966).

351. Titles selected from Carl Heine, *Der Roman in Deutschland von 1774 bis 1778* (Halle, 1892), and Price, *Literature*. On the context in which this kind of novel must be placed, see Eva D. Becker, *Der deutsche Roman um 1780*, Germanistische Abhandlungen, 5 (Stuttgart, 1964); Marion Beaujean, *Der Trivialroman im ausgehenden 18. Jahrhundert*, Abhandlungen zur Kunst-, Musik- und Literaturwissenschaft, 22 (Bonn, 1964); and Beaujean, "Das Lesepublikum der Goethezeit—Die historischen und soziologischen Wurzeln des modernen Unterhaltungsromans," in *Der Leser als Teil des literarischen Lebens . . .* (Bonn, 1971), pp. 5–32.

352. See Prüsener, "Lesegesellschaften" (note 304), col. 519.

353. These terms were suggested by Rolf Engelsing, "Die Perioden der Lesergeschichte der Neuzeit," in *Zur Sozialgeschichte* (note 335), pp. 112–54. This and the following two paragraphs are based on Engelsing's excellent account.

354. For an expression of the contemporary attitude toward the role of periodicals see *Berlinisches Archiv der Zeit und ihres Geschmacks*, 1 (1796), 1.

355. *Der Vernünfftler. Das ist: Ein teutscher Auszug aus den Engeländischen Moral-Schrifften des Tatler und Spectator, vormahls verfertiget; mit etlichen Zugaben versehen und auf Ort und Zeit gerichtet von Joanne Mattheson* (Hamburg, 1721). The first edition of 1713–1714 does not seem to survive. The entry in Price, *Literature*, p. 245, is misleading. See Beekman C. Cannon, *Johann Mattheson: Spectator in Music*, Yale Studies in the History of Music, 1 (New Haven, 1947).

356. The standard work is Wolfgang Martens, *Die Botschaft der Tugend: Die Aufklärung im Spiegel der deutschen Moralischen Wochenschriften* (Stuttgart, 1968). A detailed study of the reception of the genre is Pamela Currie, "Moral Weeklies and the Reading Public in Germany 1711–1750," *Oxford German Studies*, 3 (1968), 69–86.

357. No. 36, 7 September 1724.

358. *Der Patriot* was acutely aware of this aspect, as no. 36 shows.

359. "Er [der Romandichter] soll uns den Menschen zeigen, wie er ihn, nach der eigenthümlichen Einrichtung seines Werks, zu zeigen vermag. Das übrige alles ist Verzierung und Nebenwerk. Die verschiedenen Formen, die der Roman haben kann, müssen alle von einer Materie seyn. . . . Und ich ehre die nackte Menschheit, die, von allem, was ihr Sitten und Stand, und Zufall geben können, entblößte Menschheit so sehr; ich möchte sie so gern in ihr wahres Vorrecht wieder eingesetzt sehen." Ed. Eberhard Lämmert (Stuttgart, 1965), pp. xv f.

360. See Spiegel, *Der Roman* (note 270). Albert Ward, *Book Production, Fiction,*

and the German Reading Public, 1740–1800 (Oxford, 1974) has recently explored this topic more fully.

361. Michaelis' note of description, which does not appear to be preserved otherwise, is quoted from the manuscript in Ruprecht, *Väter und Söhne* (note 69), pp. 48 f. What Ruprecht quotes from the contract with the translator supplements and partly corrects Lawrence Marsden Price, "On the Reception of Richardson in Germany," *Journal of English and Germanic Philology*, 25 (1926), 21 f.

362. Manuscript 5k/2 No. 6, fol. 3, University Archives, Göttingen.

363. *Anthropologie in pragmatischer Hinsicht*, §47.

364. Price, *Humaniora*, pp. 205–6, lists 105 authors of "Travels" and 57 authors of "Voyages, Discoveries, Explorations."

365. See the library lists as published by Milstein, *Reading Societies* (note 304).

366. In 1784 the *Berlinische Monatsschrift* complained: "Fast niemand macht ja itzt in Deutschland eine Lustpartie mehr, einen Spatzierritt, eine Fußpromenade für sich; Nord und Süd muß es erfahren, muß lesen was dem theuren Mann begegnet, und (noch schlimmer!) was ihm dabei eingefallen ist. . . . Kinder und Unmündige, Weiber und Jungfrauen, Unwissende und Unstudierte, Menschen ohne Kopf und Sinn und Kenntniß und Beobachtungsgeist, lassen Reisebeschreibungen drukken" (4, 1784, 321).

367. Rolf Engelsing, "Die Perioden der Lesergeschichte" (note 335), p. 140.

368. Around 1800 many of the classic English authors were apparently obsolete since the "extensive" reader had turned to more current and topical material. Ernst Brandes, a friend of Edmund Burke and then curator of the University of Göttingen, made a conservative comment on the situation: "Sehr viele unserer jungen Leute beiderlei Geschlechts kennen nicht Wielands und Göthens Meisterwerke, . . . aber sie haben alle Musenalmanache der letzten Jahre . . . gelesen. Fieldings und Richardsons Romane sind ihnen ganz fremd. Desto größer ist ihre Belesenheit in zahllosen Ritterromanen, und, wenns hoch kömmt, etwa in Jean Pauls Schriften. . . . Aeltere Männer, die sich mit etwas ernsthafteren Gegenständen beschäftigen wollen, lesen das Heer von Reisebeschreibungen, wie es von Messe zu Messe erscheint, ohne je die vorzüglichsten Werke in dieser Art . . . gelesen zu haben. In der Geschichte wird nicht Hume, nicht Robertson, nicht Gibbon, nicht was wir Deutschen darin von Joh. Müller und Spittler trefliches besitzen, gelesen, sondern die Uebersetzungen der wahren Geschichten der französischen Revolution. . . . Wie viele sind unter uns, die in dem Fache der politischen Oekonomie, worüber doch die meisten schwatzen wollen, Büschens Meisterschriften, den Steuart, den Smith studirt haben?" "Ueber die Leserei der Modebücher und ihre Folgen in einigen Klassen der höhern Stände," *Neues Hannöverisches Magazin*, 9 (1800), cols. 139–40.

369. Letter to Johann Peter Uz, 5 October 1762. Quoted from Martin Sommerfeld, *Friedrich Nicolai und der Sturm und Drang: Ein Beitrag zur Geschichte der deutschen Aufklärung. Mit einem Anhang: Briefe aus Nicolais Nachlass* (Halle, 1921), p. 331.

370. 1775, no. 1, p. 7. About that time Richter, the Altenburg reprinter (see above, p. 131), was planning to reprint a collection of Sterne's works. Details of the subscription process are found in *Frankfurter Gelehrte Anzeigen*, 1774, no. 62, p. 520.

371. See Walther Rumpf, "Das literarische Publikum der sechziger Jahre des 18. Jahrhunderts in Deutschland," *Euphorion*, 28 (1927), 540–64.

372. "An die Freunde der englischen Litteratur und Sprache," *Neue Litteratur und Völkerkunde*, 1 (1787), 344–45 (translation).

373. See Rudolf Stadelmann und Wolfram Fischer, *Die Bildungswelt des deutschen Handwerkers um 1800: Studien zur Soziologie des Kleinbürgers im Zeitalter Goethes* (Berlin, 1955), pp. 158–68.

374. On the history of the teaching of English on the university level see Konrad

Schröder, *Die Entwicklung des Englischunterrichts an den deutschsprachigen Universitäten bis zum Jahre 1850* . . . (Ratingen bei Düsseldorf, 1969).

375. No study has yet been made of the various anthologies and textbooks, etc. that were compiled for the student. Their interest should be considerable.

376. See Wilhelm Ebel, *Catalogus Professorum Gottingensium, 1734–1962* (Göttingen, 1962), p. 104. The principles for the selection of foreigners as teachers of their mother tongue were formulated early by Johann David Michaelis, *Räsonnement über die protestantischen Universitäten in Deutschland* (Frankfurt and Leipzig, 1773, rpt. Aalen, 1973), III, 63 ff.

377. *Lettre sur la littérature allemande: A Son Altesse Royale Madame La Duchesse Douairiare de Brunswick-Wolfenbuttel* (Berlin, 1781), p. 34.

378. See, respectively, Friedrich Ruof, *Johann Wilhelm von Archenholtz: Ein deutscher Schriftsteller zur Zeit der Französischen Revolution und Napoleons (1741–1812)*, Historische Studien, 131 (Berlin, 1915); Imendörffer, *Johann Georg Hamann* (note 22); Max Kalbeck, "Johann Heinrich Merck an Christoph Martin Wieland," *Goethe Jahrbuch*, 27 (1906), 116; Forster, "Edward Young in Translation I" (note 16), p. 483; Goethe's letters of 11 May and 27 September 1766 to his sister, and James Boyd, *Goethe's Knowledge of English Literature*, Oxford Studies in Modern Languages and Literature (Oxford, 1932), pp. ix–xvii; Wilhelm Bode, *Der weimarische Musenhof, 1756–1781*, 3rd ed. (Berlin, 1917), p. 247; *Voltaire's Correspondence*, ed. Theodore Besterman, XXIV (Geneva, 1957), 162 (no. 5100, 26 March 1754).

379. *Historisches Journal*, 1 (1772), 274.

380. Theodor Vetter, *Zürich als Vermittlerin* (note 69), p. 17.

381. *Correspondence of Thomas Gray*, ed. Paget Toynbee, Leonard Whibley, and H. W. Starr (Oxford, 1971), I, 424 (no. 197, 27 June 1755).

382. Karl Bulling, *Die Rezensenten der Jenaischen Allgemeinen Literaturzeitung im ersten Jahrzehnt ihres Bestehens, 1804–1813*, Claves Jenenses: Veröffentlichungen der Universitätsbibliothek Jena, 11 (Weimar, 1962), 339–84.

383. 3rd ed. (Berlin and Stettin, 1776), I, 99.

384. *Lettre sur la littérature allemande* (note 377), pp. 33 f.

385. There were frequent complaints about the quality of translations. Nicolai spoke of "das Manufakturmäßige beym Uebersetzen" (*Sebaldus Nothanker*, I, 101). See also Knufmann (note 75).

386. For a detailed account see Eric A. Blackall, *The Emergence of German as a Literary Language, 1700–1775* (Cambridge, 1959). The German translation (Stuttgart, 1966) adds a "Bericht über neue Forschungsergebnisse, 1955–1964" by Dieter Kimpel.

CONTRIBUTORS

ROBERT DARNTON is Professor of History at Princeton University. He holds the A.B. degree from Harvard University, was a Rhodes Scholar at and holds the D. Phil. from Oxford University, and was a Junior Fellow of the Society of Fellows at Harvard University, 1965–1968. He is the author of *Mesmerism and the End of the Enlightenment in France* (1968) and has written many articles and reviews in learned journals in the United States, England, and France.

BERNHARD FABIAN is Professor of English at the University of Münster. He holds the D. Phil. from the University of Marburg, and has lectured widely at foreign universities. He has written *Alexis de Tocquevilles Amerikabild* (1957), has edited the works of Alexander Gerard and Francis Hutcheson, and is the coeditor of the *Anglistica & Americana* series of reprints.

PAUL J. KORSHIN is Associate Professor of English at the University of Pennsylvania and Executive Secretary of the American Society for Eighteenth-Century Studies. He holds his advanced degrees from Harvard University. He edited *Studies in Change and Revolution, 1640–1800* (1972) and is the author of *From Concord to Dissent: Major Themes in English Poetic Theory, 1640–1700* (1973). He was the program chairman of the American Society for Eighteenth-Century Studies' Fifth Annual Meeting (1974) at which these essays were originally presented.

ROY McKEEN WILES (1903–1974) was, at the time of his death, Professor Emeritus of English at McMaster University. Educated at Dalhousie University, he held the Ph.D. from Harvard University; he spent his entire career (1935–1974) at McMaster. He was the author of the standard works *Serial Publication in England before 1750* (1957) and *Freshest Advices: Early Provincial Newspapers in England* (1965), several popular guides to the humanities, and many articles and reviews in learned journals. In 1973/74, he was President of the American Society for Eighteenth-Century Studies.

INDEX OF NAMES